THE NEW CAMBRIDGE SHAKESPEARE

FOUNDING GENERAL EDITOR
Philip Brockbank

GENERAL EDITOR
Brian Gibbons, *Professor of English Literature, University of Zürich*

ASSOCIATE GENERAL EDITORS
A.R. Braunmuller, *Professor of English, University of California, Los Angeles*
Robin Hood, *Senior Lecturer in English, University of York*

THE TWO GENTLEMEN OF VERONA

Professor Schlueter approaches this early comedy as a parody of two types of Renaissance educational fiction: the love-quest story and the test-of-friendship story, which by their combination show high-flown human ideals as incompatible with each other and with human nature.

A thoroughly researched, illustrated stage history of *The Two Gentlemen of Verona* reveals changing conceptions of the play, which nevertheless often fail to come to terms with its subversive impetus. Since the first known production at David Garrick's Drury Lane Theatre, it has tempted major directors and actors, such as John Philip Kemble, William Charles Macready, Charles Kean and Samuel Phelps, who established a tradition of understanding which cast its shadow even on such modern productions as Denis Carey's famous staging for the Bristol Old Vic and Robin Phillips's for the Royal Shakespeare Company.

THE NEW CAMBRIDGE SHAKESPEARE

Romeo and Juliet, edited by G. Blakemore Evans
The Taming of the Shrew, edited by Ann Thompson
Othello, edited by Norman Sanders
King Richard II, edited by Andrew Gurr
A Midsummer Night's Dream, edited by R.A. Foakes
Hamlet, edited by Philip Edwards
Twelfth Night, edited by Elizabeth Story Donno
All's Well That Ends Well, edited by Russell Fraser
The Merchant of Venice, edited by M.M. Mahood
Much Ado About Nothing, edited by F.H. Mares
The Comedy of Errors, edited by T.S. Dorsch
Julius Caesar, edited by Marvin Spevack
The Second Part of King Henry IV, edited by Giorgio Melchiori
King John, edited by L.A. Beaurline
King Henry VIII, edited by John Margeson
The First Part of King Henry VI, edited by Michael Hattaway
Antony and Cleopatra, edited by David Bevington
The Two Gentlemen of Verona, edited by Kurt Schlueter

THE TWO GENTLEMEN OF VERONA

Edited by
KURT SCHLUETER
Professor of English, University of Freiburg

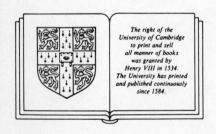

The right of the
University of Cambridge
to print and sell
all manner of books
was granted by
Henry VIII in 1534.
The University has printed
and published continuously
since 1584.

CAMBRIDGE UNIVERSITY PRESS

Cambridge
New York   Port Chester
Melbourne   Sydney

Published by the Press Syndicate of the University of Cambridge
The Pitt Building, Trumpington Street, Cambridge CB2 1RP
40 West 20th Street, New York, NY 10011, USA
10 Stamford Road, Oakleigh, Melbourne 3166, Australia

First published 1990

Printed in Great Britain at the University Press, Cambridge

British Library cataloguing in publication data

Shakespeare, William, *1564–1616*
The two gentlemen of Verona. – (The New Cambridge
Shakespeare)
I. Title II. Schlueter, Kurt
822.3'3

Library of Congress cataloguing in publication data

Shakespeare, William, 1564–1616.
The two gentlemen of Verona / edited by Kurt Schlueter.
    p.   cm. – (The New Cambridge Shakespeare)
ISBN 0-521-22222-2. – ISBN 0-521-29406-1 (pbk.)
I. Schlueter, Kurt. II. Title. III. Series: Shakespeare,
William, 1564–1616. Works. 1984. Cambridge University Press.
PR2838.A2S54 1990
822.3'3 – dc20   89-34309   CIP

ISBN 0 521 22222 2   hardback
ISBN 0 521 29406 1   paperback

THE NEW CAMBRIDGE SHAKESPEARE

The *New Cambridge Shakespeare* succeeds *The New Shakespeare* which began publication in 1921 under the general editorship of Sir Arthur Quiller-Couch and John Dover Wilson, and was completed in the 1960s, with the assistance of G.I. Duthie, Alice Walker, Peter Ure and J.C. Maxwell. *The New Shakespeare* itself followed upon *The Cambridge Shakespeare*, 1863–6, edited by W.G. Clark, J. Glover and W.A. Wright.

The New Shakespeare won high esteem both for its scholarship and for its design, but shifts of critical taste and insight, recent Shakespearean research, and a changing sense of what is important in our understanding of the plays, have made it necessary to re-edit and redesign, not merely to revise, the series.

The *New Cambridge Shakespeare* aims to be of value to a new generation of playgoers and readers who wish to enjoy fuller access to Shakespeare's poetic and dramatic art. While offering ample academic guidance, it reflects current critical interests and is more attentive than some earlier editions have been to the realisation of the plays on the stage, and to their social and cultural settings. The text of each play has been freshly edited, with textual data made available to those users who wish to know why and how one published text differs from another. Although modernised, the edition conserves forms that appear to be expressive and characteristically Shakespearean, and it does not attempt to disguise the fact that the plays were written in a language other than that of our own time.

Illustrations are usually integrated into the critical and historical discussion of the play and include some reconstructions of early performances by C. Walter Hodges. Some editors have also made use of the advice and experience of Maurice Daniels, for many years a member of the Royal Shakespeare Company.

Each volume is addressed to the needs and problems of a particular text, and each therefore differs in style and emphasis from others in the series.

PHILIP BROCKBANK

Founding General Editor

To Wolfgang Clemen

CONTENTS

ILLUSTRATIONS

Illustrations 4–10 are from the Art Collection of the Folger Shakespeare Library, by whose kind permission they are reproduced

ACKNOWLEDGEMENTS

I am indebted to previous editions of *The Two Gentlemen of Verona*, especially to the work of Clifford Leech (Arden), Norman Sanders (New Penguin) and the Riverside edition.

For my own approach, the response and contributions of students who attended my seminars at Freiburg University and the University of Massachusetts at Amherst have been most helpful, mainly for the study of the First Folio text of the play, its interpretation and the history of its criticism and stage productions. I especially thank Ian Coates and Michael Brake for the energy with which they tackled the study of the New Bibliography, and Annette Melcher, Birgit Hundrieser, Sabine Weyand and Sybill Hülsewig for their careful analyses of promptbooks. Other staff members of my chair in Freiburg also assisted me in many ways, among them Angelika Gutmann, who produced a neat copy on the wordprocessor after many rewritings and proof-readings of earlier drafts.

I am grateful to the Birmingham Reference Library, the Folger Library, the Henry E. Huntington Library, the Shakespeare Institute of the University of Birmingham and the Shakespeare Centre at Stratford-upon-Avon for permission to use their resources as a reader, and I would also like to thank the librarians for their friendly help.

With the deepest gratitude I will always cherish the memory of Philip Brockbank, the General Editor of this series and wonderful friend, who during the years of my research was willing to listen patiently to my still tentative ideas, always giving encouragement and useful advice. As Associate General Editor, Brian Gibbons saw through the finished manuscript and suggested improvements. It is due to him and the meticulous reading of Paul Chipchase of the Cambridge University Press that many mistakes, inconsistencies and stylistic faults could be eliminated. Sarah Stanton was most helpful in obtaining the rights for some of the illustrations.

Finally, I thank my wife Anne R. Schlueter, who has co-operated with me in all stages of the project.

K. S.

University of Freiburg

ABBREVIATIONS AND CONVENTIONS

Shakespeare's plays, when cited in this edition, are abbreviated in a style modified slightly from that used in the *Harvard Concordance to Shakespeare*. Other editions of Shakespeare are abbreviated under the editor's surname (Rowe, Sanders) unless they are the work of more than one editor. In such cases, an abbreviated series title is used (Cam.). When more than one edition by the same editor is cited, later editions are discriminated with a raised figure (Collier^2). All quotations from Shakespeare, except those from *The Two Gentlemen of Verona*, use the text and lineation of *The Riverside Shakespeare*, under the general editorship of G. Blakemore Evans.

1. Shakespeare's plays

Ado	*Much Ado About Nothing*
Ant.	*Antony and Cleopatra*
AWW	*All's Well That Ends Well*
AYLI	*As You Like It*
Cor.	*Coriolanus*
Cym.	*Cymbeline*
Err.	*The Comedy of Errors*
Ham.	*Hamlet*
1H4	*The First Part of King Henry the Fourth*
2H4	*The Second Part of King Henry the Fourth*
H5	*King Henry the Fifth*
1H6	*The First Part of King Henry the Sixth*
2H6	*The Second Part of King Henry the Sixth*
3H6	*The Third Part of King Henry the Sixth*
H8	*King Henry the Eighth*
JC	*Julius Caesar*
John	*King John*
LLL	*Love's Labour's Lost*
Lear	*King Lear*
Mac.	*Macbeth*
MM	*Measure for Measure*
MND	*A Midsummer Night's Dream*
MV	*The Merchant of Venice*
Oth.	*Othello*
Per.	*Pericles*
R2	*King Richard the Second*
R3	*King Richard the Third*
Rom.	*Romeo and Juliet*
Shr.	*The Taming of the Shrew*
STM	*Sir Thomas More*
Temp.	*The Tempest*
TGV	*The Two Gentlemen of Verona*
Tim.	*Timon of Athens*

Tit.	*Titus Andronicus*
TN	*Twelfth Night*
TNK	*The Two Noble Kinsmen*
Tro.	*Troilus and Cressida*
Wiv.	*The Merry Wives of Windor*
WT	*The Winter's Tale*

2. Other works cited and general references

Abbott	E.A. Abbott, *A Shakespearian Grammar*, 1870, republished 1966 (references are to numbered paragraphs)
Alexander	*William Shakespeare, The Complete Works*, ed. Peter Alexander, 1951
Allen	M.S. Allen, 'Brooke's "Romeo and Juliet" as a source for the Valentine–Silvia plot', *University of Texas Publication: Studies in English* 18 (1938), 25–46
Bond	*The Two Gentlemen of Verona*, ed. R. Warwick Bond, 1906 (Arden Shakespeare)
Bullough	*Narrative and Dramatic Sources of Shakespeare*, ed. Geoffrey Bullough, 1957
Cam.	*The Works of William Shakespeare*, ed. W.G. Clark, J. Glover and W.A. Wright, 1863–6 (Cambridge Shakespeare)
Capell	*Mr William Shakespeare his Comedies, Histories, and Tragedies*, ed. Edward Capell, 1767–8
Collier	*The Works of William Shakespeare*, ed. J. Payne Collier, 1844
Collier²	*The Plays of Shakespeare*, ed. J. Payne Collier, 1853
corr.	corrected
Craig	*The Complete Works of Shakespeare*, ed. Hardin Craig, 1908
Delius	*Shakespeares Werke*, ed. N. Delius, 1854–60
Dyce	*The Works of William Shakespeare*, ed. Alexander Dyce, 1857
edn	edition
ELR	*English Literary Renaissance*
E&S	*Essays and Studies*
F	*Mr William Shakespeares Comedies, Histories, and Tragedies*, 1623 (First Folio). The Norton Facsimile, ed. Charlton Hinman, 1968
F2	*Mr William Shakespeares Comedies, Histories, and Tragedies*, 1632 (Second Folio). Published according to the true original copies, reproduced in facsimile, by D.S. Brewer, 1985
F3	*Mr William Shakespeares Comedies, Histories and Tragedies*, 1663–4 (Third Folio). Published according to the true original copies, reproduced in facsimile, by D.S. Brewer, 1985
F4	*Mr William Shakespeares Comedies, Histories and Tragedies*, 1685 (Fourth Folio). Published according to the true original copies, reproduced in facsimile, by D.S. Brewer, 1985
Franz	W. Franz, *Shakespeare-Grammatik*, 1924 (references are to numbered paragraphs)
Genest	John Genest, *Some Account of the English Stage from the Restoration in 1660 to 1830*, 10 vols., 1832
Hanmer	*The Works of Shakespear*, ed. Thomas Hanmer, 1743–4
Hinman	Charlton Hinman, *The Printing and Proof-Reading of the First Folio of Shakespeare*, 2 vols., 1963

Johnson	*The Plays of William Shakespeare*, ed. Samuel Johnson, 1765
Kittredge	*The Two Gentlemen of Verona*, ed. George Lyman Kittredge, rev. Irving Ribner, 1969
Knight	*The Pictorial Edition of the Works of Shakespeare*, ed. Charles Knight, 1838–42
Kökeritz	Helge Kökeritz, *Shakespeare's Pronunciation*, 1953
Leech	*The Two Gentlemen of Verona*, ed. Clifford Leech, 1969 (Arden Shakespeare)
Munro	*The London Shakespeare*, ed. J. Munro, 1958
NS	*The Works of Shakespeare*, ed. Arthur Quiller-Couch and John Dover Wilson, 1921 (New Shakespeare)
OED	*The Oxford English Dictionary*, ed. Sir J. A. H. Murray, W. A. Craigie and C. T. Onions, 13 vols., 1933
PBSA	*Papers of the Bibliographical Society of America*
PMLA	*Publications of the Modern Language Association of America*
Pope	*The Works of Shakespeare*, ed. Alexander Pope, 1723–5
Rann	*The Dramatic Works of Shakespeare*, ed. Joseph Rann, 1786
Riverside	*The Riverside Shakespeare*, ed. G. Blakemore Evans, 1974
Rowe	*The Works of Mr William Shakespear*, ed. Nicholas Rowe, 1709
Sanders	*The Two Gentlemen of Verona*, ed. Norman Sanders, 1968 (New Penguin Shakespeare)
SB	*Studies in Bibliography*
SD	stage direction
SEL	*Studies in English Literature 1500–1900*
SH	speech heading
Singer	*The Dramatic Works of William Shakespeare*, ed. S.W. Singer, 1826
Sisson	*William Shakespeare. The Complete Works*, ed. C.J. Sisson, 1953
SJ	*Shakespeare Jahrbuch*
SP	*Studies in Philology*
SQ	*Shakespeare Quarterly*
S.St.	*Shakespeare Studies*
S.Sur.	*Shakespeare Survey*
Staunton	*The Plays of Shakespeare*, ed. Howard Staunton, 1858–60
Steevens	*The Plays of William Shakespeare*, ed. Samuel Johnson and George Steevens, 1773
subst.	substantively
Tannenbaum	S.A. Tannenbaum, *The New Cambridge Shakespeare and The Two Gentlemen of Verona*, 1939
Theobald	*The Works of Shakespeare*, ed. Lewis Theobald, 1733
TLN	through line numbering
uncorr.	uncorrected
Var. 1803	*The Plays of Shakespeare*, with the corrections and illustrations of various commentators; to which are added notes by Samuel Johnson and George Steevens: revised and augmented by Isaac Reed, 1803 (First Variorum)
Var. 1821	*The Plays and Poems of Shakespeare*, with the corrections and illustrations of various commentators, ed. John Boswell, 1821 (Third Variorum)
Warburton	*The Works of Shakespeare*, ed. W. Warburton, 1747
Young	*The Two Gentlemen of Verona*, ed. K. Young, 1924 (Yale Shakespeare)

INTRODUCTION

Date

The date for the composition of *The Two Gentlemen of Verona* cannot be given with certainty. Before the posthumous publication of the text in the Folio of 1623, there is only one contemporary reference to it, in the form of Frances Meres's praise of Shakespeare as a consummate writer of comedies and tragedies in his *Palladis Tamia* (1598): 'for Comedy, witness his *Gentlemen of Verona*, his *Errors*, his *Loue labors lost*, his *Loue labors wonne*, his *Midsummers night dreame*, his *Merchant of Venice*'. Though the title given by Meres is not quite complete, it is unreasonable to doubt that it refers to our play. A look at his list of tragedies shows that the sequence of titles does not reliably inform us about the order of composition. Nor does the fact that the play relies heavily on a section of Montemayor's *Diana* offer help in dating it.[1] This prose romance, written in Spanish, first appeared in 1542 and was translated into French by Nicholas Collin in 1578. Yong's English translation only appeared in 1598 but is known to have been completed by 1582. There was also an anonymous play acted before the court in early 1585, but now lost, whose title, *The History of Felix and Philiomena*, suggests that it may have relied on the same story-insert as Shakespeare did. This drama, if it really was a treatment of Montemayor's story, may have contributed the initial idea to Shakespeare's play. However, in view of the mass of detailed correspondences between the story and Shakespeare's text, it seems best to assume a direct knowledge of Montemayor in its English translation.

The limited dramatic technique in *The Two Gentlemen* – its heavy reliance on monologue and duologue, the artificial balancing of pairs of lovers and pairs of servants, the lyrical qualities of some of its speeches and other features of its style – has been taken to indicate an early place for it in the Shakespearean canon, but the actual dating and placing remain more or less informed guesswork. E.K. Chambers proposed that it was written in 1594 or 1595 after *The Taming of the Shrew* and before *Love's Labour's Lost* and *Romeo and Juliet*.[2] E.A.J. Honigmann suggested that its composition was as early as 1587, assuming it to be Shakespeare's first attempt at comedy.[3] His dating is not founded on new material relating specifically to this text but derives from a general pre-dating of Shakespeare's beginnings as a writer of plays. He has convincingly demonstrated that Chambers's chronology of the apprenticeship plays needs to be challenged.

[1] To be consulted in Judith M. Kennedy (ed.), *A Critical Edition of Yong's Translation of George of Montemayor's 'Diana'*, 1968.
[2] E.K. Chambers, *William Shakespeare*, 2 vols., 1930, I, 270.
[3] E.A.J. Honigmann, *Shakespeare's Impact on his Contemporaries*, 1982, p. 88.

He opposes to the orthodox 'late start' theory an 'early start' theory which attempts to redefine the relation of some early Shakespearean plays to those which have traditionally been taken as their 'source plays'. He maintains that these need not have preceded their Shakespearean counterparts but may have been competing with theatrically successful Shakespearean productions. Honigmann regards *The Troublesome Reign* (published in 1591) – which in his view follows Shakespeare's *King John* as well as *Richard III* – as the new keystone of the chronology of the early plays. In consequence of a later reference by Ben Jonson to the period of Senecan tragedies, he tentatively attributes the composition of *Titus Andronicus* to the year 1586 and thinks this play was then followed by *The Two Gentlemen* in 1587. However, the traditional view that Shakespeare began his career as a comic writer with *The Comedy of Errors*, a play in which he could use the experience gained by reading Latin comedies in his school-days, seems more plausible than to see him start out with the more original venture *The Two Gentlemen*, in which he found the basis of his own peculiar kind of comedy and to which he returned for devices to be reused and redeveloped in many of his maturer works. The dating and ordering of Shakespeare's experimental comedies remain a matter of conjecture, but it is not impossible that the creation of our play must be sought in the late 1580s, whatever the sequence of these early plays may be. Unfortunately, no records of Elizabethan performances of *The Two Gentlemen* have come down to us.

Themes and criticism

With *The Two Gentlemen of Verona* Shakespeare, for the first time, turned to the matter and motifs of romance, making them the vehicle of his comedy. Since similar material would become the basis of his later and more appreciated comedies, his earlier venture has tended to be misjudged. Criticism of the play has too often been based on the assumption that the author intended, or should have intended, to write something like *Twelfth Night* or *As You Like It* but, being young and newly apprenticed to the playwright's trade, had not known how to achieve this and had therefore failed. Attempts to reconstruct a direct line of development from the young to the mature Shakespeare have so far served only to denigrate the early play and put critics into the dangerous position of offering their belated advice as to what he should have done. A case in point is H.B. Charlton's treatment of the play, which, after offering much pertinent information about the background of the materials used, concludes: 'Clearly, Shakespeare's first attempt to make romantic comedy had only succeeded so far that it had unexpectedly and inadvertently made romance comic.'[1] The easiest way out of this self-forged dilemma would be simply to accept that what seems to be ridiculous in the play was meant to be so and was intended to be enjoyed as such. But bardolatry and ingrained convictions about the high educative mission of poets seem to have made

[1] H.B. Charlton, *Shakespearian Comedy*, 1938, p. 43.

the acceptance of such a position difficult. John Vyvyan offered the last great attempt to disregard what had been disturbing to other critics and bury it in his own allegorical reading of the play as an arcane exposition of highest Platonic and neo-Platonic wisdom.[1] In doing this, he has commanded some admiration but in recent times very little following.

To the mind of the purist, a mixture of the literary modes of romance and satire seems as inconceivable as that of fire and vinegar. But since Miguel de Cervantes has shown that out of such ingredients even masterpieces of world literature can be made, we should not think it impossible that the young Shakespeare started out on his career as a writer of comic plays by attempting to present a quixotic hero to his audience. Though traditional Shakespeare criticism has chosen not to admire the young writer for this daring attempt, we should not continue the practice of holding his later achievements against him when dealing with his early beginnings. We know something about the theatrical conditions under which the mature comedies were meant to be performed, but we know nothing about the stage and the audience for which this early piece was invented. The history of its later productions shows that the official theatre was likely to run into trouble with its presentation and that it was more likely to exert an immediate appeal when played by young actors or semi-professionals to young audiences in university theatres or under circumstances similar to these.[2] It is therefore not inconceivable that the play was meant to be performed under such conditions and before such audiences.

An explanation for this state of affairs may perhaps be found in the fact that the play uses educational matters more specifically than others. Two recent studies have dealt with this issue in detail. Peter Lindenbaum describes the action of the play as a series of educational processes that can be finally resolved by a happy ending when the more limited educational goal of the perfect courtier and gentleman is accommodated within a more comprehensive Christian view of man as an essentially fallible entity.[3] His paper has provoked a very subtly argued defence of the play as illustrating a successful education of the hero according to the ideals propounded in the courtesy book tradition. Camille Wells Slights's paper is particularly strong in relating the discussion of the role of the gentlemanly art of language in Castiglione's *The Courtier* to the conduct of the characters in Shakespeare's play, but it seems weaker in distinguishing between the conceptions of the nature of love and friendship and the different roles attributed to them in the works of Castiglione and Shakespeare respectively.[4] In C.W. Slights's view,

---

[1] John Vyvyan, *Shakespeare and the Rose of Love*, 1960, pp. 98–135.
[2] Numerous productions at English and American universities would testify to this if only we were able to document them all. But we have the corroboration of Arthur Holmberg, who confessed that a student production of the Royal Scottish Academy on the fringe of the Edinburgh Festival, and especially the youthfulness of the two actors playing Valentine and Proteus, inspired him to a new understanding of the play ('*The Two Gentlemen of Verona*: Shakespearean comedy as a rite of passage', *Queen's Quarterly* 90 (1983), 33–44).
[3] Peter Lindenbaum, 'Education in *The Two Gentlemen of Verona*', *SEL* 15 (1975), 229–44.
[4] Camille Wells Slights, '*The Two Gentlemen of Verona* and the courtesy book tradition', *S.St.* 16 (1983), 13–31.

Valentine lives up to the teachings he has received. Faced with the task of squaring these ideals with the exigencies of life, he encounters their inherent ambiguities, finally succeeding, by a process of trial and error, in solving all the problems with perfect *sprezzatura*. This includes the reconciliation with his former friend by offering him, in a magisterial courtly gesture, his own contracted bride, who, as a thoroughly educated lady, understands this artful ruse and beamingly stands by in approval of it. But against this interpretation one could hold that Castiglione must be seen as a practical educationist whereas Shakespeare was a writer of comic romance. Their standards in love and friendship differ accordingly. Castiglione's expectations with respect to love and friendship remain far more within the realm of what is practical and attainable than the phantoms the hero of romance finds himself pursuing.[1]

Working towards a closer understanding of the play, we should set aside the fact that the play has been described as a store-house for dramatic devices and motifs to which the dramatist later returned again and again – except that we may note in passing that he must have liked his early inventions enough to reuse them so often, dressing them up according to his later needs. But primarily we should look for such ideas as are unique to this text. Let us begin by observing that the play contains its own formulation of the primary goal of all education, the perfect gentleman:

> He is as worthy for an empress' love
> As meet to be an emperor's counsellor. (2.4.69–70)

Other plays by Shakespeare offer different descriptions of ideal manhood, but none is more comprehensive, more basic and more idealistic. In 'an emperor's counsellor' we can easily detect the goal educationists such as Sir Thomas Elyot and Baldassare Castiglione aimed at, namely to fashion the young nobleman into an able and competent adviser to his monarch. Shakespeare implies that the highest-ranking monarch deserves the highest-qualified advisers. The other qualification for the ideal gentleman – 'an empress' love' – may seem a bit more strange to many modern readers since it goes back to pre-Renaissance ideas of education. The exercise of courtly love was developed in the Middle Ages both to promote the knight's erudition in the literal sense of the word and to ensure his loyalty in service. Its ennobling effect was closely connected with the fact that this devotion was directed towards a lady of higher rank. The empress presumably deserves such courtly lovers as show the highest capability of being so ennobled. By the time Shakespeare wrote his play, the ideas of courtly love belonged primarily to the realm of romance and poetry rather than to real life, but it is just possible that the queen attempted to revive and reintroduce such ideas into practical politics in order to ensure the loyal service of her highest servants. Shakespeare's reaching back to medieval ideas of education may serve to render

---

[1] If it should be argued against this differentiation that Castiglione allows his treatise to end with the exposition of Cardinal Bembo's highly idealistic views about love, it will be necessary to recall that these are meant for the benefit of elderly gentlemen rather than for neophytes of Valentine's type.

the goal more remote and more romantic, but we should not overlook the fact that the young playwright seasoned the heady wine of romance with considerable doses of vinegar. The formulation of the ideal goal is put into the mouth of the Duke, a character who, with respect to his own daughter, shows very little trust in the ennobling effect of love and seems to favour a suitor more for his money than for his capacities of mind and character. Moreover, the definition of the perfect gentleman is tentatively applied here to Proteus, a character who is later to play the part of the villain.

Romance rewards its heroes by letting them reach the goal they are seeking. In Shakespearean comedy, where this quest always takes the form of a love-quest, the prize to be won is represented by a superior lady. But in this play she is marked in such a way as to render her a more highly stylised idealisation of a woman than any of her much-admired successors in the later comedies. Not only does she receive – as does no other Shakespearean heroine – a public demonstration of general homage in a song praising her excellence, but she is also characterised by a trinity of qualities Shakespeare was never to use again. The standard characterisation of the perfect lady 'wise, fair and true', which not even the very fastidious Benedick in *Much Ado* dares to exceed when fantasising about the qualities of ideal womanhood, is here overtopped by 'holy, fair and wise' (4.2.39) or, alternatively, 'too fair, too true, too holy' (4.2.5). In addition to all this, she is credited with a quality that is rare in the love poetry of these times, namely 'kindness' (4.2.43). The two male leads, therefore, move through a world so highly idealised that reality must fall short of it. We learn little more about their past than that they were childhood companions. They may have attended the same school or shared tutors. Their age is nowhere precisely stated, but one of them thinks it is yet too early for them to fall in love and the other – already smitten by love – recognises that his father is unlikely to consent to an early marriage. Indeed his education-conscious relatives make it clear that he should enter into what we would nowadays call tertiary education. If the heroes of romance can be subjected to the realities of age at all, Proteus and Valentine should be around sixteen years old. But more revealing, perhaps, is the fact that in some educational systems their status would be described as 'sophomores'. Valentine starts out for the world in a way that could win the approval of all his teachers. The blame he heaps on his companion in the very first scene makes us recall the fruitless warnings old Eubulus offers to the young Euphues at the beginning of Lyly's famous novel. While Proteus unscrupulously suits all his actions to what his immediate interest seems to require, we must credit Valentine with an inspired enthusiasm for the pursuit of an 'angel-like perfection' (2.4.59) which he so generously but wrongly attributes to his companion. No wonder, then, that he should fall for Silvia and that Silvia should recognise his potential.

The situation of a young *ingénu* in a world that professes and teaches very high ideals without really making the effort of living up to them will always offer matter for mirth. But his position must become abysmally grotesque when the ideals taught not only differ widely from the reality they are meant to enhance and illuminate but in addition prove mutually exclusive. Romance usually perpetuated the medieval idea of elevating heterosexual love to a primary educative force, but Renaissance thought also revived the classical idea of friendship and, by idealising it, turned it into an alternative educative power. The romance of friendship differs from commonplace friendship as much as courtly love from the everyday experience. Both claim a union of two in one, expressed as 'one soul in bodies twayne' in the case of friendship and by the conceit of the exchange of hearts in the case of love. In this theory of friendship the emotional and practical benefits are clearly of secondary importance. Friendship is first and foremost seen as an institution that enables man to develop his mental and moral potential to the highest possible degree. But educationists, though they are concerned with the full development of the individual, also consider the relation of the individual to society. In the romance of friendship true friends therefore serve the society in which they live by offering an example for ordering all human relationships. They point the way to establishing the golden rule of ethics, which should regulate all interpersonal connections. Only if we recognise the public value of the Renaissance ideal of friendship – which has been replaced by modern substitutes such as fraternity or solidarity – can we appreciate its supreme educational significance. In his play Shakespeare creates an enthusiastic hero who shows himself so much impressed that, without hesitation, he literally imitates an act of heroic generosity by offering his bride to his friend. But his own circumstances fit those of his adopted model only in his own imagination: he disregards the fact that he has been cast or has cast himself in the role of the hero of a conflicting educational fiction, the love-questing knight. Shakespeare lets his action work up to a climax in which an act seen in one context as the supreme test of idealism must be judged from the other context as abject desertion of all ideal endeavour.

Structure and sources

The best way to understand how Shakespeare arrived at tying the knot just described is to discuss the structure of his play in relation to his sources.[1] Edmund Spenser created the poetically most important educational fiction of his time by building on the knight-in-quest story, but Shakespeare started out by drawing on the tale of 'Felix and Felismena', a story-insert in Montemayor's pastoral novel *Diana*,[2] told for the greater part by the heroine herself. The story

---

[1] Geoffrey Bullough prints as relating to *The Two Gentlemen*: the 'Titus and Gisippus' story from Sir Thomas Elyot's *The Governour* (1531), Book II, chapter xii, which retells Boccaccio's tale of 'Tito and Gisippo' (*Decamerone*, X, 8), the story of 'Felix and Felismena' from J. de Montemayor's *Diana*, excerpts from John Lyly's *Euphues* and from Sir Philip Sidney's *Arcadia*, a scenario of Flaminio Scala's *Flavio Tradito* and excerpts from the German play *Julio and Hyppolita*, a text used by English actors in Germany and published in 1620 (Bullough, I, 203–66). Added to these must be Arthur Brooke's poem *Romeus and Juliet* (1562), reprinted by Bullough in the section related to Shakespeare's *Romeo and Juliet* (I, 284–363); a newly edited text of substantial parts is found in G. Blakemore Evans (ed.), *Rom.*, 1984, pp. 213–47.

[2] For a close study of these correspondences see T.P. Harrison Jr, 'Shakespeare and Montemayor's *Diana*', *Texas University Studies in English* 5 and 6 (1925–6), 72–120.

begins with a prelude in which competing supernatural powers foreordain that she will be unhappy in love but endowed with a special gift of fortitude. Having grown up, the lady finds herself insistently and elaborately courted by the son of a high-ranking neighbour. Being conscious of what fate has decreed for her, she is reluctant to fall in love. At length her suitor succeeds in bribing her maid to give her his letter. Shakespeare's 1.2 closely imitates its counterpart in the novella, except for the fact that Julia shows herself much less reluctant to accept her suitor since she lacks Felismena's motivation. Her letter, which Proteus reads in 1.3, is much more binding than the answer Felismena sends to her Don Felix, who only succeeds in winning her love by continuing his ostentatious courtship for about another year. When Felismena has finally committed herself, the father of Don Felix intervenes by sending him to a foreign court on the pretext that he should carry out some business there. When Don Felix sets out, his broken heart does not allow him to take leave of his beloved, but Felismena, being doubtful about his constancy, immediately follows him in the guise of a page. On her arrival she finds him already fallen in love with the lady Celia, and she overhears him courting her with a nightly serenade. For his play Shakespeare shortened the time of Proteus's courtship and substituted his avowal on the occasion of his leave-taking. He also changed the motivation of the father for sending his son to a place far from home and, in so doing, stressed the theme of education. Furthermore he lengthened the stretch of time between Proteus's departure and Julia's resolution to follow him. But in spite of her greater trust Julia fares as badly as Felismena. Both manage to get employment from their faithless lovers, both reason with them and are subjected to the ignominy of being sent on errands to their rivals. Within these parallels, however, we find significant differences: Felismena, reasoning in disguise with her former lover, wins his full consent and yet finds him unable to change his intentions. Presumably, this is to be ascribed to her foreordained unhappiness in love, which relieves the unfaithful lover, at least partly, of the burden of personal guilt for his faithlessness. In this situation, out of pity for the suffering caused by his unsuccessful suit, Felismena tries to induce Celia to show him some favour. Celia, who has fallen in love with the disguised Felismena, at first complies with her wishes. But this creates more grief – not only for Felismena but for Celia, too, who must see the page's attempts to help his master as the rejection of her own love for him. Felismena is caught in a double bind in which every move can only engender new suffering. Felismena suffers most – out of pity for Felix when he yearned for tokens of Celia's love and for her own sake when he seemed to receive them. The only way out is opened by the death of Celia, while Felismena survives, presumably because of her special endowment of fortitude. Felix despairingly absconds. Felismena follows in search of him, roaming the world, and, becoming an Amazon, uses her fortitude to rescue many from mortal dangers. One of those so helped turns out to be her beloved Felix. Their reunion takes place far from courts and cities in a sort of green world. There is hope that they will be united. But the full flowering of their reunion still depends on the suspension of the supernatural decree which ordained that she should be unhappy in love.

Turio   Proteus

Host: "Hark, what fine change
is in the music!"

Host   Julia

① "...That's her chamber. Tell my lady
I claim the promise for her heavenly picture."

Ursula   Silvia   Julia

② "Ursula, bring my picture there—
Go, give your master this."

Julia   Proteus

1 Possible ways of staging Silvia's chamber, by C. Walter Hodges. The design for Act 4, Scene 2 locates the chamber on an upper level of the stage; the design below shows two successive moments of Act 4, Scene 4 simultaneously: (1) the internal stage direction 'That's her chamber' and (2) the handing over of the picture, which necessitates Julia and Silvia meeting on the same level. See the notes on the locations at pp. 113 and 121 below

Since Silvia, Celia's counterpart, is firmly pledged to Valentine, she neither accepts the advances of Proteus nor falls in love with the page he employs on his errands. For the favours shown by Celia to Don Felix, the dramatist substituted the motif of the begged-for portrait. Julia's sufferings are focused in her tale of having impersonated Ariadne, the mythical prototype of the woman abandoned by a faithless lover. Julia shows more sense and a clearer determination than Felismena to further her own interest. She is determined to use the advantage of her disguise to cross the suit of her deviant lover to her rival. To reach her ends she even feels inclined to reveal herself to Silvia for what she is, but abstains when this does not prove necessary. Neither Celia's death nor Silvia's firm rejection of Proteus solves the fixation of the lovers. In the end Julia's quest surprisingly succeeds through her own initiative far from the court in an area roughly corresponding to that of the source. We must conclude, then, that the plot of the Felix-and-Felismena novella offered Shakespeare a love-quest story in which the normal roles of the male and the female were reversed. He even strengthened these traits by shortening the period of Julia's reluctance to accept her lover's suit and by making her more determined in the pursuit of her aims. He also added a scene of leave-taking (2.2), in which Julia tries to secure her lover by initiating a betrothal that Proteus seems not to have foreseen, however eagerly he enters into the bond offered him.

In accordance with the fashion of double plots, Shakespeare then found, or rather invented, a love-quest story to mirror the earlier one. At first sight the Valentine–Silvia plot seems to be the less original version in so far as it is the male who is sent on the quest. But, as a quest-hero, Valentine shows considerably more lyrical than epic or dramatic qualities. The best one can say of him is that his good intentions can never be doubted. His lack of interest in love creates a parallel to Julia's initial reluctance. On meeting Silvia, he falls in love but remains strangely passive. According to his page, he spends his time oafishly gazing at her and displaying all the signs of the conventional lover. And it is by her initiative to make him write a letter for her to himself that the decisive connection between the lover and his lady is brought about (2.1). Even this stratagem would have failed without the servant's explanation of its significance. When we next see Valentine (2.4), he is involved in a skirmish of words with a rival who has little chance to supplant him except for the fact that he is favoured by the lady's father. The father's opposition is so formidable that the lovers choose to evade it rather than to overcome it. A plan for an elopement is made. We are not told who initiated it, but we must think it likely that most of it goes back to Silvia. It involves climbing her tower by means of a rope-ladder. This seems to have been thrown in to give Valentine some semblance of a romantic hero and as an instrument by which he can be found out. The execution of the plan is foiled partly because he blabs it out to his former companion – who in rivalry reveals it to Silvia's father – and partly because the hero walks blindly into a trap the father has set for him. When the culprit is convicted on the evidence of the ladder and a quite unnecessary poetic missive to his bride, the petty domestic tyrant misuses his powers as a territorial ruler by banishing him. On his way home he has the good fortune to fall into the hands of a band of outlaws who abstain from robbing him of the little he owns and elect him to be their leader, putting all their treasures at his disposal. Instead of energetically using this power now to further his own aims, he spends his time in sighing for Silvia and in improving the morality of his men. When Silvia has followed him into the forest and he also has the good fortune to gain control over his two rivals and the opposing father, he exerts himself so far as to save the longed-for bride from being raped but, soon after, shows himself ready to give away the coveted prize in order to emulate the antique model of ideal friendship. This remains an empty gesture since through Julia's intervention neither Silvia, the prize, nor the potential prizewinner Proteus is given the chance to accept or to reject the offer. The happy ending is then completed by the Duke, who declares that, contrary to his former judgement, the hero must be thought worthy to fulfil the ideal of the perfect gentleman as laid down in his earlier definition. Thus most of the hero's success in his quest does not depend on his own decisions and actions but is given to him by chance and his lady's goodwill and initiative. This parallel plot, therefore, does not only mirror the first with significant differences; it also offers a burlesque of that type of quest story which served as the vehicle in Spenser's educational fiction.

In combining his parallel plots, Shakespeare used the already-mentioned test-of-friendship motif. This derives from Boccaccio's novella 'Titus and Gisippus', which we find retold in Sir Thomas Elyot's *The Governour*, the leading treatise on education in Tudor times.[1] In this tale Boccaccio combined the two tests of heroic friendship which world literature had developed: the giving away of one's bride to one's friend and the giving of one's life for the sake of a friend. The latter motif appears singly in stories of the Damon-and-Pythias type or in the Orestes–Pylades myth. In the wonderfully apt tripartite structure of Boccaccio's tale, however, Titus's risking his life is used as the final proof that he worthily received the bride whom Gisippus had earlier ceded to him in testimony of his friendship. The gift of the bride is presented as a case to be argued for and against. It meets with opposition from the bride and her family but is publicly defended by both friends. The Roman Titus is made to win his argument against the Greek relatives of his bride, presumably because the Romans understood the lore of friendship better than the Greeks. As if to forestall feminist criticism, the author has the story told by a female narrator, whose approval is shared by the female as well as the male listeners among her audience. It is surely important that the action takes place in the days of classical antiquity, when the relations between men and women had not been influenced either by ideas of courtly love or by Platonic and neo-Platonic reinterpretations of it. Elyot's version of the story keeps the antique setting but eliminates the argumentative elements, probably because he could not imagine that any of his readers might be tempted to prove their mettle by literally imitating the marvellous test of friendship his story tells about.

[1] See Ralph M. Sargent, 'Sir Thomas Elyot and the integrity of *The Two Gentlemen of Verona*', *PMLA* 65 (1950), 1166–80.

(a)   *(b)*   *(c)*

2   An Elizabethan actor in the role of Julia: (a) in rehearsal, (b) costumed for the woman's part in Acts
    1 and 2, and (c) in disguise as a page in Acts 4 and 5, by C. Walter Hodges. Julia would have been
    played by a male actor, probably an apprentice, since the Elizabethan theatre knew no actresses.
    This fact may have led to Shakespeare's frequent use of the motif of a woman putting on a male
    disguise

But Shakespeare's hero chooses to follow Gisippus's example, an act which
is made to look even stranger by having all the other circumstances radically
changed. Almost throughout the play Valentine and Proteus are seen as no more
than friends in the modern attenuated sense of the word. When they first appear
before the audience taking leave of each other, they certainly do not qualify as
candidates for heroic friendship since, compared with Titus and Gisippus, they
are divided by their values and their diverging intentions. Even the affectionate
form of address used in the exchange does not indicate a unique sort of bond:
Proteus addresses Turio later in almost the same terms. Nor are the two young
men recognised by the people round them as being bound together by very special
inclinations and obligations. Proteus's father describes them as companions rather
than friends; and instead of discerning an equality, which is essential to ideal

friendship, he seems to be inclined to look down on Valentine's social status. Indeed, the word 'friend' appears more often in the text of the play when a breach of friendship is involved. Earlier uses of the word refer to relatives and acquaintances rather than to friends in the sense of either ideal or common friendship. It is typical of the disparity between such realities as the play presents and the language used to describe them that the term 'friend' appears when Proteus deceptively offers his friendly services to the banished Valentine. Conversely, when Valentine tries to pacify the Outlaws by addressing them as 'friends', they reject it and declare themselves his 'enemies' but show him their love and admiration by laying themselves and their treasures at his feet. Nowhere in the play is the *alter ego* formula, so often used to characterise ideal friendship, applied to the relationship between Valentine and Proteus, nor are they ever called 'two souls in bodies twayne'; however, the formula for identity may be contained in Valentine's complaint at his banishment, which describes his union with Silvia:

> To die is to be banished from my self,
> And Silvia is my self; banished from her
> Is self from self, a deadly banishment.   (3.1.171–3)

Consequently, he sees the enforced separation as ending in his own annihilation. Though Lance's offer to strike him and Proteus's report about Silvia's stead-fastness comically reduce his annihilation fantasy, Valentine only shows grief at being separated from Silvia, not at being separated from his supposed friend.

The *alter ego* formula is not even drawn upon immediately before the spectacular offer of the bride. In his complaint about Proteus's breach of friendship, Valentine uses the image of a division between the organs of the same body: the 'right hand ... perjured to the bosom' (5.4.67–8). Indubitably, the play shows that Valentine misjudges reality if he expects his friend to conform even to a description of friendship greatly inferior to the essence of friendship described by the *alter ego* formula. Though the image contains organic unity, it conveys it by using unequal parts of the body. It appears in the literature of friendship when practical benefits are to be stressed. Both the moments of inequality and practicality render such alliances inferior to the highest concepts of friendship. But even this lower idea of friendship is nowhere applicable in this play as Valentine has not been shown to rely on the assistance of Proteus. Critics have occasionally dealt with the fact that, in comparison with Titus, Proteus scarcely deserves to receive the benefit offered to him by Valentine,[1] but the gist of the matter lies in the changed attitude towards the woman concerned. Though Sophronia is loved, esteemed and valued by Gisippus, she is for him second in importance to his friend, whom he holds to be the only person who is unique and irreplaceable. But everything leads us to believe that, in Valentine's case, it is Silvia who is unique and necessary for his continued existence, whereas all the actions of the play seem to prove that he could well do without his so-called friend.

[1] See, for instance, William Rossky, '*The Two Gentlemen of Verona* as burlesque', *ELR* 12 (1982), 210–19.

Analysing the play in the light of the test-of-friendship motif, we thus find that
Shakespeare created the imitation of a faithful friend and coupled him to an
unfaithful and undeserving friend. This leads us to consider another contemporary
fiction, ostensibly concerned with education and with love and friendship in
particular, as a possible source, or perhaps analogue, of the play. Lyly's *Euphues*
can be read, at least in parts, as a different sort of reworking of Boccaccio's tale.
Euphues and Philautos style themselves friends far more consciously than Proteus
and Valentine are ever allowed to do. They intend to lead their lives according to
the examples of heroic friendship, including Titus and Gisippus, but since they
deceive themselves about the true essence of it, they naturally fail the test. They
take friendship to be an institution for the joint pursuit of pleasure rather than
virtue. Lyly adds to the irony by giving, at least morally, a far lower status to the
woman concerned than Boccaccio allowed Sophronia. Philautos is subjected to the
same self-tormenting soliloquies as Titus when confronted with the fact that he
has fallen in love with the fiancée of his friend. Even some of the same arguments
reappear. Proteus's monologues, which end with the resolution to deceive
Valentine, are analogues of the torments both of Philautos and Titus. Since
Proteus, like Philautos, adopts those arguments that Titus rejects, his decision can
be said to be based on the example of Philautos. It is at least conceivable that
contemporary audiences would have seen the story of *The Two Gentlemen* as much
in the light of Lyly's *Euphues* as in the light of Boccaccio's tale of 'Titus and
Gisippus'.[1]

Since some critics have created the impression that Elizabethan audiences were
used to looking upon the cession of the bride to the friend as an unfailing test of
the hero's magnanimity, attention should be drawn to Robert Greene's novella
Tullies Love, another reworking of Boccaccio's tale.[2] Here the young Cicero, chief
propounder of the idea of friendship, is shown to have lived what he preached – as
understood by those of his readers who saw friendship in terms of Boccaccio's tale.
Therefore Greene's romance casts the young Cicero in the role of Titus. As this
tale pretends to be biographical, the setting of Boccaccio's story in the times of
Roman antiquity is preserved. But the heroine, quite unlike Sophronia, is con-
ceived in terms of the ladies in the romances of courtly love. She is described
as a wonder of beauty and virtue. Her fame spreads far and wide and reaches the
ears of a young Roman commander who lays down his military command to win
this wonderful woman. Indeed, in showing herself reluctant to accept the suit of
this splendid young man of military fame and impeccable social credentials, she is
far more like the heroine of the courtly love story than Shakespeare's Silvia. The
suitor, therefore, befriends the young Cicero, already noted for his powers of
persuasion though still occupying only a comparatively low rank in society, who
repeatedly meets the heroine in order to plead for his friend. The lady falls in love

[1] For a fuller discussion of the relation of Lyly's *Euphues* to Shakespeare's *The Two Gentlemen* see
Bond, pp. xvi–xix.
[2] Charles Howard Larson, *A Critical Edition of Robert Greene's 'Ciceronis Amor: Tullies Love'*, Salzburg,
1974.

with the go-between and encourages him to claim her for himself. Although Cicero shares the admiration of the world for this paragon, he refuses to pursue his own interest against that of his friend. But having fallen deeply in love with the lady himself, he feels the same torments Titus feels in a similar situation. In both stories the first lovers get to know of the calamity of their friends – quite against the intention of these second lovers, who would rather die than tell their friends about it. In both, the first lovers step back and renounce their earlier claims and actively assist their friends to gain or to keep the ladies they desire. But there is a difference: in the Boccaccio–Elyot version the first lover cedes a contracted bride who has accepted him as her husband and must be deceived about the identity of the person she admits to the consummation of her marriage. The Greene version eschews any violation of emotional, moral or legal proprieties. The young Roman warrior is not ceding what he may regard as his own, nor is the lady tricked into accepting what she has not desired. There is no need to argue for or against the conduct of either of the friends, and yet in the author's eye their behaviour is marvellous enough to build a story of ideal friendship around it as if they were Titus and Gisippus. To clinch the argument, a third suitor appears. He too is of a vastly superior social standing to the favoured Cicero but has hitherto shown himself strangely boorish in his unwillingness to love and to learn. On meeting the lady who favours Cicero, he is miraculously transformed and soon becomes a perfectly learned model courtier. Since the desired lady cannot be won by his entreaties, he at last resorts to military force. In the ensuing civil war, the first lover adds his powers to those of the favoured second one against the third. Thus venturing their lives and testifying to their friendship, they triumphantly vindicate the right of the lady to exercise her freedom of choice. Together they not only defeat the mighty rival but, in doing so, also win the unanimous approval of the Roman community.

If we see Shakespeare's Valentine–Silvia–Proteus plot and Greene's story as more modern reworkings of Boccaccio's tale than Elyot's version of it, we note that both agree in elevating the position of the woman concerned but differ in the representation of the male characters. Greene keeps them both as deserving as Boccaccio's figures are meant to be but frees them of all possible blame and of what may seem unacceptable to his readers, whereas Shakespeare puts additional blemishes on both of them: treachery on the one, folly on the other. Viewing *The Two Gentlemen* from this perspective we can hardly claim that Shakespeare did not intend to write a burlesque of the romance or that he meant Valentine's offer as a sign of gentlemanly behaviour and an acquired capability of handling his rival friend.

Speed and Lance

Two of the figures of the play do not derive from the sources so far discussed. Indeed, earlier critics complained that they had no discernible function in the plot till Harold Brooks explained their parodistic use.[1] Speed seems to be modelled on the pert pages of Lyly's comedies. Only in *Love's Labour's Lost* did Shakespeare continue this line of comedic characters. But Lance presents the fully-fledged Shakespearean clown to such a degree that he has been taken for a later addition. Actors and their dogs playing the parts of Lance and Crab have often tended to monopolise the stage. Lance has usually been played as the touchstone of stern reality to the emotional and idealistic follies of his betters. One can hardly deny that this is part of his function, which climaxes in the anti-encomium of his own intended bride (3.1.262–347). But surely this is only one side of the figure. There is another which typifies an even more exaggerated kind of high-flown idealism than that of his master. His comic report of his leave-taking from his family (2.3) is a one-man play-within-a-play which parodies the parting of Proteus and Julia. Even more important than the finished dramatic re-enactment of the scene he succeeds in putting on are the difficulties he encounters in casting himself, his dog and the properties (his shoes, his hat and his staff) in their respective roles. The unresolved confusion of the dramatic identity of his dog amounts to a metadramatic statement about the dangers of an over-optimistic expectation that a fellow creature should act as one's *alter ego*. In such cases disappointment will necessarily follow. Crab fails in this test of ideal friendship because it is not in his nature to cry. In his last monologue or rather dialogue with his dog (4.4.1–32), Lance returns to the comedy of misplaced expectations by dealing more extensively with problems of nature and nurture. He manages to project the droll picture of a teacher whose high idealistic expectations fail because they are the reverse side of abject folly. Lance's conception of the teacher as the best friend of his pupil is nothing short of the ideal pedagogic relationship. His method of teaching acceptable behaviour by providing the exemplary conduct himself and having his pupil observe him is admirable beyond all questioning. But something must have gone wrong if the teacher, in spite of all this, ends up as the whipping-boy for his own pupil. Students of Renaissance educational theory get a momentary glimpse of the reason for this failure when Lance tells the audience how Crab intruded among the 'gentlemanlike dogs' only to misbehave under the Duke's table (4.4.14–17). The dog simply lacks the gentlemanly nature educationists required as a pre-condition for good results. Surely the point of all this is to parody all kinds of misplaced idealisms in the world of this play. If the other 'idealists' are not as frequently punished as Lance is, this is owing to the author's foreordained happy ending of the play, the very arbitrariness of which comically questions the value and the necessity of all educational efforts.

The Outlaws

The society of the Outlaws in the forests somewhere between Milan and Mantua has been described as Shakespeare's first in a series of attempts to incorporate

---

[1] Harold F. Brooks, 'Two clowns in a comedy', *E&S*, 1963, pp. 91–100.

3 The meeting of Speed and Lance in Act 2, Scene 5, by C. Walter Hodges. Of the two clowns, Speed is the typical, pert page, but Lance is Shakespeare's highly unusual development of the traditional rustic fool

the so-called 'green world' into his plays, into which maltreated members of a disordered society flee and from where the movement for the necessary improvement of this victimising society derives. In each of these Shakespeare provides a different version of the pastoral mode of writing, at least in his choice of the occupation of the people who figure as the main inhabitants. In this respect, the shepherd world in *The Winter's Tale* shows the most conventional form of pastoralism. But other kinds of *métier* are drawn upon in Shakespeare's plays – as they are in other forms of bucolic writing – to represent the 'simple man' stripped of the trappings and supports of a more complicated – and often overcomplicated – society. The hunters and woodmen in *As You Like It* and the cave-dwellers in

Cymbeline are fairly conventional as compared to the bandits in *The Two Gentlemen*; but, in whatever guise pastoral man appears in Shakespeare's plays, he is likely to be outlawed, banished or under the threat of severe penalties or danger. The qualification of a gang member as representative pastoral man would depend upon his opposition to a world of unbearably despotic rulers and institutions; but the tyranny of the Duke of Milan is shown only in aspects of petty domesticity. Apart from his whimsical arbitrariness in his choice of a son-in-law, his realm seems a much sought-after place where serious-minded young gentlemen flock together in order to complete their education, whereas the gentlemen of the forest find themselves under a cloud because of kidnappings, manslaughter and other such peccadilloes.

Shakespeare can thus be seen to start out on his series of 'green world' versions with a parody, just as he began his series of love-quest comedies with a combination of burlesque versions. Even the subject of education, which is not a necessary ingredient of a 'green world', is introduced mockingly here, though admittedly with far less subtlety than in Lance's monologue. But there is matter for laughter in seeing how the Outlaws put a premium on scholastic effort in dealing with Valentine. Their astonishing turnabout in the treatment of their prisoner is probably the most ironic comment on the value of learning foreign languages that can be found in world literature, and the most progressive of educationists will not be able to outdo Valentine in thinking that the period of internship the gentlemen served in the forest will qualify them for public offices. In spite of the fact that the lack of knowledge about the lore of courtly love and even more so of idealised friendship will impair the enjoyment of the play for modern audiences, spectators who have just come out of any kind of educational institution are still the most likely people to enjoy it.

Stage history

An essential part of the comicality of *The Two Gentlemen of Verona* is created by the necessary conflict between highly stylised concepts of love and friendship. The lasting effectiveness of such a play may therefore be seen as depending upon the continuity of cultural traditions which secure at least a lively knowledge of texts in which these ideals are embodied. In the history of thought and feeling, the two ideals have fared differently. Attempts at romanticising love have had a more lasting cultural success than attempts to romanticise friendship. This difference is arguably reflected in the fact that, among the decisive sources of the play, the one related to the ideal of love was already identified in the eighteenth century, whereas the one exemplifying ideal friendship was only recognised very recently – in spite of its higher literary value. Although the friendship discussion was never again carried on in later periods with the intensity of the Renaissance, advocacy of ideal friendship has revived from time to time. But the supremacy of the ideal of romantic love excluded the revival of stories of the Titus-and-Gisippus type, and poets and writers wishing to extol ideal friendship have confined themselves to the

Damon-and-Pythias type of story. This seems to go a long way to explain the play's limited success on the stage.

By the time of the first recorded performance of *The Two Gentlemen of Verona* (1762), the ideal of heroic friendship and the story that embodies it were so little known that Valentine's offer of his bride could only be seen as an irritating oddity better got rid of in the performance text prepared by Benjamin Victor. His rewriting of the final scene is more momentous for the history of the play's reception than his rearranging or conflating of scenes. The latter served primarily to adapt the free-flowing action, which had been written for performances without scenery, to the conditions of a theatre that had progressed a good deal towards the picture-frame stage with a front curtain and painted flats and wings. With the offer of the bride gone, there was no sure sign left to indicate that the friendship of the two leads was meant to be of the heroic type. This changes both the status of the hero and the main thematic concern of the play. Since the emphasis is shifted from the clash of two ideals, so highly stylised that they must necessarily cancel each other out, to a comparison between faithfulness and unfaithfulness in love, Valentine's character is changed from the well-intentioned but bewildered hero to a model courtier, at least in comparison with his counterpart. To underline this change, the curtain at Drury Lane dropped on a last line averring 'That lovers must be faithful, to be bless'd'. This is not Shakespeare's thematic emphasis, nor would he have moralised his comedy by such means. The whitewashing of the hero is complemented by a blackening of the villain. Proteus's puzzling use of Speed as his go-between to Julia is now motivated as a ruse which, if his designs were detected, would direct suspicion towards Valentine. This excludes the possibility of seeing Proteus as a victim who, overpowered by a sudden infatuation for Silvia, turns willy-nilly against his friend. From the beginning he is a miserable schemer. The contemporary desire for intrigue in drama also affected Victor's reading of other characters. Shakespeare's Julia in her first scene suggests a young

4 *Mr Yates in the character of Lance.* Engraving by Henry Roberts after a design by Thomas Bonner. Richard Yates (1706?–96) played the part of Lance in the first recorded production of *The Two Gentlemen* at Garrick's Drury Lane in 1762, which used Victor's adaptation. Though the portrait claims to have been taken from life, it is hardly an accurate theatrical record so much as a product of the artist's studio with some features reminiscent of the actual performance. The engraving is furnished with a caption relating it to Act 2, Scene 3 and with a full quotation of Shakespeare's monologue. Victor had revised this speech and transferred it from Verona to Milan, fixing the undetermined location of the original as a street scene; the picture, however, suggests a woodland setting. Various items of stage property, used by Lance in his dramatic demonstration to represent the persons in his tale of the leave-taking, are seen spread out before the actor. The sticking of the staff into the stage boards seems to reflect stage practice. Reviews indicate that Macready still made use of this method in 1841. But without the pieces of stage property, which are enumerated here rather than dramatically integrated, the picture would serve well as an illustration of the first of the additional scenes introduced by Victor in Act 5, where, in a further monologue addressed to the audience, the actor points to his dog, and says: 'See – the hardened wretch – he discovers no fears.' Instead of the sour dog of the first monologue, the artist presents a sweet, trusting, even self-satisfied-looking dog. It would therefore be best to regard the design as a composite picture, intended to remind theatregoers of the actor in two different scenes: one basically of Shakespeare's making, the other of Victor's

Mʳ YEATES in the Character of LAUNCE in the TWO GENTLEMEN of VERONA with his Dog Crab.

Tho. Bonner ad vivum delin.ᵗ

Hen. Roberts sculp.ᵗ

ACT II. SCENE III.

Laun. Nay 'twill be this hour ere I have done weeping; all the kind of y.ᵉ Launces have this very fault: I have receiv'd my proportion, like the prodigious son, and am going with Sir Protheus to the Imperial court. I think Crab my dog be the sowrest-natur'd dog that lives: my mother weeping, my father wailing, my sister crying, our maid howling, our cat wringing her hands, & all our house in a great perplexity; yet did not this cruel hearted cur shed one tear! he is a stone, a very pebble-stone, & has no more pity in him than a dog: a Jew would wept to have seen our parting; why, my grandam having no eyes, look, you, wept herself blind at my parting. Nay I'll shew you the manner of it: this shoe is my father; no this left shoe is my father; no, no, this left shoe is my Mother; nay, that cannot be so neither; yes it is so, it is so, it hath the worser soles: this shoe with the hole in it is my Mother; and this my father; a vengeance on't, there 'tis: now Sir, this staff is my sister; for look you, she is as white as a lilly, & as small as a wand; this hat is Nan our maid; I am the dog; no, the dog is himself; and I am the dog: oh, the dog is me, and I am my self: ay, so so: now come I to my father; father, your blessing; now should not the shoe speak a word for weeping; now should I kiss my father; well he weeps on: now come I to my mother; oh that she could speak now like an ould woman! well I kiss her; why there 'tis; here's my mother's breath up & down: now come I to my sister; mark the moan she makes: now the dog all this while sheds not a tear, nor speaks a word; but see how I lay the dust with my tears.

Publish'd as the Act directs by C. G. DYER, Antient & Modern Print Warehouse 7. Compton Street Soho.

J.Roberts del.   Publish'd for Bells Edition of Shakespeare March 7.ᵗʰ 1776.

Mr VERNON in the Character of THURIO.
Then to Sylvia let us Sing,
That Sylvia is excelling.

girl as yet inexperienced in love who, when confronted with her first love-letter, feels so alarmed in spite of her amatory curiosity that she finds it difficult to acknowledge her feelings to herself – let alone to the maid, who kindly intends to minister to her wishes. Victor's adaptation excludes this interpretation. His rearrangement of scenes makes Julia take the initiative in her affair with Proteus, and her antics before her maid can only appear as a deliberate covering-up of her forwardness. Lucetta for her part is turned into a girl who pries into her mistress's affairs in order to gain influence. She voices a rather cynical view of men; and, according to Speed, she is lascivious.

It is possible that Victor adapted the text not only in view of the stage conditions at Garrick's theatre but also in foreknowledge of the cast. If he had expected the 34-year-old Mrs Yates to play the part of Julia, the thought that this character could be seen as a young girl maturing into womanhood through suffering might never have entered his head. It is even more likely that the alterations concerning the figure of Turio were due to his anticipation that Mr Vernon, a well-known singer, was to create this part, for he not only assigned him the execution of the nightly serenade but also made him appear throughout the play as showing a foolish pride in his poetical and musical gifts and interests (see illustration 5). Whether Victor fully understood the use of Shakespeare's clowns in this play cannot be exactly determined. As the more quixotic and ridiculous features of the hero are toned down, Speed loses much of his function of pointing them out and Lance of parodying them. Victor then tried to make good the comic loss by adding two new scenes, one involving only Lance, the other both clowns. The new scenes provide another comic intrigue and give the clowns a chance to witness the happy ending when the curtain falls. But as the fun derives entirely from the foolishness of Lance, these additional scenes add very little point to the meaning of the whole play.

Genest scorned Victor's alterations, and critics have tended to follow him. But the historian must register that Victor's influence on the perception of Shakespeare's play and its parts well exceeded the six performances it received on Garrick's stage. These may not have had the kind of success both Garrick and Victor had hoped, but the creation of new stage characters was a more con-sequential event then than in our time. It is quite possible that stage traditions perpetuated at least some of the peculiar traits of these figures beyond the days when Victor's text or its derivatives were in use. In this connection an engraving by Fuseli comes to mind which can be called the most widely-publicised graphic

5   *Mr Vernon in the character of Turio.* Engraving by J. Roberts. Joseph Vernon (1738?–82), a well-known singer, played Turio in 1762. In Victor's adaptation Turio appears as foolishly vain and proud of his musical talents. It is possible that Victor made him so in the expectation that this actor would fill the role. The caption in particular relates the figure of Turio to the song in praise of Silvia, which he performed in this production as a solo singer. As this engraving conforms even more closely than that of Mr Yates to the souvenir pictures sold in close connection with a particular production, the costume, which is more elegant than foppish, can be deemed historically correct. See 4.2.37–51 n.

design relating to *The Two Gentlemen*; it was created to adorn a Shakespeare edition of 1803 (see illustration 6). It is almost certain that Fuseli did not see the Drury Lane production, but the artist's conception of the scene between Julia and Lucetta, without doubt, bears a greater likeness to what was offered on the stage then than what we visualise when we read Shakespeare's text today. Although the scene is not set in Julia's chamber as Victor's text indicates, the figures confronting each other seem to represent in their relative ages and temperamental relationship what probably appeared before the audience when the middle-aged Mrs Yates played opposite the twenty-year-old Miss Pope. Five years after the performance, the *Dramatic Censor* wrote in a general characterisation of Mrs Yates: 'regular but haughty features and a powerful voice carry her well through rage and disdain, but she is deficient of tender feeling . . . she has not a trace of comedy about her'. A third parallel between Fuseli's design and Victor's conception can be found in the translation of Julia's forwardness into the emblem of a huge urn, which the artist put into the picture to characterise her.

Covent Garden first performed *The Two Gentlemen* in 1784. The play was announced as 'SHAXESPEARE's with alterations'. Genest concludes his short entry on this production: 'this was not Victor's alteration but the original play with slight alterations. r.b.' Entries ending with these initials have been taken to mean that the source of the information was a regular playbill. In calling the alterations 'slight' and in declaring that they were not Victor's, Genest seems not to have paid enough attention to this source. A more careful inspection of the playbill suggests that the adapter used at least some of Victor's ideas because it announces, as a special treat, 'A Frighten'd Song' in Act 5 by Mr Quick (Lance). The words may not have been Victor's, but the idea is derived from his adaptation and the first of the two scenes he added to the end of the play provides the appropriate place for the song. There are other puzzles to be solved in connection with this production, which was clearly intended to have a run but was discontinued after the first performance. If the fact that it was announced as a benefit for Mr Quick meant that this actor had a larger than usual say in the production, one would have expected the comedian to have availed himself of the additional appearances Victor's conception of this part made possible. On the other hand, the 'Theatrical Intelligence' in the *Public Advertiser* makes it known that Valentine's part at least was embellished with purple passages from other Shakespearean plays, which was not Victor's practice.[1] The suppression of his name on the playbill may indicate that not all the alterations in the performance text were due to him. There is an engraving showing Quick as Lance (illustration 7). If this represents him in costume, the performance would

[1] *Public Advertiser*, 15 April 1784.

6 *Two Gentlemen of Verona* Act 1, Scene 2, by John Henry Fuseli (Füssli). First published in London in 1803. That Fuseli's illustration is directly influenced by first-hand theatrical experience is more than doubtful in spite of his well-known drawings of Garrick in Shakespearean parts. The artist cannot have seen the Drury Lane production of 1762–3, since he first visited England in 1764. Yet his conception of Julia and her relationship to Lucetta curiously resembles Benjamin Victor's rather than Shakespeare's representation of it. See pp. 21–2 above

Act 1. TWO GENTLEMEN OF VERONA. Sc.1.

Fuseli del.   Bromley sculp.

Julia. *Go, get you gone; and let the papers lie:*

Publish'd by F & C. Rivington, London. Jan.8.1803.

Act 4. TWO GENTLEMEN OF VERONA. *Scene 3ᵈ*

Rhamberg delt.   *Grignion sculpt.*

M.ʳ QUICK in LAUNCE.
here I have brought him back again.

Printed for J.B. British Library, Strand London Janʸ 12. 1785.

have shown the actors in contemporary dress. Such costuming was at that time by no means unusual, but it will puzzle the reader to find the critic for the *Public Advertiser* giving especial praise to the new costumes and the fresh scenery of this production.

John Philip Kemble was connected with Covent Garden as one of its actors at the time of the 1784 production and may therefore have seen it. He himself staged the comedy in 1790 at Drury Lane and in 1808 at Covent Garden. In his first production he gave the parts of Silvia and Proteus to his sister-in-law, Mrs Stephen Kemble, and Mr Wroughton, who had already filled these roles in 1784. In 1790 Mr Barrymore played the part of Valentine, which in 1808 Kemble decided to perform himself. About the performance text of 1790 nothing can be said with certainty, but the prompt-book of 1808 has been published in facsimile.[1] This shows that Kemble worked out a comprehensive version of his own but, in doing so, paid Victor the great compliment of adopting more than half of his ideas and elaborating on them. Kemble's dependence shows up most strikingly in the reappearance of Victor's conflation of 2.2 and 2.4, because this involves absurdities in the sequence of the ensuing action. Silvia enters upon the scene with a paper containing a plan for elopement and marriage which she must have drawn up before Valentine had declared his love for her; and in order to be able to tell Proteus about it later, Valentine has to read it on a stage where he is never alone. Thus it is reasonable to assume that the 1790 performance was based on a text half-way between Victor's version and Kemble's prompt-book of 1808. This view may find some support in the casting as well as in reviews of the production. The 25-year-old Mrs Goodall must have portrayed a quite different Julia from either Mrs Yates in 1762 or the 38-year-old Mrs Mattocks in 1784. By 1790 the actress was already famed for her pleasing feminine appearance in breeches roles, and one critic testifies to her softness and suavity.[2] The Kemble text of 1808 differs most significantly from Victor's version in dissolving the

[1] Charles H. Shattuck (ed.), *John Philip Kemble Promptbooks*, IX, 1974.
[2] *The Times*, 16 January 1790.

7 *Mr Quick as Lance.* Engraved by Charles Grignion after a design by Johann Heinrich Rhamberg. First printed for J. Bell, London, 1785. The design shows John Quick (1748–1831), a well-known comedian, who played Lance in 1784 at the first Covent Garden production of *The Two Gentlemen.* When this was used as a book illustration, a quotation from the Folio's Act 4, Scene 4 was added: 'here have I brought him back again'. The correctness of this addition needs to be questioned as the design shows neither an interlocutor nor a background appropriate to the scene. In editions up to 1784, the scene quoted from is set by editors in or under Silvia's apartment. Victor's adaptation finds room for this occasion in 'Sir Protheus Lodgings'. But the setting in the picture need not be purely fanciful: Rhamberg may have remembered Mr Quick's performance of his 'Frighten'd song' and the situation leading up to it, which probably derived from Victor's additions to Act 5. See pp. 22–5 above.

One may also question how well Grignion succeeded in transmitting the essence of Rhamberg's design to his engraving. The publisher John Cawthorn embellished an 1806 edition of Shakespeare with a slightly different engraving. Though neither designer nor engraver is named, the image clearly relates to the one shown here. But Lance is presented more clearly as if suddenly arrested by fear; and the quotation is missing, though there may have been reasons for this other than the intention to correct an error in relating the illustration to the text

scene conflations of Victor's first act and in restoring the original order of 1.2 and 1.3. Kemble, moreover, cancelled all suggestions of lasciviousness, cynicism and proneness to intrigue which Victor had attributed to Lucetta. It is only Victor's text, not Kemble's, which calls for a domineering type of Julia involved in the defence of her own intrigue against an intriguing servant. Indeed, if there was a major difference between Victor and Kemble at all, it would be that between the play seen through the eyes of, on the one hand, a reader of the comedy of intrigue and, on the other, a reader of the comedy of sentiment.

This is perhaps most visible in Kemble's continuation of Victor's efforts to straighten out Shakespeare's comically naïve hero. Like practically all eighteenth-century readers, Kemble did not consider that Shakespeare could have meant the quixotic offer of the bride as climaxing the theatrical revelation of Valentine's character; he therefore dispensed with it, basing the final scene more on Victor's than on Shakespeare's text. He makes Valentine a steadier character by following Victor in mitigating the sudden swing from mocker of love to ardent devotee, elaborating on what appears in Shakespeare's text only as the faintest foreshadowing of the turn-about. As in Shakespeare's 2.1, Kemble's Silvia is allowed to tempt Valentine's understanding; but, immediately afterwards, he is given the opportunity to pose as her strong protector. Kemble also tones down Valentine's exuberance as a lover – both in the passages about the enjoyable punishment he receives from 'Lord' Love and in the lines of his over-enthusiastic praise of Silvia, which Proteus rejects as braggartism. In 3.1 Valentine's speech is freed both of the fulsome praise of Turio and the cynical views with which he advises the Duke on how to win a woman. The pathetic monologue expressing Valentine's emotional reaction to his banishment is cut by half, with the effect that the point of Lance's subsequent jokes is lessened. When first encountering the Outlaws, Speed's fear is stressed to point up the calm bearing of the hero. Proteus's attempted rape is witnessed by Valentine at the head of a little host of Outlaws, leaving Proteus no chance to resist the interference. Silvia, being afraid of the bandits, gives Valentine the opportunity to appear as an all-powerful protector and leader, who can bid the treacherous Proteus prepare himself for death. It is this event that triggers off Sebastian's swoon, which leads to Julia being revealed. In watching her coming to terms with Proteus, both Valentine and Silvia express how much they are touched by the spectacle of the reunion. This emotional experience then causes Silvia to initiate the reconciliation between Valentine and Proteus.

As we already know, Victor attempted to blacken Proteus from the beginning by supplying a sinister motive for his use of Valentine's servant as his go-between to Julia. Kemble removes this blame, though he cannot succeed in whitewashing the 'villain' altogether. So he allows him to say at the end that he had been operating under a magic spell, and the other characters are shown to believe this. Accordingly, the two monologues given him before he enters upon his treacherous plan are cut severely by Kemble. Any traces of a struggle in Shakespeare's Proteus are eliminated here, together with almost all signs indicative of consideration for his friend. Kemble seems to shift the thematic concern further away from the

conflict in friendship to mere unfaithfulness in love. In both versions, the reconciliation between the friends is relegated from the central position in Shakespeare's
last scene to a secondary matter, following the reconciliation between Julia and
Proteus. Kemble clearly works towards an edifying morality, which avers that true
virtue wins through in the end and even error can be forgiven – at least when
committed under the influence of magic spells which, as the villain proves by his
closing speech, have been removed. Kemble therefore lengthens the speech that
Victor had originally provided for Proteus to end the play.

Even textual changes with regard to minor figures affect the conception of
the play. The treatment of Sir Eglamour calls for special attention as it shows
Kemble's conviction that idealism must never be treated comically. His Eglamour
is not allowed to run off nimbly on encountering the Outlaws but has to stand and
defend Silvia staunchly till struck down by the outnumbering enemies and left for
dead on the battlefield. His resilience, however, allows him to reappear at the
end to act as a guide for the Duke's party which has come in search of Silvia
(illustration 8). Kemble's treatment of Sir Eglamour is all the more striking as
his alterations elsewhere seem, wherever possible, to be governed by the law of
probability. This makes itself felt also in the revisions that concern the Outlaws,
whom Kemble individualised by naming them and rearranging their speeches. In
differentiating between leading and minor figures among them by a more unequal
distribution of lines than the Shakespearean text provided, he also distinguishes
more genial Outlaws from more objectionable ones. The more brutal or otherwise
offensive utterances are relegated to the lesser speakers. In the end, Kemble
recommends them to the Duke not for 'great' but for 'brave' employment in order
to include them in the general reconciliation. These small though meticulous
changes show the adapter's endeavour to make his text close the credibility gap
and also to approach more nearly the ideas of poetic justice prevalent in the theatre
of his age.

According to the tastes and convictions of their age, both Victor and Kemble
prune the Shakespearean text of its wordplay and coarse or bawdy expressions.
Kemble goes much further in this than Victor; indeed, in the latter field he
seems to compete directly with Dr Bowdler. On the whole, the play must have
appeared much less funny to Kemble's audience than, one might suppose, to the
Elizabethans. Since it seems that it had become anathema to satirise or parody the
capers of youthful idealism, the clown scenes are relegated to a thematically
superfluous by-play. It is significant that this relegation outlasted the Kemble text
well into the twentieth century, when their original function was redetected. The
fact that the eighteenth and early nineteenth centuries chose not to see the
comically naïve hero in Valentine, but rather viewed him naïvely, may explain
much of the casting in these performances. Extreme youthfulness in Shakespeare
does a good deal to mitigate the capers of Proteus and, even more so, of Valentine.
Though actors and actresses well beyond the age of the figures they have to
represent may, to a certain extent, succeed in enacting 'youthfulness', there are
limits to the art of concealing the wrong theatrical signals nature provides.

SHAKSPEARE

TWO GENTLEMEN OF VERONA.
Sil. ———— go on, good Eglamour,
Out at the postern by the abbey wall;
I fear I am attended by some spies.
Egl. Fear not: the forest is not three leagues off.
Act V. Sc. 2.

J. Thurston del.

A. Smith. A.R.A. sculp.

London, Publish'd by Geo. Kearsley, April 30. 1803.

Whether such considerations have any relevance to the earlier performance, we do not really know. But we know that they do apply to the staging of the 1808 production when Kemble, then about fifty years old, undertook to play Valentine. He clearly saw that the text did not fit his appearance and thought it possible to remedy the discrepancy by changing indications of age in the text. It is well known that the 'youthful lover' was changed into a 'confident' one. Other parts had to be adapted accordingly – for example, references to the clowns as 'boys'. Critics may find that in all these changes Kemble did not reach a very high degree of consistency, but this must be deemed true for all his alterations, which indicate tendencies rather than completely successful realisations. For all his effort, Kemble was less successful than Victor in making a bid to re-establish the play on the English stage. Both his productions reached only half the number of the six showings of Victor's version. Victor found a Kemble to follow him, but Kemble seems to have had no followers. And yet this is possibly only half the truth, for Kemble's version may have influenced the conception of Valentine's part well beyond its use as a performance text.

The greater emphasis on the military prowess of the hero, which Victor introduced and Kemble greatly stressed, was reflected by painters in their designs relating to Act 5 of the comedy. Whereas earlier illustrations show Valentine rushing to the rescue of Silvia armed only with a rapier or even empty-handed (illustration 9), artists now let him appear heroically clad in steel and furnished with a weapon that looks like a broadsword. Typical of this new pictorial tendency is the painting by Thomas Stothard, which found its way into several Shakespeare editions as an engraving with the caption *The recognition of Julia* (see illustration 10). Even productions of the play by Macready (1841) and Charles Kean (1846, 1848), who both returned to a play text based more closely on the Shakespearean original, continued the idealisation of Valentine. Holman Hunt's famous picture of 1851, first called *Valentine rescuing Sylvia from Proteus*, then renamed *The Two Gentlemen of Verona*, presents this tendency at its height (illustration 11).

In terms of the number of performances, the most successful nineteenth-century production was Covent Garden's lavish 1821 staging of an operatic version of the play, based on a co-operation between Reynolds and Bishop. It even

8 *Two Gentlemen of Verona* Act 5, Scene 1, by John Thurston. As published in London, 1803. Thurston's watercolour (now in the Huntington Library), of which this engraving by A. Smith is a fairly faithful rendering, shows Sir Eglamour leading Silvia out of what presumably represents the 'postern by the abbey wall'. Silvia is drawing his attention to a noise she has heard and which she thinks may have been caused by spies following her. Eglamour's coat is covered with a breastplate, and he has his sword drawn as if ready to fight their way out, though Shakespeare's text contains little to indicate that this would be necessary. Thurston casts an elderly gentleman in the role of Eglamour as if his belief in the latter's idealism did not go far enough to entrust Silvia's honour into the keeping of a younger man; yet he idealises the fighting knight beyond what Shakespeare tells us about him. The artist has given Eglamour a build that would make him more apt to stand staunchly in the later fight with the Outlaws than to run off nimbly. This conception seems to be closer to J.P. Kemble's than to Shakespeare's. See p. 27 above. The quotation used as a caption ascribes the engraving to Act 5, Scene 2, which is Act 5, Scene 1 in the conventional act and scene division

TWO GENTLEMEN OF VERONA.

Act.V *Scene IV*

E.Edwards del. M.Liart sculp

Ruffian let go that rude uncivil Touch

Publish'd according to Act of Parl.t May 1. 1774. by John Bell, Strand.

outdistanced their versions of other Shakespearean comedies that in the legitimate theatre had usually been more successful; it was surpassed only by the number of performances later to be reached by the Bristol Old Vic's *The Two Gentlemen* of 1952. Since this theatrical entertainment used the story of Shakespeare's play merely as a vehicle for music and half an hour of stupendous stage effects, culminating in the appearance of Cleopatra's galley on the occasion of a carnival celebration on the 'Great Square of Milan', it would not be strictly necessary to deal with this production if it did not testify to the continuing influence of John Kemble's version.

Though the libretto is not known except for the words of the additional songs, various pointers from the playbill, from the text and distribution of the songs and from the reviews, make it seem likely that the librettist used Kemble's text. Frederick Reynolds's main task appears to have been to concoct the text of the songs from lines he culled from other Shakespearean plays and poems. Beyond that, he had to cut the text severely to gain time, partly for the music and songs (some of which would have to be encored on demand) and the stage-spectacle, and partly to relieve an audience easily bored by long speeches. The playbill shows that Reynolds used Kemble's Italian names for his Outlaws, though sometimes their spelling is entirely his own. The *Weekly Dispatch* tells us that Act 1 concluded with a duet between Miss Tree (Julia) and a boy singer playing a page.[1] This arrangement suggests that Kemble's act division was followed, where Act 1 ended with Shakespeare's 2.7. The *Examiner* mentions that scenes were transposed from one act to another and that speeches even changed places within the same scene.[2] Both practices also occurred in Kemble's version, though we cannot be absolutely sure that Reynolds's text reproduced all these features exactly. *The Times* observed two other textual peculiarities, namely that the part of Turio had been extended and that an additional scene was devoted to Lance and his dog.[3] These are Victor's inventions, partly preserved and passed on by Kemble. One of the critics warned Miss Hallande (Silvia) not to fall into ranting when among the Outlaws.[4] Undoubtedly, Kemble's version of Shakespeare's 5.2 provides a greater temptation to do this than the original. It is possible that the influence of Kemble's

---

[1] *Weekly Dispatch*, 1821, p. 381.
[2] *Examiner*, 1821, pp. 761–2.
[3] *The Times*, 30 November 1821.
[4] *Theatrical Observer*, 21 January 1821.

---

9 *Two Gentlemen of Verona* Act 5, Scene 4, by Edward Edwards. Edwards was employed by the publisher John Bell for his Shakespeare edition of 1773–4. Bell provided reasonably priced and copiously illustrated texts of Shakespeare and other classics. Although the title claims that the plays are given 'as they are now performed at the Theatres Royal in London, regulated from the Promptbooks of each House', the design shown here relates to a purely pictorial tradition that started with an illustration of the same subject in Rowe's edition of 1709. Edwards introduced some kind of stage-Elizabethan costume into book illustrations of Shakespeare's plays: he clad his figures almost uniformly in round hose and codpiece. The artist must have been so fond of this that, not heeding Julia's expressed rejection, he seems to have furnished even her with this gear. In Victor's adaptation Lucetta's joking suggestion is altogether eliminated

Stothard.

THE TWO GENTLEMEN OF VERONA.

ACT V. SCENE 4.

version on the libretto extends beyond the text to specific points peculiar to Kemble's production. In his prompt-book a handwritten note shows that he employed five singers for the nightly serenade.[1] This unusual precedent was followed by the 1821 production. Bishop's version of the song in praise of Silvia is described as a quintet, with the melody of the first stanza borrowed from Ravenscroft and that of the second stanza from Morley. It is possible that Bishop's eclectic composition originally served Kemble. In any case, the reviews indicate that characters appeared according to Kemble's conception: the gently-enduring Julia, the stronger-minded Silvia, who nevertheless does not impair the spirited image of Valentine as a true lover and bold outlaw, and a Proteus too treacherous to be really redeemable under normal conditions.

Let it be said in passing that the comments of two critics are of particular interest with regard to the topographical veracity of theatrical settings demanded of producers at that time. Though Cruikshank's design of Lance and his dog shows them in front of a town identifiable neither as Verona nor Milan, one critic of the Reynolds–Bishop production remarked that Venice, not Milan, was the place best known for carnival celebrations;[2] another noted that the stage-set, rather than showing the 'Great Square of Milan', presented a view of the Piazza di San Marco complete with the façade of the cathedral, part of the Piazzetta and part of the Ducal Palace.[3] This critic did not remark on the change of place, only on the wrong number of arches on the face of the church. Modern academic critics like to quote reviews averse to turning Shakespeare into spectacle,[4] but it is only fair to add that such critical voices were a small minority in the chorus of acclaim.

When William Charles Macready produced the play in 1841 at Drury Lane, the performance text came closer to the Folio than any of the foregoing productions. There was no attempt to attract visitors by means of lavish spectacle, though Macready seems to have tried to do so (introducing Cleopatra's galley) when he staged the play at Bristol in 1822. The prompt-book, preserved in the Folger Library (Washington, DC), shows that he did to the text almost everything that can be done. He added lines of his own making (though only a few); he transposed speeches from one scene to another and from one speaker to another; he changed the act division and the sequence of scenes, excising 3.3 and 5.1 entirely. The claim to have restored the genuine text rests chiefly on the fact that, by using Shakespeare's 5.4, he reintroduced the offer of the bride. The prompt-book shows how this was played: Valentine is discovered seated on a bank near the opening of

---

[1] Shattuck (ed.), *Kemble Promptbooks*, IX, 45.
[2] *European Magazine*, 17 December 1821, in G. Salgādo, *Eyewitnesses of Shakespeare*, 1975, p. 81.
[3] *The Drama or Theatrical Pocket Magazine*, II (December 1821–May 1822), 81.
[4] See, for instance, Salgādo, *Eyewitnesses of Shakespeare*, pp. 78–85.

---

10 *The recognition of Julia*, by Thomas Stothard. At the end of the eighteenth century, artists' designs began to appear that distinctly emphasised the heroic status of Valentine. Perhaps the most widely published of these is the painting Thomas Stothard provided for Boydell's *Shakespeare Gallery*, 1792. The engraving of it by John Osborne was used in several Shakespeare editions. It shows Valentine in shimmering armour and furnished with a rather unwieldy longsword, which must have been difficult to handle in a forest. See p. 29 above

11 *Valentine rescuing Silvia from Proteus*, also known as *The Two Gentlemen* or *Valentine and Proteus*, 1851, by Holman Hunt. Hunt's well-known painting presents many puzzling problems, but the position, stance and costume of his Valentine clearly document the continuance of the tendency to idealise Shakespeare's quixotic hero. Contrary to his part in the play, Valentine has been singled out by being placed in the middle of the picture, calmly controlling the other figures. His head is raised higher than those of all the others. This fact is further stressed by the arching out of the upper border of the painting, as if the position of the head could not otherwise have been comfortably accommodated on the canvas. In comparison with earlier designs by other artists, the idealising tendency of armour and weaponry is toned down by covering the figure with a long mantle of nearly royal red, which has led one critic to speak of this picture as an icon of kingly forgiveness; for the more observant viewer, Valentine remains clad in steel from neck to toe. The importance of this becomes clearer when we realise that a man with a foot and leg thus armoured would hardly be able to walk freely on the stage, let alone in a forest. The painter has further invested his hero with that piece of real-life stage property that to his contemporaries signified virility: Valentine alone is furnished with a beard – a youthful one, it is true, but complete with whiskers; on the stage such a beard would surely provide the wrong theatrical signal. But the acme of idealisation is reached by the totally unnatural control of emotion shown by all the figures, especially by Valentine. The emotional turmoil of people involved in a case of attempted rape should be totally different from the decorously expressed feelings shown here. The way they are represented may be found useful if we read didactic tendencies into the play as Kemble did, but they fall short of expressing the grotesque compound of horror resolved in hilarity at which the play seems to aim.

Apart from the idealising tendency of the picture, the opposition of the two dominating gestures made by the hero presents a paradox: with his hands he seems to be joining Proteus to the main group, but he has his foot set firmly down to separate him from Silvia. Art historians could explain this paradox by recurring to the genesis of the picture. Sketches indicate that the painter started with an image of separation, as the title still avers. He first intended to produce a version of the pictorial design usually accompanied by the quotation 'Ruffian let go …' but changed the conception by attributing to Valentine's hands and arms not the work of separation but that of tentatively uniting Proteus to himself and Silvia. At the same time he used the slightly changed

his cave. When he has delivered his monologue, he withdraws to the mouth of the cave, from where he watches Proteus importune Silvia. When Proteus seizes Silvia by the waist and swings her round, threatening rape, Valentine orders him to let her go. Upon this Proteus instantly quits her and, drawing his sword, turns against him. When Proteus recognises that it is Valentine who confronts him, he staggers back and drops his sword. Confounded by Valentine's accusation, he goes to him and kneels before him, asking his forgiveness. Valentine, having raised Proteus to his feet and embraced him, takes both Silvia and Proteus by the hand and leads Proteus towards her. As Julia faints, Valentine catches her in his arms. The whole sequence was spoken and acted rapidly. While Proteus is engaged with the newly-revealed Julia, Silvia moves towards Valentine and they go upstage together. Finally Valentine turns to Proteus, takes his hand and joins it to Julia's.

The production was not unfavourably received by the reviewers. *The Times* expressly defended the genuineness of the text against Charles Knight, who in his *Pictorial Shakespeare* had suggested that the lines of the offer should be spoken by Silvia to Valentine, though the reviewer's defence of Shakespeare sounds rather flimsy – namely, that after Valentine's unaccountably quick forgiveness of Proteus another improbability could be admitted without difficulty.[1] As acted in Macready's production, the earlier part of the situation at least was singled out for praise by the same reviewer: 'when Valentine rescues Silvia, and Proteus at the sight of his injured friend starts back in horror – this fixed group was admirably executed by both performers, and caused tumultuous applause'. He also points out that Miss Fortescue presented a rather girlish Julia, but the *Spectator* seems to blame her for playing the embarrassment initially caused by Proteus's letter as having been real rather than merely pretended. Yet he praised her for her display of passion and later of pathos.[2] The reviewer did not realise that the principals of the play should be adolescents nor did the actors seem to have aimed at conveying this impression. Macready, who played Valentine, stressed his nobility of character and the heartiness of his friendship with Proteus – though the final curtain dropped on a tableau showing Valentine paired with Silvia and Proteus with Julia. The *Spectator* criticised the casting of both Valentine and Proteus, Macready having too stern a character for the placable Valentine and Anderson's Proteus

---

[1] *The Times*, 30 December 1841.
[2] *Spectator*, 1842, pp. 9–10.

---

stance of the hero to separate Silvia from Proteus. The result is a more original version, which now includes more of the spirit of the play than any of its predecessors by indicating at least the possibility of future reconciliation. From the beginning, Hunt's intention seems to have been to tone down the angry aggressiveness attributed to the hero by other pictorial artists. In the final form of the design, his Proteus is made to feel less threatened than in the earlier sketches: he no longer draws in his head but, feeling it no longer necessary to guard it, merely bows it in shame. Thus the possibility of reconciliation has been advanced even on Proteus's side. But would Hunt's Valentine be capable of clinching the reacceptance of his former friend by offering him his bride? Neither his right hand, reassuringly reaching down towards the girl who is seeking his protection, nor his separating foot and leg seem to convey any promise of this. Nor would they need to if Hunt had in mind Kemble's rather than Shakespeare's Valentine showing too robust a passion for Julia to make his inconstancy credible. The same review comments favourably on the harmony of the fifteenth-century Italian costumes and the venerable architecture of the settings painted by Tomkins and Marshall. The first set, announced on the playbill as the tombs of the Scaliger family, represented a view of the Piazza dei Signori in Verona with the Romanesque façade of Santa Maria antica. The second set, Julia's garden, showed the Castel Vecchio in the background. There were three sets involving the Duke's palace in Milan (represented by an unidentified building of classical design): a courtyard of the palace, a view from a loggia of the palace on to the gardens, and a palace front with balcony and city gate in the background. The first two prospects involved the Duomo in Milan as an emblem of locality. Care was taken to have the escutcheons of the Sforzas and Viscontis correctly represented.

Macready's production ran for thirteen performances. Furthermore, it was brought to America by Charles Kean with the help of a copy of Macready's prompt-book, which George C. Ellis, an assistant prompter at Drury Lane, had made for the purpose, complete with sketches of the scene designs. It was performed in 1846 at the Park Theatre, New York. When in 1848 Kean brought the production back to the Haymarket Theatre, London, the play got a polite but rather cold reception from the reviewers. The chief attraction seems to have been Ellen Tree (Mrs Charles Kean) as Julia, who in the same season also appeared as Viola. The review in *The Times* shows that she still relied, at least partly, on the stage business that Macready had devised for Miss Fortescue.[1] Besides her Julia, only Rob Keeley's Lance found whole-hearted approval. Kean did not include the play in the series of his more famous Shakespeare revivals at the Princess's Theatre.

In 1849 the Olympic Theatre chose *The Two Gentlemen* for its opening production. Henry Compton, Macready's Turio, now had the opportunity to appear as Lance. The play was followed by the pantomime *Laugh and Grow Fat*, which the reviewer for *The Times* considered to be the main piece.[2] The *Examiner* noted that the audience, in consideration of what was to follow, sat through the performance of the comedy 'with a rare patience',[3] though all the critics concurred in lauding the management for selecting this play as a showpiece of good taste. The addition to the play's title – 'from the text of Shakespeare' – may suggest that the text had been cut considerably.

Samuel Phelps, who had played the Duke in Macready's production, himself staged the play at Sadler's Wells in 1857. Little is known about his production, though Theodor Fontane, who saw it, wondered why it had not been performed in Berlin. He was so pleased that he intended to recommend its staging there. Unfortunately, he did not give details in his report because he did not expect his German readers to be able to compare them with their own theatrical experience. The lack of a fuller knowledge of Phelps's production is all the more to be

---

[1] *The Times*, 15 December 1848.
[2] *Ibid.*, 27 December 1849.
[3] *Examiner*, 29 December 1849.

regretted because of a sentence in the introductory remarks on the play in the 1858 edition that went under his name: 'The ridiculous is not only a step from the sublime, but is often blended with it, and the distinct currents of the humorous and the heroic are apt to flow together from the same lips.'[1] But whether his production dared to go the whole way with the insight expressed here must remain doubtful because of a note on Valentine's offer of his bride. It rejects, it is true, Knight's treatment of the text, but it also states: 'We rather incline to the belief that this surrender, which has been described as "an overstrained and too generous act of friendship", may have been intended by Valentine merely as a test of the sudden penitence of Proteus.'[2]

In the first half of the twentieth century, various efforts were made to keep the play before the public, as for instance Harley Granville-Barker's Court Theatre production in 1904, about which much less is known than about his later and more famous stagings of Shakespearean comedies at the Savoy Theatre. William Poel's various experiments with the play culminated in the production Sir Herbert Beerbohm Tree invited him to put on at His Majesty's Theatre in 1910. The Old Vic had its first go at the play in 1916–17 and revived it in 1923 in Robert Atkins's production. But, indubitably, the theatrical activities at Stratford-upon-Avon did most to keep the discussion about this play going, though obviously with only limited success.

For the Stratford Festival season of 1910, F.R. Benson chose to present *The Two Gentlemen* as the so-called 'revival-play', although Osmond Tearle had shown it in 1890, while other plays (*All's Well*, *Troilus and Cressida*, *Titus Andronicus*) still waited to have their first staging there. The reviewer of the *Birmingham Gazette and Express* remarks on the cutting and adaptation that were necessary.[3] In particular, Lance seems to have been made more respectable by not allowing him the scatological and bawdy elements in his humour. On the other hand, we can be sure that the offer of the bride was left to stand. The reviewer of *The Stage* avers: 'The best scene was that in which, in the excess of his rapture for the repentance of Proteus, Valentine gives up to him all his right to Sylvia.' He then continues: 'Miss Norah Lancaster's impersonation of Sylvia was exceedingly natural; it revealed a woman of much charm and tenderness.'[4] The conjunction of these two statements leaves us to wonder just what the actress did to show how her natural charm and tenderness helped her to cope with this difficult situation. Shakespeare's Silvia is not at all a passive woman. But the nineteenth-century ideal of passive womanhood, which persisted well into the twentieth century, corresponds to the idealisation of Valentine and falsifies the Shakespearean balance. All the reviewers failed to realise that the principal characters were adolescents, which, in view of the fact that Julia was played by Constance Benson,

---

[1] *Complete Works of Shakespeare*, revised, with introductory remarks, and copious notes by Samuel Phelps, Esq., 1858, p. 34.
[2] *Ibid.*, p. 62.
[3] *Birmingham Gazette and Express*, 25 April 1910.
[4] *The Stage*, 28 April 1910.

then aged fifty, may have been difficult to imagine. At the Stratford Festival season in the summer of 1916, Ben Greet and the Royal Victoria Repertory Company gave three performances of *The Two Gentlemen* with Sybil Thorndike as Julia. This was probably based on an unabridged text and seems to have been the production later shown at the Old Vic in London.

When William Bridges-Adams produced the play in 1925 for the Stratford-upon-Avon Festival Company, he too seems to have used an unabridged text. From reviewers who remarked on Valentine's 'hearty laugh and buoyant manner' and Lucetta's 'infectious laughter, [which] set the audience tittering',[1] we can at least infer that an impression of the characters' youthfulness was projected. Production details are scarce, but one critic notes that Crab appeared costumed: Randle Ayrton (Lance) had put his Pomeranian into a keep-me-warm.[2] The invention not only underlines the owner's care for his 'friend' but also his attribution of human qualities to him. But the most important detail is only recorded in Gordon Crosse's private notebook, which reveals how Valentine's surrender of Silvia was played: 'At this point Silvia buried her face in her hands and did not come to the surface again until Valentine calmly resumed possession of her some thirty lines later.'[3] Although this difficult event can be performed in a number of ways, Crosse approved of this version: 'As she [Silvia] has nothing to say at either point this was about the best thing she could do.' The impact of Bridges-Adams's production can be gauged from the fact that most reviewers praised it, and a few even said they were surprised that the play should be so seldom performed; one predicted: 'it is safe to say that the comedy has come back to stay'.[4] But there were also voices of dissent, most violently that of A.K.C. of the *Stratford-upon-Avon Herald*, who found it necessary to blast the moderately favourable appreciation which had appeared earlier in the same paper.[5] Obviously embarrassed by the play's eroticism ('immature flounderings' 'of aphrodisian birth') and the bad form shown by both the male leads, he thought it highly undesirable that the play should be shown to the foreigners who found their way to the Memorial Theatre.

Iden Payne's Stratford production in 1938 did not convince reviewers that the play was important enough to deserve performance. But its well-documented settings, which look forward to the heavy reliance on pictorial effects in Peter Hall's staging at the same place in 1960 and to the Old Vic production in 1957, give it a place in the stage history of this comedy. Its simple, dominating design, which made the action seem remote from reality, relates it also to the masque-like setting used at the Bristol Old Vic in 1952 and to the 'theatre-within-the-theatre' device of John Barton's production in 1981. In 1938 the stage was walled off by a

[1] *Stratford-upon-Avon-Herald*, 17 April 1925.
[2] *Birmingham Mail*, 16 April 1925.
[3] Gordon Crosse's manuscript notebook on Shakespeare performances he had seen, preserved in the Birmingham Reference Library, p. 49.
[4] *Stratford-upon-Avon Herald*, 17 April 1925.
[5] *Ibid.*, 28 August 1925.

screen showing a harmonious classical façade reminiscent of the Venetian window in Palladian architecture; its openings could be fitted with various backdrops, revealing street perspectives, gardens, palatial interiors, and so forth. Only the forest setting for Act 5 was relieved of the heavily harmonising effect of this classical screen. Actors, costumed in dresses cut according to fashions which appear in Giotto's murals, but more highly coloured, enacted before the screen a tale of the sort that can be found in children's picture-books. Within the colourful and harmonising framework, everyone seemed rather nice. Reviewers saw in Valentine a real gentleman, and Proteus was played in such a way 'that one never had to think too seriously about his villainy';[1] he 'skims gracefully over the treachery, and tactfully gives an air of dalliance to deception'; in his betrayal of Julia he seemed charming enough 'to popularise philandering'.[2] When he threatened to rape Silvia, Valentine managed to get between them well ahead of real danger. The prompt-book reveals that even the Outlaws were nice enough not to blab out that Eglamour had taken to his heels. Lance, played by Jay Laurier, a variety comedian, brought to Stratford his technique of audience address which was still unusual enough there to make him seem to pop out like a cardboard figure from a two-dimensional surface. But he was not allowed to state in plain English for what offence Crab was thought to deserve whipping, which left the audience with the impression that it was merely for pushing his presence into the company of more gentlemanlike dogs. The most important reflection of this production is found in the private notebook of Gordon Crosse, although he exaggerates the amount of cutting applied to the performance text, which concerned puns and comic syllogisms, coarse expressions, and references to articles of dress unknown to Giotto like doublets, jerkins, farthingales and codpieces. But he was right in saying, though no other reviewer found it necessary to remark upon it, that 'one omission was about the most notable thing in the performance. They cut the knot of Valentine's surrender of Silvia by the simple expedient of leaving out the lines in which he makes it. This left no particular reason for Julia's swoon, unless . . . it is merely a trick to call attention to herself. But apart from this the scene ran with perfect smoothness and no one who did not know the story would have guessed that anything had been left out.'[3] In view of this flattened-out production, one could wish that Shakespeare had made the subversive elements of the play less easily eradicable.

Denis Carey's light-hearted production, first shown at the Bristol Old Vic in 1952, was a milestone in the stage history of *The Two Gentlemen* for two reasons: firstly, because the play, known in theatrical slang as 'The Walking Gentlemen', proved to be an unexpected financial success there, as it was later when it was transferred to the London Old Vic – and, secondly, because it won the whole-hearted acclaim of the critics. The production made the play known nation-wide, at least in the papers. Reviewers, who had too often filled the newspaper space

[1] *Birmingham Mail*, 20 April 1938.
[2] *Birmingham Post*, 20 April 1938.
[3] Notebook, pp. 15–19.

allotted to them with facetious remarks about the 'actor' who had taken on the role of Crab, now started to talk about the actual production; and at least some of them confessed that they wanted to read the text. The degree of success can also be gauged from the fact that since then reviewers have been less often inclined to belittle the play.

The fame this production achieved seems in many respects to have been well earned and, what is more, well earned by the whole ensemble. The producer did not treat it simply as a straight play; instead he enlisted all the arts of the theatre to provide a lively spectacle involving song, mime and dance, as well as incidental music, all of which interpreted and connected an excellently acted series of scenes, played continuously on a permanent set. The number of songs attributed to professional singers and singing actors amounted almost to the number of musical additions to be found in the operatic version by Reynolds and Bishop which stage historians have so often treated derisively. But here they were added with a lighter touch, and the style of the music strengthened the impression of the Elizabethan roots of the theatrical experience.

Turning to the actors and their acting, one must mention the success with which they managed to create the impression of being adolescents. This has always been a crucial problem which former productions so often failed to solve or even to recognise. The solution cannot be found in costuming: the difference between teenage fashions and fully adult dress is only a very recent invention, and stage Elizabethan costuming lacks the idiom to express it. Directors who later tried to solve the problem by casting found critics complaining that the actors lacked sufficient professional experience to execute their tasks adequately. The principal actors of the 1952 production were young men and women, but none of them was still adolescent or looked so in stage pictures; yet it seems that they played their roles convincingly, for one critic called the spectacle 'all carols and capers'.[1] There must have been numerous little inventions in the staging to project this quality of adolescence. A handwritten stage direction in the prompt-book says that 'VAL plays "ringel-ringel-roses" with PRO' after their reconciliation. This emphasis on adolescence is Shakespearean and serves to exonerate – at least to some extent – the faults in the behaviour of both heroes.

But, in aiming to present a celebration of youthful love, the production went too far in depriving the play of its problematic nature. The most notable sign of this, of course, is the omission of Valentine's offer of his bride. In this respect, Gordon Crosse's reaction is interesting.[2] An inveterate viewer of Shakespeare's plays, he was full of admiration for this particular production, which he found praiseworthy all round, but especially for the balance it struck between the comic and romantic parts of the play – something he had never seen before. Crosse was so enchanted by the performance that the omission of Valentine's offer, which he had criticised in other productions, seemed to him acceptable now as the only possible way

[1] *Observer*, 24 February 1952.
[2] Notebook, p. 93.

towards a modern staging of the play, in spite of his conviction that it clearly ran against the author's intentions. Not having to account for the problematical action implied in the lines omitted, it became easier to present Valentine as a sort of born winner. Indeed, reviewers praised the actor for his manliness and aristocratic airs in conducting his love-affair. A most telling element in the portrayal of Valentine's character was offered by the specially arranged fights which allowed him to demonstrate his superior swordsmanship when encountering the Outlaws and later saving Silvia from being violated. In these features, elements of Kemble's staging of the play and of his conception of Valentine's character seem to shine through. But Carey's production differed sharply from Kemble's in not choosing to deepen Proteus's faults into downright villainy; these were instead treated as lightly as possible. Indicative of this tendency is the bit of mime that introduced his second monologue in 2.6: playing a game of blind-man's-buff with some courtly ladies, Proteus, during the decisive monologue, held in his hands his blindfold, which was naughtily made to resemble a piece of women's underwear. Chasing girls in an almost childlike fashion exonerated the villain, who seemed to grow aware of the seriousness of his betrayal of Julia only in the course of his monologue in 2.6. The situation was further conditioned by cuts in the monologue ending 2.4, where all references to Valentine were deleted. Proteus's recognition that his betrayal of Julia also involved the breaking of his friendship with Valentine was even further delayed than Shakespeare intended. Another mimed scene was interposed between Shakespeare's 5.1 and 5.2. When Silvia has eloped, her maid Ursula is left behind to enjoy the amorous attentions Turio now directs to her. Shakespeare's Turio is not necessarily an amorous turncoat; but, since the mimed incident introduces a dialogue that reveals his insatiable and injudicious desire to be appreciated, it may not be entirely amiss. It also serves to lighten the atmosphere at this court, creating a background of amorous activities against which Proteus's lack of constancy does not stand out glaringly. Proteus's character was thus tilted towards adolescent irresponsibility and youthful excess rather than villainy, making it much easier to accept his inclusion in an entirely happy ending.

It is pleasant to think that it was the great success of the Bristol Old Vic production which caused the London parent company to invest so much care, ingenuity and taste in its own version of the play in 1957. The wonderful elegance of its décor can perhaps be best illustrated by noting that a golden Labrador was brought in to play Lance's cur. The charms of Regency and Empire fashions provided a feast for the eyes and served to support the exhibition of excessive emotions, which was satirised here and even subjected to a broadly burlesque treatment. The play's tricky balance between laughing with the characters and laughing at their actions, which had tipped towards sympathy in the 1952 production, now moved towards the derisive. The Shakespearean emphasis on adolescence was submerged in the emotionalism of the Romantic period. This showed up most clearly in the treatment of the always difficult figure of Sir Eglamour, Shakespeare's emblem of high idealism and the limitations set by reality. Contrary to conventional interpretation and practice, he was promoted from 'agent in

12 Act 4, Scene 3, with John Morris as Eglamour and Ingrid Hafner as Silvia at the Old Vic, 1957. It was characteristic of this production that Eglamour appeared as one of Silvia's suitors. See pp. 41–3

Silvia's escape' to 'suitor to Julia and to Silvia', which was, of course, only possible by cancelling Silvia's lines about his unswerving devotion to his lost lady. When called to Silvia, Eglamour appeared as an old gentleman offering a posy with the intention of furthering his own suit to her. Silvia then heartlessly misused the old fool's devotion in order to be safely conducted to her other lover. Proteus, costumed and made up to remind the audience of Byron, opposed a Shelleyan Valentine. But when it came to betraying his rival's elopement, he was not only intoxicated by his infatuation with Silvia but also by alcoholic drink. The play's difficult dénouement was to provide the climax for satiric laughter, a climax that was not reached when Valentine offered to renounce his bride but when Proteus formulated his newly-won insight that man would be perfect if only he were constant. Though Valentine's offer may have been only a temporary measure specifically motivated by Proteus's threat to shoot himself, Silvia fell into a swoon on hearing it, making all further reactions from her unnecessary. Fainting and pistol point also proved useful for the completion of the happy ending: Sebastian swooned to be recognised as Julia, and the Duke was induced to yield his daughter to Valentine and to pardon the Outlaws under the threat of being shot. As to the question whether the production worked well or not, there were divided opinions, especially between the *Shakespeare Survey*[1] and *Shakespeare Quarterly*.[2]

Peter Hall's Stratford production of 1960 was even less of a success, in spite of the fact that Diana Rigg played one of the Outlaws for him. His intention of representing the play as the first effort in a series of comedies gradually becoming more mature paralleled theatrically a time-honoured exercise among scholars and critics. Such a method misleads by tending to obscure the feature which marks this play as radically different from the so-called happy comedies: its emphasis on the satirical criticism directed at the limited concepts under which the characters of the comedy labour. Trying to reconstruct the production from all the accessible sources, the stage historian is immediately struck by the fact that this must have been an extremely ambitious endeavour to vie with the pictorial effects of the London Old Vic and to surpass the Bristol Old Vic in its reliance on additional songs, incidental music, mime and dance. To the technical resources of the theatre were added a turntable and a newly-constructed apron stage. Not only was the original list of *dramatis personae* filled with additional dancers, musicians and singers, but there was also provision for giving Valentine's father an onstage appearance, for a blind beggar led by a child to roam the streets of Verona and for the town guards to open and close the gates for everyone who left there. There were additional figures for a procession and a tableau, and even the Host was given a female companion. There were undeniable deficiencies in the costuming and the casting of the play. It is always regrettable when critics largely agree that the four central parts were the least well-acted ones, especially when the parts of Speed and Turio are singled out for praise. Moreover, the director's experiments with the

---

[1] Richard David, 'Actors and scholars: a view of Shakespeare in the modern theatre', *S.Sur.* 12 (1959), 85–6.
[2] Muriel St Clare Byrne, 'The Shakespeare season at the Old Vic, 1956–57', *SQ* 8 (1957), 469–71.

speaking of Shakespearean verse misfired. His intention of stressing the suffering in Shakespearean comedy either did not get across or was misunderstood. Reviewers, who wistfully recollected the spring freshness of the Bristol Old Vic production, complained about the impression of autumn sadness they felt to exude from the colours of the stage-set and its emblematic indications of architectural objects, which appeared to them as sad romantic ruins. Suffering is indeed among the essential ingredients of the play; at one time or other, almost everyone concerned experiences it, even Proteus, but most of all Julia. But was it necessary to highlight her suffering by literally overburdening her with an oversized portrait of Silvia, awkwardly moved back and forth between the ladies and obstinately resistant to all her efforts to break it?

The production was based on a practically uncut text. The lines in which Valentine offers Proteus his bride were this time spoken on stage. But since almost all the reviewers failed to comment on them, it is impossible to reconstruct how the lines were spoken, what they conveyed and how they were received. The one critic who did note them says: 'Valentine's embarrassing, impossible, generous "All that was mine in Silvia" was spoken so that it was hardly noticed.'[1] On the whole, the ending seems to have been too broadly burlesque: 'the director also missed the romantic climax of the play. The last scene was dominated by laughter – at Silvia's "Oooh!" as Proteus unblindfolded her (an interpolated incident), at the trotting Julia's comic faint, and at Proteus' high-pitched "were man/But constant, he were perfect".'[2] Even the threatened rape of Silvia seems to have been treated as a broad joke and Proteus's repentance as a sentiment to laugh at. A proper balance between the positively and the ludicrously romantic elements was not found.

Ten years later the RSC made a radically new departure in the staging of *The Two Gentlemen* – radically, that is, if we discount an earlier modern-dress version shown in 1930 at the People's Theatre, Newcastle. Since the 1920s and early 1930s, the public has become used to this device, but it remains difficult to see what this play in particular can gain by being laid out as a contemporary event. It is far easier to grasp what it has to lose: the peculiar connection between love-code and caste on the one hand and the idea of heroic friendship on the other, which in Shakespeare's play present additional obstacles to growing up smoothly. Robin Phillips's production put a heavy emphasis on adolescence, perhaps more successfully than ever before. But it was not looked upon with good-humoured and amused tolerance, as it had been in the case of the Bristol Old Vic production, but rather with a sort of head-shaking disgust, only faintly relieved by the conviction of its almost necessary awfulness.

One of the possible ways of showing up this difference is to study the figure of Lance, the embodiment of much of Shakespeare's own criticism. The Bristol Lance was still young and genial, turning his own perplexities and those of others into humour; in this production Lance was an ever-present touchstone of stern

[1] John Russell Brown, 'Three directors: a review of recent productions', *S.Sur.* 14 (1961), 132.
[2] *Ibid.*

13   Patrick Stewart as Lance in the Royal Shakespeare Company production, 1970. See pp. 44–5

reality, more a menacing than a tolerant judge of his betters. Shakespeare's play satirises ruling ideas by depicting behaviour which tries to conform to them, but it touches problems of psychological veracity only very lightly; a modern-dress production will necessarily try to clarify the psychological implications or even supply a psychological aspect missing in the drama. Since the producer saw adolescence essentially as a young person's search for his own identity, he could dismantle the song praising Silvia as one of the wonders of the world and flatten out its opening question: 'Who is Silvia?' by extending it to ask: 'Who is Proteus, who is Valentine?' A version of this extended song was sung both at the beginning and the end of the performance. It is true that, for instance, Shakespeare's Valentine has a hard time understanding himself and his own relations to others. His spectacular offer of his bride can be taken to indicate that, at this particular moment, he does not understand his relationship to either Proteus or Silvia. But Shakespeare seems to be content to let his characters find and define themselves by their final pairings.

This production added a modern complication to the problem of self-definition: the choice of mate was additionally made dependent on the sexual preferences of these young people. (This problem played no role in Boccaccio's 'Titus and Gisippus' story and was quite unlikely to have been foreseen by Sir Thomas Elyot

14   Peter Egan as Valentine and Ian Richardson as Proteus in the Royal Shakespeare Company
production, 1970. The actors are costumed as they appeared in Act 1, Scene 1. See pp. 46–7.

when he retold the tale.) The burden of motivation was shifted from Valentine's enigmatic behaviour to an explanation of Proteus's aberrations. Those readers who see evil-doing out of sheer motiveless malignity even in the later Shakespeare will find this change quite unnecessary. But this is how it was played out: the conventionally heroic image of Valentine was brought up to date by relating it to the dubious peer-prestige created by the excessive appreciation of athletic talent in some undergraduate societies. The bouncing of balls and the wearing of beachwear were made to demonstrate Valentine's superior prowess and physique, which the less gifted Proteus was made to admire in spite of the signs of mindlessness that are sometimes found to accompany these advantages and that Valentine shows by deriding his companion's crush on the teenage Julia and by bouncing his ball on the head of his mate before taking off to Milan (illustration 14). Proteus's inclination to admire a male body better developed than his own was brought out again in his meeting with Turio, who was played as a well-oiled and well-bronzed Italian beach-lizard ready to offer *amore*. The picture was completed by Proteus's annoyed rejection of the kiss Julia offered on the occasion of their leave-taking. His interest in Silvia did not draw upon the convention of love at first sight but seemed to begin when he was slighted by Valentine, who belittled his friend's love by extolling his own. The plan to get Valentine banished and pinch his girl was made to appear as a psychological obsession on Proteus's part – the result of his need to be revenged on his friend and free himself of his own deep sense of inferiority. Some reviewers felt that it was to achieve this end that Proteus deliberately tried to put himself in the shoes of his friend and rival. His madness reached a dramatic climax in a graphically staged attempt to rape Silvia. But finding himself caught by his friend, he felt utterly defeated and despondent. Valentine's handling of him was calmly superior: he appeared to offer his bride as a cure for Proteus's madness. The offer was not to be understood in the traditional way. The prompt-book reveals that Valentine kissed Silvia before speaking his two momentous lines and afterwards kissed Proteus. Valentine's offer seems to have been understood as a declaration of equality and of his acceptance of Proteus on equal terms, as balm to his deeply-felt inadequacy. If there is a psychological theory that allows the action to be read in this light and that allows Valentine to appear as a master psychologist who instinctively provides remedies for his friend's inferiority complex and unclarified sexual preferences, the producer did not trust it all the way. He chose to doubt the convincingness of the conventional sign of a happy ending by reintroducing at the end the song that questions the identity of the leading characters. In the dark and grey world of this production, idealism could only be understood as foolishness. Sir Eglamour appeared as a super-annuated bare-kneed boy scout, over-officious but ridiculously ineffective in his intent to help Silvia. But, if the four principals and their scoutmaster refused to become mature, can we really blame them when the world they would grow up to is as unattractive as the one depicted here? Proteus's father was played so unsympathetically that at least some of Proteus's psychological problems could be traced back to an emotionally deprived home. Julia could carry her problems only to a gin-sodden cynical Lucetta, who seemed to have been deeply disappointed by life. And who would respect a Vice-Chancellor/Duke who was bent on forcing his daughter to marry a narcissistic *pappagallo* rather than one of the mainstays of his baseball team?

Even less successful productions may help to clarify our conception of a play. In 1981 John Barton presented a heavily-cut version of *The Two Gentlemen* in a double bill together with *Titus Andronicus* at Stratford-upon-Avon. These two disparate Shakespearean products were held together by both being played as fit-up productions by the same group of strolling players. But the advantages offered by this unusual dramatic fiction were not sufficiently realised. Emphasising everything modern audiences and critics have ever found difficult to accept in *The*

Two Gentlemen could have served to stress the very Elizabethanness of the comedy; on the contrary, the 'Elizabethan' actors were made to present an astonishingly modern and commonsensical reading of the story. The heroes, instead of presenting two kinds of abomination, the one by breaking all codes of honour, the other by blindly striving to fulfil whatever such codes seem to demand, were turned into images of the usual kind of adolescent who cuts loose from male companions when he falls in love for the first time, quickly changes his attachment when encountering a more attractive woman (the Julia of this production never appeared more pathetic than when comparing her advantages to Silvia's) and pursues his aims in ruthless rivalry with his former companion. The sane message this production thought to convey – that is, that male friendships should be preserved beyond marital attachments – takes the satirical bite out of Shakespeare's play. The delivery of the two lines in which Valentine offers his bride to Proteus marks the crucial point. Although the text of the play had to be extensively cut, these lines were not omitted and laudably so. But it is impossible to reconstruct what their function was meant to be in this production. One reviewer notes: 'in the final scene the genuineness of his [Valentine's] concern for both Silvia and Proteus carries us surprisingly well through this notoriously difficult dénouement'.[1] The oft-questioned phrase was robbed of its impact by 'deliberately running it over with action'. It seems that the actors had first tried to let not only Julia but also Silvia swoon on hearing the offer, which would be quite understandable after the realistically staged violent attack upon her by Proteus. But, according to the prompt-book, Silvia was comforted after the assault by a draught of some strong potion from Valentine's hip-flask. Thus fortified, she was able to speak a half-line of text newly given to her, by which she quickly deflected attention from Valentine's words. Near the end Silvia went off in the company of her father, leaving Valentine alone for his last lines with Proteus. The commentary in the programme did not clarify the situation; it suggested that the offer was perhaps only intended to test Proteus's reaction. But as he was not allowed to convey his reaction effectively to the audience, the difference between cutting the lines and having them played in this way is negligible. Otherwise, the cutting of the text necessary for the double bill worked marvellously well in preserving the story line. No scene was cancelled entirely, and their traditional sequence was preserved. One may wonder that so much of the play survived when more than a quarter of the original text was stripped away. And yet it may be felt that the abbreviations made an essential contribution to the strange modernisation of the play. Given very elaborate and highly artificial codes of love, the process of fitting an adolescent's natural instincts to them inevitably involves a certain excess in wordiness, gesturing and even attitudinising. Anyone who sees this situation as Shakespeare's occasion for mirth will regret that passages relevant here were cut short. They should have been made to stand out by cutting elsewhere, especially for an audience not subject to such codes and only faintly aware of them.

[1] Stanley Wells, 'Elizabethan doublets', *Times Literary Supplement*, 18 September 1981.

Modernising the story is indubitably one way of making the play more acceptable to a contemporary audience, but it remains to be asked if today's spectator would not be more deeply touched and more reflective when confronted with these matters in their specific Elizabethan form. The moulding of human behaviour by foreign codes of conduct and their possibly disastrous consequences could have proved a valuable thematic link in a performance that yoked this comedy to *Titus Andronicus*.

NOTE ON THE TEXT

The Two Gentlemen of Verona was first published in the First Folio (F) as the second play among the comedies; there is no other authoritative text. For a discussion of the possible copy-text for F see the Textual Analysis, pp. 147–52 below. It is a relatively clean text, which requires few substantive or semi-substantive emendations. These, including variants of lineation, are recorded in the collation; significant alterations are also discussed in the Commentary, with an asterisk before the lemma calling attention to a word or phrase that has been emended. In the collation the authority for this edition's reading comes immediately after the square bracket, followed by the reading in F; alternative readings, if any, follow in chronological order. Emendations not adopted by this edition are recorded if they are likely to give information on the transmission and interpretation of the text. The form *This edn* is used for emendations without precedent. For a full list of abbreviations used and editions cited, see pp. x–xii above.

Spelling has been modernised in this edition, and punctuation has been kept as light as possible. Alterations to spelling and punctuation have only been recorded if they affect the meaning. Contractions ('tis, lov'st, and so on) have been retained, but elided *-ed* endings (betray'd, deserv'd) are silently expanded. Where the metre requires a syllable to be pronounced, it is marked with a grave accent (vanquishèd).

Act and scene divisions correspond with those in F. Locations are presented and discussed in the Commentary. Additional entrances and exits not found in F are supplied, inserted in square brackets, as are the descriptive stage directions, which are entirely missing in F.

The Two Gentlemen of Verona

LIST OF CHARACTERS

DUKE *of Milan, 'father to Silvia'*
VALENTINE, }
PROTEUS,　　} *'the two gentlemen' of Verona*
ANTONIO, *'father to Proteus'*
TURIO, *'a foolish' suitor to Silvia, favoured by her father*
EGLAMOUR, *a Milanese courtier, who assists 'Silvia in her escape'*
SPEED, *page 'to Valentine'*
LANCE, *servant 'to Proteus', with his dog Crab*
PANTINO, *'servant to Antonio'*
HOST *of the inn in Milan 'where Julia lodges'*
OUTLAWS, *who elect Valentine to be their captain*
JULIA, *a lady of Verona, 'beloved of Proteus'*
SILVIA, *the Duke's daughter, 'beloved of Valentine'*
LUCETTA, *'waiting-woman to Julia'*
SERVANTS
MUSICIANS

Notes

A list of 'The names of all the Actors' appears at the end of the F text, though its authority is highly doubtful (see p. 150 below). It has been rearranged and completed. Those parts of the character-descriptions which have been taken from F are in single quotation marks. They have been amplified following the practice of other editors.

Shakespeare experimented in this play as in other comedies with telling names (see Francis Griffin Stokes, *A Dictionary of Characters and Proper Names in the Works of Shakespeare*, 1960). Lance, for instance, introduces his dog Crab by name to his audience and immediately explains its appropriateness (2.3.4), and Julia and Lucetta present a review of suitors who are characterised by their names (1.2.7–19). Therefore it is most likely that hints at personal qualities or the functions of characters or a combination of both are intended by all the names in the cast.

DUKE For the alternative naming of the ruler as 'emperor' in this play, see 1.3.27 n. In Shakespeare's early comedies, with the exception of *LLL*, the territorial ruler ranks as 'duke'. A higher-ranking ruler seems to be more typical of the problem comedies and the romances. Most often these rulers are given personal names, but there are exceptions in the Shakespearean canon like the Duke of Venice in *MV* and Duke Senior in *AYLI*.

VALENTINE The name suggests the ideal lover, as is pointed out by Lance in 3.1.191–2, Valentine being the patron saint of lovers.

PROTEUS Named after a god in Greek mythology known for his ability to change shapes; widely used in English literature as a symbol of unreliability and deceit. (Compare for example 'Change shapes with Proteus for advantages' (*3H6* 3.2.192).) In view of the sheer ubiquity of the unfavourable associations of this name, the trust other figures of this comedy put in Proteus seems highly ironic.

TURIO This figure functions as the typical rival. Though only slightly characterised, he professes a taste for fashion and military prowess. The type returns later as Osric in *Ham*.

and as Aguecheek in *TN*, but there are also affinities with Tybalt in *Rom.* and others. This character may have been influenced by the 'capitano' of the *commedia dell'arte*, a typical and always defeated rival of young lovers. If that were the case, the name may have derived from the Latin *centurio*. Other suggested derivations – 'Curio' from Lyly's *Euphues* and 'Thyreus' from North's Plutarch – seem less convincing. The 'h' of F's 'Thurio' has been dropped in accordance with modern editors' handling of the name Proteus (F Protheus).

EGLAMOUR Besides this speaking character, there is a man of the same name mentioned in the review of suitors (1.2.9). Such doubling of names is not unusual (see Murray J. Levit, *What's in Shakespeare's Names*, 1978, p. 24). The name first appeared in the medieval romance *Sir Eglamour of Artois*, and Spenser in *The Faerie Queene* used it as a model for coining the names 'Blandamour' and 'Scudamour'. 'Eglamour' suggests either a person who is always in love or who is always constant in love. The former sense seems uppermost in the character named in 1.2, who can be understood as the knightly lover of medieval romance with a somewhat ridiculous air of unreality. The latter sense is uppermost in the gentleman chosen by Sylvia to escort her in her escape. His particular qualification for this task is expressed at 4.3.18–21.

SPEED Though he has a quick wit and tongue, there is also a pointedly ironic use of the name at 1.1.72–3 and 3.1.355–6. As page (1.2.38) he should be considerably younger than Lance. The latter is only once called a 'boy' by Proteus, probably in his capacity as servant. Speed, however, is not only frequently called 'boy' by his master Valentine but also by Lance (3.1.361). The seeming contradiction between Speed's age and his versatility in matters of love is an inheritance from the pages in Lyly's comedies.

LANCE Probably a short form of 'Lancelot', which Levit explains as meaning 'servant' from Old French *l'ancelot*, 'attendant or adherent' (*What's in Shakespeare's Names*, p. 80). 'Launcelot' and 'Lancelot', 'launce' and 'lance' were variant spellings. F's 'Launce' has been modernised accordingly.

PANTINO Though the character appears in the list appended to the F text and in two of the stage directions as 'Panthion', he is twice called 'Panthino' in the text (if we regard 'Panthmo' as a misreading) and also in one of the stage directions. Bond suggests a derivation from 'Pandion' in Lyly's *Sapho and Phao*, but it may be only the scribe Ralph Crane's subconscious awareness of this character that produced the variation 'Panthion' in his transcript. The name may have been developed from the word 'pantler', meaning a sort of butler, with the addition of an Italian diminutive. The dropping of the 'h' follows the principle adopted for Proteus and Turio.

JULIA Editors have thought that the name was suggested by that of Juliet in Arthur Brooke's poem *Romeus and Juliet* (see 2.4.185–8 n. below), but the reference to the hottest month of the year appropriately indicates her occasionally passionate temper.

SILVIA With its reference to woodland, the name points towards the pastoral setting of the resolution of the play.

LUCETTA Diminutive of Lucy.

THE TWO GENTLEMEN OF VERONA

1.1 *Enter* VALENTINE *and* PROTEUS

VALENTINE Cease to persuade, my loving Proteus;
Home-keeping youth have ever homely wits.
Were't not affection chains thy tender days
To the sweet glances of thy honoured love,
I rather would entreat thy company   5
To see the wonders of the world abroad
Than, living dully sluggardised at home,
Wear out thy youth with shapeless idleness.
But since thou lov'st, love still and thrive therein,
Even as I would when I to love begin.   10
PROTEUS Wilt thou be gone? Sweet Valentine, adieu.
Think on thy Proteus when thou happ'ly seest
Some rare noteworthy object in thy travel.
Wish me partaker in thy happiness

Act 1, Scene 1   1.1] *Actus primus, Scena prima.* F   0 SD] *Rowe; Valentine: Protheus,* and *Speed.* F   12 happ'ly] *Riverside;* hap'ly F   13 travel] F4; trauaile F

Act 1, Scene 1

Location Locations will possibly be of interest to readers trying to follow the fictional narrative, but they were not visually presented in the Elizabethan theatre, which had no system of movable scenery; it did, though, use large stage properties, such as furniture, arbours and mossy banks, as isolated formal emblems to represent place.

The geographical location 'Verona' for this and some of the following scenes can only be deduced from the title of the play. The text itself does not indicate whether this is an indoor or an outdoor scene. The traditional street setting is derived from Roman, Italian and Italianate comedies. Modern productions usually convey the idea that Valentine is preparing for embarkation by having luggage transported to the exit he is later to take. Whether Elizabethan actors availed themselves of this possibility is not known.

1–54 The witty dissent between Valentine and Proteus concerning the opposition of love and reason and the educative value of travel differs significantly from the harmonious agreement between Titus and Gisippus and even Euphues and Philautus at the beginning of their stories (see pp. 11–13 above).

1 loving This adjective used to address a person may simply be conventionally polite, but there is possibly a reference to Proteus's love for Julia. See also 'sweet' at 11.

1 Proteus Here trisyllabic, but often disyllabic in the play.

3 tender young.

8 shapeless purposeless.

9 still constantly.

10 This line is hardly in keeping with character and situation; it functions as exposition.

11 Sweet For the range of applicability of this adjective in forms of address compare 1.2.123; 2.4.33, 100, 103; 2.5.2; 3.2.89; 5.2.46.

12 happ'ly with pleasure. The possible meaning 'perchance' would be spelt 'haply', but this is excluded here as the express purpose of the journey is to 'see the wonders of the world' (6).

When thou dost meet good hap; and in thy danger,   15
If ever danger do environ thee,
Commend thy grievance to my holy prayers,
For I will be thy beadsman, Valentine.
VALENTINE And on a love-book pray for my success?
PROTEUS Upon some book I love I'll pray for thee.   20
VALENTINE That's on some shallow story of deep love,
How young Leander crossed the Hellespont.
PROTEUS That's a deep story of a deeper love,
For he was more than over shoes in love.
VALENTINE 'Tis true; for you are over boots in love,   25
And yet you never swam the Hellespont.
PROTEUS Over the boots? Nay, give me not the boots.
VALENTINE No, I will not; for it boots thee not.
PROTEUS   What?
VALENTINE To be in love: where scorn is bought with groans,
Coy looks with heart-sore sighs, one fading moment's mirth   30
With twenty watchful, weary, tedious nights;
If haply won, perhaps a hapless gain;
If lost, why then a grievous labour won;
How ever, but a folly bought with wit,
Or else a wit by folly vanquishèd.   35
PROTEUS So, by your circumstance, you call me fool.
VALENTINE So, by your circumstance, I fear you'll prove.

26 swam] *Singer*, swom F, swum *Cam.*

15 **hap** fortune.
17 **Commend** Entrust, commit.
18 **beadsman** One bound to pray for another person – that is, to tell the beads of the rosary.
19 **love-book** love story, romance. Time-honoured source of instruction about love.
22 **Leander** Marlowe's poem *Hero and Leander* circulated in manuscript, and Shakespeare knew it before it was published in 1598; it was licensed in 1593. It tells of the legendary Greek lover who not only had to swim the Hellespont to reach his love Hero but also to scale a tower. In Shakespeare, Leander is one of the prototypal lovers. Rosalind in *AYLI* mentions him together with other 'patterns of love' (4.1.100). Valentine later becomes an imitator of the pattern he here scorns. This dramatic irony is pointed out at 3.1.119–20.
24 **over shoes in love** A now obsolete saying, 'over shoes, over boots', expresses reckless con-

tinuance in a course already begun (*OED* Boot sb^3 1b). The phrase is suggested by Leander's drowning. Proteus's resort to the idiom shows his ineptitude, since he lays himself open to an even more forceful attack by Valentine at 25.
27 **give me not the boots** i.e. don't make a fool of me. Proverbial (Tilley B537).
28 **boots** profits.
29–35 Valentine's argument, drawing upon conventional warnings against love, is logically convincing and elegantly worded, but it does not save him from falling in love later.
31 **watchful** wakeful.
34 **How ever** In either case.
36 **circumstance** argument. Often approaching the form of syllogism, though it is here incomplete; Proteus draws the conclusion for himself. Compare 83–91.
37 **circumstance** state of affairs. With a pun on 'circumstance' as used at 36.

PROTEUS 'Tis Love you cavil at, I am not Love.

VALENTINE Love is your master, for he masters you;
 And he that is so yokèd by a fool,   40
 Methinks, should not be chronicled for wise.

PROTEUS Yet writers say: as in the sweetest bud
 The eating canker dwells, so eating love
 Inhabits in the finest wits of all.

VALENTINE And writers say: as the most forward bud   45
 Is eaten by the canker ere it blow,
 Even so by love the young and tender wit
 Is turned to folly, blasting in the bud,
 Losing his verdure, even in the prime,
 And all the fair effects of future hopes.   50
 But wherefore waste I time to counsel thee
 That art a votary to fond desire?
 Once more adieu. My father at the road
 Expects my coming, there to see me shipped.

PROTEUS And thither will I bring thee, Valentine.   55

VALENTINE Sweet Proteus, no; now let us take our leave.
 To Milan let me hear from thee by letters
 Of thy success in love, and what news else
 Betideth here in absence of thy friend;
 And I likewise will visit thee with mine.   60

PROTEUS All happiness bechance to thee in Milan.

57 To Milan] To *Millaine* F; At *Millaine* F2

38 **'Tis Love you cavil at** Proteus does not yet admit defeat but weakly tries to shift the argument.

41 **chronicled for wise** recorded as an example of wisdom.

42–4 It is ironic that Proteus, trying to defend his wit, resorts to commonplaces; furthermore, his choice of image betrays him since it supports by implication Valentine's position that love is destructive (45–50).

43 **canker** cankerworm, caterpillar.

46 **blow** blossom.

48 **blasting** withered. Present participle used in a passive sense (Abbott 372).

49 **prime** springtime of life (*OED* sv sb¹ 8).

50 **fair effects of future hopes** i.e. the wonderful realisation of the wished-for future.

52 **votary** one who has taken a vow. A religious term.

52 **fond** doting, foolish.

53 **road** anchoring-place.

54 **shipped** Both Valentine and later Proteus (2.2.14, 2.4.180) go by boat to Milan. In going on a voyage, they fulfil a requirement of romance heroes. One might surmise that Shakespeare's conception was here influenced by a book illustration of Verona showing sails on the river Adige. It has been pointed out that boat-travel between these two cities was possible because of a then existing system of inland waterways. But it is doubtful that Shakespeare knew about them. Anyhow, he treats the journey of his young gentlemen as starting on a tidal river leading to the open sea (2.2.14), much as the voyages of travellers from London began in the Thames estuary.

57 **To Milan** i.e. by letters sent to Milan. Milan is accented on the first syllable, with a short *i*, as the *ll* of the F spelling suggests.

61 **bechance to** befall.

VALENTINE As much to you at home, and so farewell.   *Exit*
PROTEUS He after honour hunts, I after love.
           He leaves his friends to dignify them more;
           I leave my self, my friends and all, for love.   65
           Thou, Julia, thou hast metamorphised me:
           Made me neglect my studies, lose my time,
           War with good counsel, set the world at nought,
           Made wit with musing weak, heart sick with thought.

                          [*Enter* SPEED]

SPEED Sir Proteus, 'save you! Saw you my master?   70
PROTEUS But now he parted hence to embark for Milan.
SPEED Twenty to one then, he is shipped already,
           And I have played the sheep in losing him.
PROTEUS Indeed, a sheep doth very often stray,
           And if the shepherd be awhile away.   75
SPEED You conclude that my master is a shepherd then and I a
           sheep?
PROTEUS I do.
SPEED Why then my horns are his horns, whether I wake or sleep.
PROTEUS A silly answer and fitting well a sheep.   80
SPEED This proves me still a sheep.
PROTEUS True, and thy master a shepherd.

65 leave] *Pope;* loue F 65 my self] my selfe F; myself *Warburton* 65 all,] *Dyce;* all F 69 SD] *Rowe; not in*
F 76–7 a sheep] a sheepe F2; Sheepe F

64, 65 friends Refers primarily to relatives. See also 1.3.68, 3.1.106.

65 *leave Pope's emendation restores the text perfectly in view of the parallelism between this line and 64, and of the following statement about the speaker's metamorphosis. A misreading of the manuscript was easily possible since modern 'leave' could be represented by a variant spelling 'leve'. Secretary hand would increase the chance of misreading it as 'love'.

65 leave my self Registering loss of self in love seems to indicate that Proteus is incapable of either love or friendship.

66 metamorphised A variant form of 'metamorphosed'. In his later plays Shakespeare prefers to use 'transformation' to describe the change caused by love. In Elizabethan literature this change was not necessarily seen as a negative one. Robert Greene in *Tullies Love* depicts the transformation of a dolt into a learned and accomplished courtier in accordance with the ennobling effect claimed in theories of courtly love.

If Proteus in his private thought expresses a less favourable view here, it must be seen as due to Valentine's abrasive commentary on love, the effect of which seems temporarily to be more shattering than Proteus could openly admit. At 2.1.25–7 Speed will make fun of Valentine being 'metamorphised' by love.

69 thought anxiety, sorrow.

70 'save you God save you. A form of greeting.

73 sheep With a pun on 'ship' supported by a possible short pronunciation of the word (Kökeritz, p. 145). Sheep jokes seem to have been popular with the young Shakespeare, as is evident from *LLL* 2.1.218–22, 4.3.6–8, 5.1.50–6.

75 And if If

76–7 *a sheep The omission of the article in F seems all the more astonishing as Hinman has determined that this page was proof-corrected and the mistake is clearly detectable without collating the copy-text (Hinman, I, 253).

SPEED Nay, that I can deny by a circumstance.

PROTEUS It shall go hard but I'll prove it by another.

SPEED The shepherd seeks the sheep, and not the sheep the   85
shepherd; but I seek my master, and my master seeks not me:
therefore I am no sheep.

PROTEUS The sheep for fodder follow the shepherd, the shepherd
for food follows not the sheep; thou for wages followest thy
master, thy master for wages follows not thee: therefore thou art   90
a sheep.

SPEED Such another proof will make me cry 'baa'.

PROTEUS But dost thou hear? Gav'st thou my letter to Julia?

SPEED Ay, sir; I, a lost mutton, gave your letter to her, a laced
mutton, and she, a laced mutton, gave me, a lost mutton, nothing   95
for my labour.

PROTEUS Here's too small a pasture for such store of muttons.

SPEED If the ground be overcharged, you were best stick her.

PROTEUS Nay, in that you are astray; 'twere best pound you.

SPEED Nay, sir, less than a pound shall serve me for carrying your   100
letter.

PROTEUS You mistake; I mean the pound, a pinfold.

SPEED From a pound to a pin? Fold it over and over,
'Tis threefold too little for carrying a letter to your lover.

PROTEUS But what said she?   105

SPEED [*Nods*] Ay.

92 baa] *Var. 1803;* baâ F   105–6] *Cam.; Pro.* But what said she? *Sp.* I. F; *Pro.* But what said she? *Speed* She nodded
and said, I. *Pope; Pro.* But what said she; did she nod? [Speed *nods.*] *Speed.* I. *Theobald;* PROTEUS But what said she?
SPEED [*nods*] PROTEUS [*looks at* SPEED *in question*] SPEED Ay. *Sisson*

83 **circumstance** argument. As at 36.
92 cry 'baa' bleat like a sheep. With a possible
pun on 'bah!' (Bond).
93–6 After the success of proving Speed a
sheep, Proteus recovers enough to pursue his
love interest. But Speed in revenge turns the
sheep image against his master's love (95). It is
not quite clear whether he is aware that he has
not delivered the letter to Julia herself but only to
her maid (1.2.39–40). Critics have wondered
why Proteus has Speed carry the letter to Julia
and not his own servant Lance.
94–137 This is an absurd messenger's report
that fails to communicate properly because the
go-between's interest lies in the reward only and
not in the content of his errand. The former is
wordily and insistently voiced, but the message,
when demanded, is only sparingly expressed and
treated with derision throughout.
95 laced mutton prostitute. With a jingle-like

pun on 'lost' (Kökeritz, p. 79). Speed's imperti-
nence is typical for a page.
98 stick her i.e. slaughter the excess sheep.
With a bawdy quibble on the sense 'have sexual
intercourse with'.
99 astray With a pun on a stray sheep.
99 pound (1) enclosure for stray cattle, (2)
beat. But Speed takes it at 100 as meaning 'give a
pound of money'.
102 pinfold pound for stray cattle.
103–4 Doggerel verse. See also 128–31.
103 Fold Double, multiply.
105–10 This difficult passage is one of the
places where editors and adapters have tried to
improve the F text by adding words or stage
directions. Perhaps one can understand it better
if one includes it in the category of spelling jokes
of the kind that also occurs in *Err.* 3.2.109–10,
where the name Nell is interpreted as 'an ell', in
LLL 5.1.47–57 and *Rom.* 2.4.36–7.

PROTEUS Nod-ay? Why, that's 'noddy'.

SPEED You mistook, sir. I say she did nod; and you ask me if she did
        nod; and I say 'ay'.

PROTEUS And that set together is 'noddy'.   110

SPEED Now you have taken the pains to set it together, take it for
        your pains.

PROTEUS No, no, you shall have it for bearing the letter.

SPEED Well, I perceive I must be fain to bear with you.

PROTEUS Why, sir, how do you bear with me?   115

SPEED Marry, sir, the letter very orderly, having nothing but the
        word 'noddy' for my pains.

PROTEUS Beshrew me, but you have a quick wit.

SPEED And yet it cannot overtake your slow purse.

PROTEUS Come, come, open the matter in brief: what said she?   120

SPEED Open your purse, that the money and the matter may be both
        at once delivered.

PROTEUS [*Gives him a coin*] Well, sir, here is for your pains. What
        said she?

SPEED [*After inspecting the coin expresses his discontent*] Truly, sir, I   125
        think you'll hardly win her.

PROTEUS Why, couldst thou perceive so much from her?

SPEED Sir, I could perceive nothing at all from her;
        No, not so much as a ducat for delivering your letter.
        And being so hard to me that brought your mind,   130
        I fear she'll prove as hard to you in telling your mind.
        Give her no token but stones, for she's as hard as steel.

PROTEUS What said she? Nothing?

108–9] *As Capell; as verse,* F   116–17] *As Capell; as verse,* F   123 SD] *Collier² subst.; not in* F   125 SD] *NS subst.;
not in* F   133] *Cam.; What said she, nothing?* F; *What, said she nothing? Pope*

107 **noddy** simpleton, fool.

116 **Marry** A mild oath.

118 **Beshrew** Curse.

123–37 Line 135 shows that the coin given
at 123 is a testern, or testril, the Elizabethan
sixpence. Although Speed is himself dissatisfied
with the amount, the tip is probably adequate.
For Pistol it signals the difference between being
in and out of money (*Wiv.* 1.3.87). Costard gets
two sixpences from Lord Berowne for delivering
a letter (*LLL* 3.1.171) but only three farthings
from Don Armado (3.1.137). Sir Andrew Aguecheek, a person of three thousand ducats a year,
gives a 'testril' for a song (*TN* 1.3.22, 2.3.33),

whereas Proteus is a young man without an
income of his own. As a messenger Speed could
expect a tip from the addressee; but since he
delivered the letter only to the maid, he got
'nothing at all from her' (128).

128 **perceive** receive.

129 **ducat** Gold coin, at least six times the
value of a testern. Jessica gives Lancelot Gobbo a
ducat when he leaves to take up service with Bas-
sanio (*MV* 2.3.4), and in *MM* a ducat appears to
be a princely payment for a prostitute (3.2.126).

132 **stones** precious stones, jewels. Perhaps
with bawdy sub-sense of 'testicles'.

SPEED No, not so much as 'Take this for thy pains.' To testify your
    bounty, I thank you, you have testerned me; in requital whereof,   135
    henceforth carry your letters yourself; and so, sir, I'll commend
    you to my master.   *[Exit]*
PROTEUS Go, go, be gone, to save your ship from wreck,
    Which cannot perish having thee aboard,
    Being destined to a drier death on shore.   140
    I must go send some better messenger.
    I fear my Julia would not deign my lines,
    Receiving them from such a worthless post.   *Exit*

1.2 *Enter* JULIA *and* LUCETTA

JULIA But say, Lucetta, now we are alone,
    Wouldst thou then counsel me to fall in love?
LUCETTA Ay, madam, so you stumble not unheedfully.
JULIA Of all the fair resort of gentlemen
    That every day with parle encounter me,   5
    In thy opinion which is worthiest love?
LUCETTA Please you repeat their names, I'll show my mind
    According to my shallow simple skill.
JULIA What think'st thou of the fair Sir Eglamour?
LUCETTA As of a knight well-spoken, neat and fine;   10
    But were I you, he never should be mine.

134–5] *As Capell; No. . .pains / . . .me* F   135 testerned] Testern'd F2; cestern'd F   137 SD] *Capell; not in* F   Act
1, Scene 2   1.2] *Scœna Secunda* F   5 parle] *Rowe,* par'le F

135 *testerned given me a testern. Tannenbaum takes F's error for a misreading because
of the close similarity of *c* and *t* in Elizabethan
Secretary hand (p. 30), but a simple foul-case
accident is more likely the cause of F's error.
138–40 wreck Alluding to the proverb 'He
that is born to be hanged shall never be drowned'
(Tilley B139).
143 post messenger. Perhaps with the underlying meaning of 'blockhead'.

Act 1, Scene 2
Location Julia's garden, as suggested by the
mention of 'stones' (109) and 'wind' (116). The
Elizabethan stage could give the sense of place
through an arbour or at least indicate it by using
garden seats. The opening lines show the two
speakers retreating into privacy.

4–32 A more elaborate list of suitors is
reviewed by Portia and Nerissa in *MV* 1.2.36–
121. There are also similarities with the presentation of the warriors returning to Troy in the
dialogue between Pandarus and Cressida in *Tro.*
1.2.177–249.
4 resort company. Perhaps with a submerged
image of courtship as a form of siege, with parleys
and discussions between the two sides under a
flag of truce.
5 parle conversation.
9 Sir Eglamour For the double use of this
name in *TGV* see p. 53 above.
10 neat and fine Lucetta probably objects to
the over-refined, dandified suitor.

JULIA What think'st thou of the rich Mercatio?

LUCETTA Well of his wealth; but of himself, so-so.

JULIA What think'st thou of the gentle Proteus?

LUCETTA Lord, Lord, to see what folly reigns in us!   15

JULIA How now, what means this passion at his name?

LUCETTA Pardon, dear madam, 'tis a passing shame
        That I, unworthy body as I am,
        Should censure thus on lovely gentlemen.

JULIA Why not on Proteus, as of all the rest?   20

LUCETTA Then thus: of many good I think him best.

JULIA Your reason?

LUCETTA I have no other but a woman's reason:
        I think him so because I think him so.

JULIA And wouldst thou have me cast my love on him?   25

LUCETTA Ay, if you thought your love not cast away.

JULIA Why, he of all the rest hath never moved me.

LUCETTA Yet he of all the rest, I think, best loves ye.

JULIA His little speaking shows his love but small.

LUCETTA Fire that's closest kept burns most of all.   30

JULIA They do not love that do not show their love.

LUCETTA O, they love least that let men know their love.

JULIA I would I knew his mind.

LUCETTA [*Gives a letter*] Peruse this paper, madam.

JULIA [*Reads*] 'To Julia'. [*To Lucetta*] Say, from whom?   35

LUCETTA That the contents will show.

JULIA Say, say, who gave it thee?

LUCETTA Sir Valentine's page; and sent, I think, from Proteus.

---

34 SD] *Dyce; not in* F   35 SD.1 *Reads*] *Dyce; not in* F   35 SD.2 *To Lucetta*] *This edn; not in* F

12 Mercatio The name characterises this suitor as a merchant who may be thought of, following a passage in the English translation of Castiglione, as 'sawsie' and full of 'wanton pride and beastlinesse' (*The Book of the Courtier*, trans. Sir Thomas Hoby (1561), Everyman's Library, 1928, p. 192), which would make the 'gentleness' of the third suitor, Proteus, a golden mean between two extremes. Castiglione (p. 34) and English educationists who followed him believed that the condition of gentleness and nobility tended most to virtuous conduct and deeds.

14 gentle well-born, well-educated.

17 passing surpassing.

23 a woman's reason Proverbial (Tilley B179).

26 cast away wasted.

27 moved made a proposal.

27–32 This abstract discussion about love is similar to the dialogue between Valentine and Proteus in 1.1.19–50. The earlier one proceeded according to literary commonplaces, the later draws on the vexingly controversial experience of being tongue-tied and on the eloquence of lovers as preserved in proverbial lore. See, for instance, 'Whom we love best to them we can say least' (Tilley L165), 'Love makes men orators' (Tilley L522) and 'Love (and business) teach eloquence' (Tilley L491). This is one example of the extensive use of proverbs in the play.

36 contents Accented on the second syllable.

He would have given it you; but I, being in the way,
Did in your name receive it. Pardon the fault, I pray.   40
JULIA Now, by my modesty, a goodly broker!
Dare you presume to harbour wanton lines?
To whisper and conspire against my youth?
Now trust me, 'tis an office of great worth,
And you an officer fit for the place.   45
There, take the paper. See it be returned,
Or else return no more into my sight.
LUCETTA To plead for love deserves more fee than hate.
JULIA Will ye be gone?
LUCETTA   That you may ruminate.   *Exit*
JULIA And yet I would I had o'erlooked the letter.   50
It were a shame to call her back again
And pray her to a fault for which I chid her.
What fool is she, that knows I am a maid
And would not force the letter to my view,
Since maids, in modesty, say 'no' to that   55
Which they would have the profferer construe 'ay'.
Fie, fie! How wayward is this foolish love
That like a testy babe will scratch the nurse
And presently, all humbled, kiss the rod.
How churlishly I chid Lucetta hence   60
When willingly I would have had her here.
How angerly I taught my brow to frown
When inward joy enforced my heart to smile.
My penance is to call Lucetta back
And ask remission for my folly past.   65
What ho! Lucetta!

[Enter LUCETTA]

LUCETTA   What would your ladyship?

---

53 fool] F4; 'foole F; a fool *Cam.*   66 SD] *Rowe subst.; not in* F

---

41 broker go-between. With implied censure as in *John* 2.1.567–8: 'that sly devil, / That broker that still breaks the pate of faith'.
50 o'erlooked read.
52 to a fault to commit an offence.
55–6 Proverbial (Tilley w660).
56 construe interpret. Accented on the first syllable.

58 testy peevish.
59 kiss the rod Proverbial (Tilley R156).
62 angerly angrily; -*ly* combined with a noun and used as an adverb also appears occasionally in other Shakespearean plays (Abbott 447).

JULIA Is't near dinner-time?

LUCETTA   I would it were,
        That you might kill your stomach on your meat
        And not upon your maid.
               [Drops and takes up the letter]

JULIA   What is't that you
        Took up so gingerly?

LUCETTA   Nothing.

JULIA   Why didst thou stoop then?   70

LUCETTA To take a paper up that I let fall.

JULIA And is that paper nothing?

LUCETTA Nothing concerning me.

JULIA Then let it lie for those that it concerns.

LUCETTA Madam, it will not lie where it concerns   75
        Unless it have a false interpreter.

JULIA Some love of yours hath writ to you in rhyme.

LUCETTA That I might sing it, madam, to a tune.
        Give me a note, your ladyship can set –

JULIA As little by such toys as may be possible.   80
        Best sing it to the tune of 'Light o'Love'.

LUCETTA It is too heavy for so light a tune.

JULIA Heavy? Belike it hath some burden then?

LUCETTA Ay, and melodious were it, would you sing it.

JULIA And why not you?

LUCETTA   I cannot reach so high.   85

69 SD] *Collier² subst.; not in* F   79 set –] *This edn; set* F; *set.* F2

68 **kill your stomach** (1) satisfy your appetite, (2) put an end to your anger. According to Elizabethan physiology, anger had its origin in the stomach.

69 **maid** Possibly a pun on 'meat', which could also be pronounced 'mate'.

69–71 There is no indication in the F text of when Lucetta dropped the letter that she now picks up. The SD to 69 follows the solution most modern productions have found. To have the letter dropped and immediately picked up again best conveys Lucetta's intention once more to draw Julia's attention to it. Leech has Lucetta drop the letter at 48 so that, ironically, it is lying about when Julia regrets not having read it (50–65). So did the BBC production, where Julia even noticed the letter, though she scrupled to collect and read it.

75 **lie** inform falsely. With a quibble on 'lie' = remain (74).

79 **note** (1) musical note, tune, (2) letter (of reply).

79 **set** (1) set to music, (2) draft (a letter).

80 **As little by** i.e. set as little store by.

81 **Light o'Love** A popular tune, which Shakespeare also used in *Ado* 3.4.44.

82 It is too important for such a trivial tune.

83 **burden** (1) load, (2) undersong or bass. With a bawdy allusion to the weight of a man's body during intercourse.

85 **I cannot reach so high** (1) It is beyond the range of my voice, (2) Proteus is too high in rank for me to aspire to marry him.

JULIA Let's see your song.
          [*Lucetta withholds the letter*]
          How now, minion!
          [*Threatens her*]
LUCETTA Keep tune there still, so you will sing it out.
          And yet methinks I do not like this tune.
JULIA You do not?
LUCETTA   No, madam, 'tis too sharp.
JULIA You, minion, are too saucy.   90
LUCETTA Nay, now you are too flat
          And mar the concord with too harsh a descant.
          There wanteth but a mean to fill your song.
          [*Lucetta yields the letter*]
JULIA The mean is drowned with your unruly bass.
LUCETTA Indeed, I bid the base for Proteus.   95
JULIA This babble shall not henceforth trouble me.
          [*Looks into the letter*]
          Here is a coil with protestation!
          [*Julia tears the letter into pieces which Lucetta tries to collect*]
          Go, get you gone, and let the papers lie:
          You would be fing'ring them to anger me.

86] *As Hanmer subst.;* Let's...Song / ...Minion F   **86** SD.1 *Lucetta...letter*] *Alexander, after NS; not in* F   **86** SD.2
Threatens her] *This edn; not in* F; *Gives her a box on the ear / Hanmer; giving chase / NS*   **93** SD] *This edn; not in*
F   **94** your] F2; you F   **96** SD] *Capell subst. (after* protestation*); not in* F   **97** SD] *This edn (after* Pope*); not in* F

86–97 Stage action is obviously needed to
motivate some of the speeches in this passage.
The text, for instance, does not indicate when the
letter passes from Lucetta to Julia. Most modern
editors let Julia take the letter at 86, but this
edition follows NS and others in having Lucetta
withhold the letter here, thus motivating Julia's
angry reaction. It can be handed over at 93. NS,
Alexander and Sisson leave it open whether it
comes into Julia's hands at all before she tears it
after 97. The music metaphors at 87–90 also
need explaining by stage action. Editors and producers have seen Julia as chasing, pinching, slap-
ping or even punching Lucetta.
   86 minion Here a term of contempt.
   87 tune (1) correct musical pitch, (2) mood,
humour.
   89 sharp Refers to (1) the musical notation, (2)
some piece of stage business performed by Julia.
   91 flat (1) below normal pitch, (2) downright,
outspoken.

   92 descant melody sung *ex tempore* upon a
plainsong ground or bass to which it forms the
air.
   93 mean middle part, tenor or alto. Hinting at
Proteus, perhaps with a pun on 'man'.
   94 *your unruly bass F2's reading – 'your
unruly base' – strengthens the musical sense of
'base' = bass without entirely excluding the
moral sense. The omission of the letter *r* in F
('you') could have been the transcriber's fault, but
it remains to be asked whether the wording of F
isn't intentional, as it blends the moral with the
musical sense.
   95 bid the base A challenge to run; a phrase
from the game called 'Prisoner's base'.
   97 coil fuss.
   97 protestation solemn declaration or promise (of love).

LUCETTA [*Aside*] She makes it strange, but she would be best
    pleased   100
    To be so angered with another letter.   [*Exit*]
JULIA Nay, would I were so angered with the same.
    O hateful hands, to tear such loving words!
    Injurious wasps, to feed on such sweet honey
    And kill the bees that yield it with your stings!   105
    I'll kiss each several paper for amends.
        [*Collects some of the fragments*]
    Look, here is writ 'kind Julia'. Unkind Julia!
    As in revenge of thy ingratitude,
    I throw thy name against the bruising stones,
    Trampling contemptuously on thy disdain.   110
    And here is writ 'Love-wounded Proteus'.
    Poor wounded name, my bosom as a bed
    Shall lodge thee till thy wound be throughly healed;
    And thus I search it with a sovereign kiss.
    But twice or thrice was 'Proteus' written down –   115
    Be calm, good wind, blow not a word away
    Till I have found each letter in the letter,
    Except mine own name. That some whirlwind bear
    Unto a ragged, fearful, hanging rock
    And throw it thence into the raging sea.   120
    Lo, here in one line is his name twice writ:
    'Poor, forlorn Proteus, passionate Proteus,
    To the sweet Julia'. That I'll tear away –
    And yet I will not, sith so prettily
    He couples it to his complaining names.   125

100 SD] *Sanders; not in* F   101 SD] F2; *not in* F   106 SD] *Capell subst.; not in* F   111 Love-] *Love-* F2; *Loue* F; *love- /
Capell*   119 fearful,] fearefull, F; fearful- *Delius*

100 makes it strange pretends indifference.
102–27 This unusually dramatic monologue
has something of the quality of a playlet within
the play. Julia, with the two names written down
in the letter as the actors, plays out the desired
course of action. The speech moves from the
comparative artificiality of denouncing the fingers
as killer wasps to the stark simplicity of the end.
It is full of concrete circumstances and gestures.
Only two of the phrases demand acting out by a
demonstrative 'thus' (114, 126–7). For further
passages in this text that convey the sense of
an internal playlet, see Lance's monologue at
2.3.11–27 and, with a different relation between

the ground level of the encompassing play and
the fiction growing out of it, 2.1.83–149. Yet
another version of the play-within-a-play is
represented by Julia/Sebastian's invention at
4.4.149–63 of having played Ariadne at Pentecost (see 4.4.158 n.).
104 wasps Referring to her fingers.
106 each several paper i.e. each piece of the
torn letter.
114 search probe (a wound). Julia keeps up
the medical image begun at 111.
114 sovereign of supreme medical efficacy.
124 sith since.
125 complaining names Compare 111, 122.

Thus will I fold them one upon another;
Now kiss, embrace, contend, do what you will.

[*Enter* LUCETTA]

LUCETTA Madam!
      Dinner is ready, and your father stays.
JULIA Well, let us go.   130
LUCETTA What, shall these papers lie like telltales here?
JULIA If you respect them, best to take them up.
LUCETTA Nay, I was taken up for laying them down.
      Yet here they shall not lie for catching cold.
            [*She collects the pieces*]
JULIA I see you have a month's mind to them.   135
LUCETTA Ay, madam, you may say what sights you see;
      I see things too, although you judge I wink.
JULIA Come, come. Will't please you go?

                                                        Exeunt

1.3 *Enter* ANTONIO *and* PANTINO

ANTONIO Tell me, Pantino, what sad talk was that
      Wherewith my brother held you in the cloister?
PANTINO 'Twas of his nephew Proteus, your son.
ANTONIO Why, what of him?
PANTINO   He wondered that your lordship
      Would suffer him to spend his youth at home,   5
      While other men, of slender reputation,
      Put forth their sons to seek preferment out:

---

127 SD] F2; *not in* F   134 SD] *NS subst.; not in* F   **Act 1, Scene 3   1.3**] *Scæna Tertia.* F   **o** SD] *Enter* Antonio *and*
Panthion. *Rowe; Enter Antonio and Panthino. Protheus.* F

126–7 A similar joke, though not involving the same stage action, appears in *Ado* 2.3.136–8.
  129 **stays** waits.
  132 **respect** value.
  132 **best to take** it would be best to take.
  133 **taken up** rebuked, reprimanded.
  134 **for** for fear of.
  135 **a month's mind** fancy, liking; 'month's' is here disyllabic.

Act 1, Scene 3
  Location There is no indication in the text as

to where Pantino and Antonio meet. In the Elizabethan theatre this would most likely be on the main stage. An interior setting could be suggested by having the stage action develop from the inner stage. Illusionistic productions, with their need for a more definite location, should not choose the study of the master of the house, else Proteus, marching into the room with his thoughts on Julia's letter, would appear more absent-minded than necessary.
  1 **sad** grave, serious.
  7 **preferment** advancement, promotion.

Some to the wars to try their fortune there,
Some to discover islands far away,
Some to the studious universities.   10
For any or for all these exercises
He said that Proteus, your son, was meet,
And did request me to importune you
To let him spend his time no more at home,
Which would be great impeachment to his age   15
In having known no travel in his youth.
ANTONIO Nor need'st thou much importune me to that
Whereon this month I have been hammering.
I have considered well his loss of time
And how he cannot be a perfect man   20
Not being tried and tutored in the world.
Experience is by industry achieved
And perfected by the swift course of time.
Then tell me whither were I best to send him.
PANTINO I think your lordship is not ignorant   25
How his companion, youthful Valentine,
Attends the emperor in his royal court.
ANTONIO I know it well.
PANTINO 'Twere good, I think, your lordship sent him thither.
There shall he practise tilts and tournaments,   30
Hear sweet discourse, converse with noblemen

12 **meet** proper, fit.

15 **impeachment** disparagement.

18 **hammering** pondering.

23 **perfected** Accented on the first syllable, as usual in Shakespeare (Kökeritz, p. 335).

27 **emperor in his royal court** At 1.1.57 Valentine suggested that Proteus should direct his communications to Milan, but there was no indication that he intended to enter the service of the court there. The territorial ruler is sometimes named emperor and sometimes duke (always the latter in speech headings). Whether Shakespeare had in mind the Spanish Emperor Charles V, who inherited the duchy of Milan when the last Sforza died, must remain a mere conjecture. A contemporary historian praises 'the company of noblemen and gentlemen' and the 'sumptuous apparel' of the ladies 'continually attendant on the Emperor's lieutenant or deputy in Milan' (George B. Parks (ed.), *William Thomas: The History of Italy (1549)*, 1963, p. 113). Charles later

gave the duchy of Milan to his son Philip, who was well-known in England as the husband of Queen Mary. Milan is mentioned in Holinshed as part of his property.

30 **tilts and tournaments** Military exercises that still smack of the world of medieval knights and the courts of love. They are drawn upon by the writers of romance: by Montemayor's *Diana*, for instance, where Felix courts Felismena with a similar display of arms. It should also be noted that, in Castiglione's *Courtier*, exercises in the use of arms and in courtly conduct are high on the list of priorities for the education of young noblemen. Spenser describes a tournament in *The Faerie Queene*, IV, iv; and Sidney twice presents Astrophil as a contender in the lists – successful in one case and unfortunate in the other – in *Astrophil and Stella*, 41 and 53. During the reign of Queen Elizabeth I, tournaments were held to celebrate the anniversary of her accession and as part of festive entertainments for foreign visitors.

And be in eye of every exercise
Worthy his youth and nobleness of birth.
ANTONIO I like thy counsel; well hast thou advised.
And that thou mayst perceive how well I like it,   35
The execution of it shall make known.
Even with the speediest expedition
I will dispatch him to the emperor's court.
PANTINO Tomorrow, may it please you, Don Alphonso
With other gentlemen of good esteem   40
Are journeying to salute the emperor
And to commend their service to his will.
ANTONIO Good company; with them shall Proteus go –

              [Enter PROTEUS*]*

And in good time! Now will we break with him.
PROTEUS *[Musing on a letter]*
Sweet love, sweet lines, sweet life!   45
Here is her hand, the agent of her heart;
Here is her oath for love, her honour's pawn.
O that our fathers would applaud our loves,
To seal our happiness with their consents!
O heavenly Julia! –   50
ANTONIO How now? What letter are you reading there?
PROTEUS May't please your lordship, 'tis a word or two
Of commendations sent from Valentine,
Delivered by a friend that came from him.
ANTONIO Lend me the letter: let me see what news.   55
PROTEUS There is no news, my lord, but that he writes
How happily he lives, how well beloved
And daily gracèd by the emperor,
Wishing me with him, partner of his fortune.

43 SD] F2 *(after 44); not in* F   45 SD] *Capell subst.; not in* F   50 O] Oh F2; *Pro.* Oh F

32 **be in eye of** see.
39 **Don Alphonso** The title characterises him and Don Antonio (2.4.47) as Spaniards. Shakespeare may have been influenced by one of his main sources, where the counterpart of Proteus's father is styled Don Felix, but it was possibly meant to classify them as members of the ruling class (see 27 n.). Shakespeare's other Spaniards in foreign countries are Don Armado in *LLL* and Don Pedro and his brother Don John in *Ado*.
44 **in good time** at the right moment.

44 **break** speak.
45–50 Julia, to judge by Proteus's reaction, must have committed herself far more deeply in this letter than Felismena did when she wrote to Felix in Shakespeare's source (Bullough, I, 232). For a comparison of the two ladies, see also pp. 6–9 above.
52–9 This is the first of Proteus's many lies, by which he tries to further his ends and protect his interests.
53 **commendations** greetings.

ANTONIO And how stand you affected to his wish?   60
PROTEUS As one relying on your lordship's will
    And not depending on his friendly wish.
ANTONIO My will is something sorted with his wish.
    Muse not that I thus suddenly proceed;
    For what I will, I will, and there an end.   65
    I am resolved that thou shalt spend some time
    With Valentinus in the emperor's court.
    What maintenance he from his friends receives,
    Like exhibition thou shalt have from me.
    Tomorrow be in readiness to go –   70
    Excuse it not, for I am peremptory.
PROTEUS My lord, I cannot be so soon provided;
    Please you deliberate a day or two.
ANTONIO Look what thou want'st shall be sent after thee.
    No more of stay; tomorrow thou must go.   75
    Come on, Pantino; you shall be employed
    To hasten on his expedition.
                        [*Exeunt Antonio and Pantino*]
PROTEUS Thus have I shunned the fire for fear of burning
    And drenched me in the sea where I am drowned.
    I feared to show my father Julia's letter   80
    Lest he should take exceptions to my love;
    And with the vantage of mine own excuse
    Hath he excepted most against my love.
    O, how this spring of love resembleth
    The uncertain glory of an April day,   85
    Which now shows all the beauty of the sun,
    And by and by a cloud takes all away.

                    [*Enter* PANTINO]

76 Pantino] *Panthino* F2; *Panthmo* F   77 SD] *Rowe; not in* F   87 SD] *Enter.* F2; *not in* F

60 **affected** disposed.
62 **his friendly wish** the wish of my friend.
63 **something** somewhat, to some extent.
63 **sorted with** in agreement with.
64–77 Shakespeare shows fathers even more angry when they have to deal with their daughters: see Old Capulet's tantrum in *Rom.* 3.5.149–57, 160–8 and 176–95, or the accusations of Egeus in *MND* 1.1.22–45.
68 **friends** relatives, family.
69 **exhibition** allowance of money for support.

71 **Excuse it not** Do not try to find excuses not to go.
71 **peremptory** resolved. Not necessarily in the modern harsh sense of 'dictatorial'.
74 **Look what** Whatever.
81 **take exceptions** object.
83 **excepted most** i.e. raised the greatest obstacles.
84 **resembleth** Pronounced here as four syllables.

PANTINO Sir Proteus, your father calls for you.
  He is in haste; therefore I pray you go.
PROTEUS Why, this it is: my heart accords thereto,   90
  And yet a thousand times it answers 'no'.

                                                              Exeunt

2.1 *Enter* VALENTINE *and* SPEED

SPEED Sir, your glove!
VALENTINE   Not mine; my gloves are on.
SPEED Why then this may be yours, for this is but one.
VALENTINE Ha, let me see. Ay, give it me, it's mine.
  Sweet ornament that decks a thing divine!
  Ah, Silvia, Silvia!   5
SPEED [*Calling*] Madam Silvia! Madam Silvia!
VALENTINE How now, sirrah?
SPEED She is not within hearing, sir.
VALENTINE Why, sir, who bade you call her?
SPEED Your worship, sir, or else I mistook.   10
VALENTINE Well, you'll still be too forward.
SPEED And yet I was last chidden for being too slow.
VALENTINE Go to, sir; tell me, do you know Madam Silvia?
SPEED She that your worship loves?
VALENTINE Why, how know you that I am in love?   15

---

88 father calls] F4; Fathers call's F; Father call's F2   91 answers] F4; *answer's* F   91 SD] *Exeunt. Finis.* F   **Act 2,**
Scene 1   2.1] *Actus secundus: Scœna Prima.* F   0 SD] *Rowe; Enter Valentine, Speed, Siluia.* F   6 SD] *Dyce; not in* F

88 *father calls Tannenbaum (p. 8), trying to preserve the F reading, understands 'your father's calls' as accompanying and explaining calls from behind the scenes. There is also the possibility of supposing a foul-case error and conjecturing 'your father's (= has) called' which would make the sense of calling Proteus from the scene more urgent.

91 *it answers Tannenbaum (p. 8) defends F's reading as meaning 'its answer is', which is not impossible if 'it' stands for 'its', as elsewhere in Shakespeare.

Act 2, Scene 1
  Location The geographical location 'Milan' for this and many of the later scenes is derived from references at 1.1.57, 61, 71. More specifically, 1.3.30–3 presented the purpose of Val-

entine's sojourn there, the emperor's court being mentioned at 27, 38, 67. Silvia's entrance (82) suggests a place inside the Duke's palace.

  1 Directors, following Dyce and later editors, usually have Speed pick up Silvia's glove here; either it is lying on the floor or Valentine loses it inadvertently on entering. In the BBC production, however, Silvia crossed the stage, dropping the glove – obviously a ruse to stir Valentine into action.

  2 one Quibble with 'on' (1), as 'one' could be spelt and pronounced like 'on' in Elizabethan English.

  7 sirrah Ordinary form of address to inferiors, but Valentine also uses the politer 'sir' (9, 13, 125, etc.) when speaking to Speed.

  11 still always.

  13 Go to Here expressing impatience.

SPEED Marry, by these special marks: first, you have learned, like
    Sir Proteus, to wreathe your arms like a malcontent; to relish a
    love-song like a robin redbreast; to walk alone like one that had
    the pestilence; to sigh like a schoolboy that had lost his ABC; to
    weep like a young wench that had buried her grandam; to fast   20
    like one that takes diet; to watch like one that fears robbing; to
    speak puling like a beggar at Hallowmas. You were wont, when
    you laughed, to crow like a cock; when you walked, to walk like
    one of the lions; when you fasted, it was presently after dinner;
    when you looked sadly, it was for want of money. And now you   25
    are metamorphised with a mistress, that, when I look on you, I
    can hardly think you my master.
VALENTINE Are all these things perceived in me?
SPEED They are all perceived without ye.
VALENTINE Without me? They cannot.   30
SPEED Without you? Nay, that's certain; for without you were so
    simple, none else would. But you are so without these follies,
    that these follies are within you and shine through you like the
    water in an urinal, that not an eye that sees you but is a physician
    to comment on your malady.   35
VALENTINE But tell me, dost thou know my lady Silvia?
SPEED She that you gaze on so as she sits at supper?
VALENTINE Hast thou observed that? Even she I mean.
SPEED Why, sir, I know her not.
VALENTINE Dost thou know her by my gazing on her, and yet   40
    know'st her not?
SPEED Is she not hard-favoured, sir?

16–27 Speed gives a conventional list of at-
titudes signalling a person in love. For a comparable list, see *AYLI* 3.2.372–81.

17 wreathe...malcontent Folded arms were
a conventional sign of love melancholy.

17 relish sing, warble.

19 ABC primer, spelling-book.

21 watch stay awake all night, have sleepless
nights.

22 puling whining plaintively.

22 Hallowmas All Saints' Day (November 1),
a feast on which paupers begged for special alms.

22 Other dramatic uses of the conventional
'character' of a lover appear in *AYLI* 3.2.372–84
and *Ado* 3.2.31–62.

23–4 like...lions This has been taken as an
allusion both to the lions kept at the Tower of
London and to the heraldic lions on the royal

standard, which may have been displayed in the
theatre.

24 presently immediately.

26 with by.

26 that Elliptical for 'so that'.

29 perceived without ye detected in your
personal appearance.

30 Without me Valentine misunderstands
Speed as meaning 'in my absence'.

31 for without you for unless you.

32 would i.e. would perceive them.

34 urinal Receptacle for inspecting urine in
medical diagnosis. This comparison relates to a
conception of love as a kind of disease.

42 hard-favoured ugly.

42–66 Speed, with the pertness of a page,
questions the beauty of his master's beloved on
the premise that a lover's view cannot be objective.

VALENTINE Not so fair, boy, as well-favoured.

SPEED Sir, I know that well enough.

VALENTINE What dost thou know?   45

SPEED That she is not so fair as, of you, well favoured.

VALENTINE I mean that her beauty is exquisite, but her favour infinite.

SPEED That's because the one is painted and the other out of all count.   50

VALENTINE How painted? And how out of count?

SPEED Marry, sir, so painted to make her fair that no man counts of her beauty.

VALENTINE How esteem'st thou me? I account of her beauty.

SPEED You never saw her since she was deformed.   55

VALENTINE How long hath she been deformed?

SPEED Ever since you loved her.

VALENTINE I have loved her ever since I saw her, and still I see her beautiful.

SPEED If you love her, you cannot see her.   60

VALENTINE Why?

SPEED Because Love is blind. O that you had mine eyes, or your own eyes had the lights they were wont to have when you chid at Sir Proteus for going ungartered!

VALENTINE What should I see then?   65

SPEED Your own present folly and her passing deformity; for he, being in love, could not see to garter his hose, and you, being in love, cannot see to put on your hose.

---

43 well-favoured] well-favour'd *Pope;* well fauour'd F   46 well favoured] well favour'd F2; well-fauourd F
47–8] *As Capell; as verse,* F   58–9] *As Capell; as verse,* F

That Silvia must be thought of as representing ideal beauty is testified by Proteus at 4.2.5 and by the song in her praise performed in the serenade scene (4.2.37–51).

43 fair beautiful.

43 well-favoured gracious, charming. Speed at 46 interprets the meaning as 'favoured', i.e. 'admired'. Valentine explains his meaning at 47–8.

47 favour charm, graciousness. But Speed takes this word up as meaning 'face' when he refers to it as being painted at 49.

49–50 out of all count uncertain.

52 counts of takes account of, values.

55 deformed misshapen. Speed means that Valentine sees Silvia under the falsifying condition of being in love.

63 lights power of seeing clearly.

64 going ungartered This was a conventional sign attributed to a lover.

66 passing surpassing.

68 cannot…hose Here a metaphorical expression to indicate a higher degree of being in love.

VALENTINE Belike, boy, then you are in love; for last morning you
    could not see to wipe my shoes.   70
SPEED True, sir; I was in love with my bed. I thank you, you swinged
    me for my love, which makes me the bolder to chide you for
    yours.
VALENTINE In conclusion, I stand affected to her.
SPEED I would you were set, so your affection would cease.   75
VALENTINE Last night she enjoined me to write some lines to one
    she loves.
SPEED And have you?
VALENTINE I have.
SPEED Are they not lamely writ?   80
VALENTINE No, boy, but as well as I can do them. Peace, here she
    comes.

[Enter SILVIA]

SPEED *[Aside]* O excellent motion! O exceeding puppet! Now will he
    interpret to her.
VALENTINE Madam and mistress, a thousand good morrows.   85
SPEED *[Aside]* O, 'give ye good even! Here's a million of manners.
SILVIA Sir Valentine and servant, to you two thousand.
SPEED *[Aside]* He should give her interest, and she gives it him.
VALENTINE As you enjoined me, I have writ your letter
    Unto the secret, nameless friend of yours;   90
    Which I was much unwilling to proceed in
    But for my duty to your ladyship.
    [He gives a letter to Silvia]

69–70] *As Rowe; as verse,* F   **76–7]** *As Pope; as verse,* F   **82** SD] *Rowe; not in* F   **83** SD] *Dyce; not in* F   **86** SD] *Var.*
1803; not in F   **88** SD] *Dyce; not in* F   **92** SD] *Capell; not in* F

69 Belike Perhaps. Used ironically.
71 swinged beat.
74 stand affected to remain in love with.
75 set seated. With a bawdy pun on 'stand'
(74), meaning to have an erection.
83–149 The little play-within-the-play underlines the conventionality of the lovers' behaviour,
which is also stressed by the ceremonious forms
of address. At the same time Silvia transcends
mere conventionality by assuming not only the
part of a puppet but also the director's function.
83 motion puppet-play.

84 interpret supply speech to the puppet.
When Speed explains the stage action as a
puppet-show, he seems to have a foreknowledge
of Silvia's ruse to have Valentine write the letter
for her in answer to his suit, that is, to make him
act as her own spokesman (128).
86 'give ye God give you.
87 servant This was a term in courtly love for
one devoted to the service of a lady.
88 i.e. he ought to outdo her in paying com-
pliments, but she outdoes him.

SILVIA I thank you, gentle servant.

[Looks at the letter]

'Tis very clerkly done.

VALENTINE Now trust me, madam, it came hardly off;
    For being ignorant to whom it goes,   95
    I writ at random, very doubtfully.
SILVIA Perchance you think too much of so much pains?
VALENTINE No, madam; so it stead you, I will write,
    Please you command, a thousand times as much;
    And yet –   100
SILVIA A pretty period! Well, I guess the sequel;
    And yet I will not name it; and yet I care not.

[Offering to return the letter]

    And yet take this again; and yet I thank you,
    Meaning henceforth to trouble you no more.
SPEED *[Aside]* And yet you will; and yet another 'yet'.   105
VALENTINE What means your ladyship? Do you not like it?
SILVIA Yes, yes; the lines are very quaintly writ,
    But, since unwillingly, take them again.

[Offers the letter again]

    Nay, take them.
VALENTINE   Madam, they are for you.
SILVIA Ay, ay; you writ them, sir, at my request,   110
    But I will none of them; they are for you.
    I would have had them writ more movingly.

[Valentine takes the letter]

VALENTINE Please you, I'll write your ladyship another.
SILVIA And when it's writ, for my sake read it over,
    And if it please you, so; if not, why, so.   115
VALENTINE If it please me, madam, what then?
SILVIA Why, if it please you, take it for your labour;
    And so, good morrow, servant.   *Exit*

---

93 SD] *NS subst.; not in* F   102 SD] *NS; not in* F   105 SD] *Rowe; not in* F   108 SD] *NS; not in* F   112 SD] *NS; not in* F   118 SD] *Exit Sil.* F

93 **clerkly** like a scholar.
94 **hardly** only with difficulty.
98 **so it stead you** if it be of use to you.
101 **period** pause.
107 **quaintly** elegantly.
109 According to Fredson Bowers, two short lines can be accepted as one divided line even if the two parts do not seem to add up to a full pentameter. The caesural pause that comes after a stressed or, though this is less frequent, an unstressed syllable as here can be thought of as making up for the missing syllable. For a full discussion, see Fredson Bowers, 'Establishing Shakespeare's text: notes on short lines and the problem of verse division', *SB* 33 (1980), 96–100.

SPEED [*Aside*] O jest unseen, inscrutable, invisible
        As a nose on a man's face or a weathercock on a steeple!   120
        My master sues to her, and she hath taught her suitor,
        He being her pupil, to become her tutor.
        O excellent device, was there ever heard a better?
        That my master, being scribe, to himself should write the
            letter!
VALENTINE How now, sir? What, are you reasoning with yourself?   125
SPEED Nay, I was rhyming; 'tis you that have the reason.
VALENTINE To do what?
SPEED To be a spokesman from Madam Silvia.
VALENTINE To whom?
SPEED To yourself. Why, she woos you by a figure.   130
VALENTINE What figure?
SPEED By a letter, I should say.
VALENTINE Why, she hath not writ to me!
SPEED What need she, when she hath made you write to yourself?
        Why, do you not perceive the jest?   135
VALENTINE No, believe me.
SPEED No believing you indeed, sir. But did you perceive her
        earnest?
VALENTINE She gave me none, except an angry word.
SPEED Why, she hath given you a letter.   140
VALENTINE That's the letter I writ to her friend.
SPEED And that letter hath she delivered, and there an end.
VALENTINE I would it were no worse.
SPEED I'll warrant you, 'tis as well.
        For often have you writ to her, and she in modesty   145
        Or else for want of idle time could not again reply,
        Or fearing else some messenger that might her mind
            discover,
        Herself hath taught her love himself to write unto her lover.

119 SD] *Sanders; not in* F   124] *As Pope;* That...Scribe / ...Letter F   125] *As Pope;* How...Sir / ...yourself
F   125 What,] *Collier;* What F   134–5] *As Capell; as verse,* F   137–8] *As Pope; as verse,* F

119–24 Doggerel verse. See also 141–2.
125 reasoning with talking to.
125–6 The dialogue uses the alliterative terms of the proverb 'There is neither rhyme nor reason' (Tilley R98 and 99). For Shakespeare's inclination to contrast the parallel terms, see also *LLL* 1.1.99 and 1.2.107–8.
130–5 The dialogue involves the double meaning of 'figure' as (1) indirect expression, (2)

symbol of arithmetic, and of 'letter' as (1) alphabetical symbol, (2) epistle.
130 by a figure indirectly, i.e. by Silvia's device of having Valentine write a letter to himself.
138 earnest (1) seriousness, (2) money paid to secure a bargain.
145–8 Regular seven-foot lines ('fourteeners').

All this I speak in print, for in print I found it. Why muse you,
   sir? 'Tis dinner-time.   150
VALENTINE I have dined.
SPEED Ay, but hearken, sir; though the chameleon Love can feed on
   the air, I am one that am nourished by my victuals and would fain
   have meat. O, be not like your mistress; be moved, be moved.

Exeunt

2.2 *Enter* PROTEUS *and* JULIA

PROTEUS Have patience, gentle Julia.
JULIA I must where is no remedy.
PROTEUS When possibly I can, I will return.
JULIA If you turn not, you will return the sooner.
   [*Gives a ring*]
   Keep this remembrance for thy Julia's sake.   5
PROTEUS Why then we'll make exchange;
   [*Gives a ring in return*]
                              here, take you this.

149–50] *As Dyce; as verse,* F   **Act 2, Scene 2**   2.2] *Scœna secunda.* F   0 SD] *Rowe; Enter Protheus, Iulia, Panthion.*
F   4 SD] *Rowe subst.; not in* F   6] *As Pope; Why...exchange; / ...this.* F   6 SD] *Dyce; not in* F

149 speak in print speak exactly, with great
detail. Speed uses this proverbial expression
(Tilley M239) to ridicule Valentine's obtuseness;
he is still explaining his phrase 'she woos you by a
figure' (130). The repetition of 'in print' in the
same line probably means 'exactly so'. Some
editors have taken this literally as a reference
to a quotation which, however, has never been
identified.
   151 I have dined For the same idea that lovers
live on love, see 2.4.134–5.
   152 chameleon The belief that the chameleon
could live on air was proverbial (Tilley M226).
The association with love and the lover on
account of their changeableness was an Elizabethan commonplace.
   153 fain gladly.
   154 be moved (1) have compassion, (2) be
persuaded (to go to dinner).

Act 2, Scene 2
   Location The text of this and many other
scenes gives no indication of a specific location.

The reappearance of the stage properties used in
1.2 would signal the return of the action to
Verona and that the leave-taking takes place in
Julia's garden. The outdoor environment would
definitely be preferable to Theobald's 'inside
Julia's house', as the place must be readily accessible to allow for Pantino's entrance at 18.
   1–2 Tilley finds that the dialogue develops
according to the proverbial expression 'Patience
perforce' and the proverb 'What cannot be cured
must be endured' (P111, C922).
   2 where is where there is.
   4 turn be inconstant.
   4–12 Editors frequently point out that the
action here constitutes a binding engagement
even in the absence of a witness. But the point
seems to be that the impulsive Julia leads Proteus
into it. Though he ends up over-enthusiastically
avowing his constancy, he may originally have
come only to take his leave. Julia's leading role in
this scene was sometimes found unacceptable
and her line 7 attributed to Proteus (Victor) or cut
(Kemble and Kean).

JULIA And seal the bargain with a holy kiss.

PROTEUS Here is my hand for my true constancy;
 And when that hour o'erslips me in the day
 Wherein I sigh not, Julia, for thy sake,   10
 The next ensuing hour some foul mischance
 Torment me for my love's forgetfulness!
 My father stays my coming; answer not.
 The tide is now – nay, not thy tide of tears;
 That tide will stay me longer than I should.   15
 Julia, farewell.

            [Exit Julia]

   What, gone without a word?
 Ay, so true love should do; it cannot speak,
 For truth hath better deeds than words to grace it.

     [Enter PANTINO*]*

PANTINO Sir Proteus, you are stayed for.

PROTEUS Go; I come, I come.   20
 [Aside] Alas, this parting strikes poor lovers dumb.

             Exeunt

2.3 *Enter* LANCE *[weeping, leading a dog]*

LANCE Nay, 'twill be this hour ere I have done weeping; all the kind
 of the Lances have this very fault. I have received my proportion
 like the prodigious son and am going with Sir Proteus to the

---

16 SD] *Dyce, after Rowe (at 15); not in* F 18 SD] *Enter* Panthion *Rowe; not in* F 21 SD.1 *Aside] Sanders; not in* F Act
2, Scene 3 2.3] *Scæna Tertia* F 0 SD] NS *subst.; Enter Launce, Panthion.* F

7–8 For the stage business involved, see p. 153
below.

9 **o'erslips** passes by.

13 **stays** waits for.

14 **The tide is now** i.e. it is time for sailing.
See 1.1.54 n.

14 **tide of tears** flood of tears. Compare the
parody of these words in the next scene (2.3.25–
46).

17–18 This irony in view of Proteus's previous
wordy enthusiasm and later unfaithfulness speaks
for his present innocence.

20–1 These lines were perhaps intended to
conclude the scene as a rhyming couplet.

Act 2, Scene 3
 Location In the Elizabethan playhouse,
Lance's monologue would have been delivered at
the front of the stage. The audience became, as it
were, gaping loiterers in a public place between
the house of Lance's family in Verona and the
roadstead.

1–27 Shakespeare turns the conventionally
extra-dramatic self-introduction of the comic
hero into a little metaplay. See p. 15 above.

1 **kind** family.

2 **proportion** Lance's malapropism for
'portion'.

3 **prodigious** Lance means 'prodigal'.

imperial's court. I think Crab, my dog, be the sourest-natured
dog that lives: my mother weeping, my father wailing, my sister   5
crying, our maid howling, our cat wringing her hands, and all
our house in a great perplexity; yet did not this cruel-hearted
cur shed one tear. He is a stone, a very pebble-stone, and has
no more pity in him than a dog. A Jew would have wept to have
seen our parting. Why, my grandam, having no eyes, look you,   10
wept herself blind at my parting. Nay, I'll show you the manner
of it. [*Taking off his shoes*] This shoe is my father. No, this left
shoe is my father; no, no, this left shoe is my mother. Nay, that
cannot be so neither. Yes, it is so, it is so: it hath the worser sole;
this shoe with the hole in it is my mother – and this my father.   15
A vengeance on't, there 'tis! Now, sir, this staff is my sister,
for, look you, she is as white as a lily and as small as a wand.
This hat is Nan, our maid. I am the dog. No, the dog is himself,
and I am the dog. O, the dog is me, and I am myself. Ay, so, so.
Now come I to my father; [*Kneels*] 'Father, your blessing.' Now   20
should not the shoe speak a word for weeping. Now should I
kiss my father; [*Kisses one shoe*] well, he weeps on. Now come I
to my mother. O that she could speak now – like a wood woman!
Well, I kiss her. [*Kisses the other shoe*] Why, there 'tis. Here's my
mother's breath up and down. Now come I to my sister. Mark   25
the moan she makes! Now the dog all this while sheds not a tear
nor speaks a word. But see how I lay the dust with my tears.

[*Enter* PANTINO]

12 SD] *NS; not in* F   20 SD] *NS; not in* F   22 SD] *NS; not in* F   23 wood woman] *Theobald;* would-woman F; ould
woman *Pope;* wode woman *Warburton*   24 SD] *NS; not in* F   27 SD] *Rowe; not in* F

4 **imperial's** For 'emperor's'.

4 **Crab** Named after the crab-apple because of
his sour nature.

8–9 **has...wept** Jews and dogs were proverbial for their lack of pity.

14 **sole** With a pun on 'soul', according to the
misogynistic view of women.

15 **this...mother** The absurdity of ascribing
sexual difference to the shoes is apparent in this
otherwise crude bawdy.

16 **A vengeance on't, there 'tis** An exclamation expressing the difficulty of casting the two
shoes in the roles of father and mother.

17 **as white...wand** Facetiously explaining
the appropriateness of casting his staff as his
sister.

17 **small** slender.

23 ***wood woman** Theobald's emendation
seems right in view of a possible misreading of
'wodd' (an alternative spelling of 'wood') as
'would'. Shakespeare uses the word in *MND*,
coining the phrase 'wood within this wood'
(2.1.192) in the sense 'frenetic' or 'mad'. The
term was often used for dogs and other animals.
A pun has been suggested with reference to
Lance's wooden shoes.

25 **breath up and down** Lance visibly reacts
to the shoe's bad smell.

25–6 **Mark the moan** NS suggests that
Lance swishes the staff through the air as he says
this.

PANTINO Lance, away, away! Aboard! Thy master is shipped, and
    thou art to post after with oars. What's the matter? Why weep'st
    thou, man? Away, ass, you'll lose the tide if you tarry any longer.   30
LANCE It is no matter if the tied were lost, for it is the unkindest tied
    that ever any man tied.
PANTINO What's the unkindest tide?
LANCE Why, he that's tied here, Crab, my dog.
PANTINO Tut, man, I mean thou'lt lose the flood; and in losing the   35
    flood, lose thy voyage; and in losing thy voyage, lose thy master;
    and in losing thy master, lose thy service; and in losing thy
    service – why dost thou stop my mouth?
LANCE For fear. thou shouldst lose thy tongue.
PANTINO Where should I lose my tongue?   40
LANCE In thy tale.
PANTINO In thy tail! [*Kicking him*]
LANCE Lose the tide, and the voyage, and the master, and the
    service, and the tied? Why, man, if the river were dry, I am able
    to fill it with my tears; if the wind were down, I could drive the   45
    boat with my sighs.
PANTINO Come, come away, man. I was sent to call thee.
LANCE Sir, call me what thou dar'st.
PANTINO Wilt thou go?
LANCE Well, I will go.   50

                                  Exeunt

---

31 tied...unkindest tied] ty'd...unkindest ty'd *Theobald;* tide...unkindest tide F   34 tied] ty'd *Rowe,* tide F   42
thy tail!] *Dyce,* thy Taile. F; thy tail? – *Theobald;* my tail? *Hanmer*   42 SD] *Conj. anon. (in Cam.); not in* F   44 and the
tied] *Knight;* and the tide F; *omitted, Capell*

29 **post** go with haste.

30–4 **tide, tied** F's 'tide' was an accepted
spelling of the past and past participle of 'to tie'.
So the wordplay is on four forms: the noun 'tide',
the finite form of 'to tie' and the past participle of
the verb in its substantival and verbal functions.

42 **In thy tail!** Dyce's conservative treatment
of the F text becomes more understandable when
we consider Cam.'s suggestion that Pantino kicks
Lance here. Editors, following Hanmer in writ-

ing 'my tail?', presuppose, as Bond explains, a
common bawdy gibe, which is also drawn upon in
Shr. 2.1.214–18.

44 **and the tied** Lance perhaps unties the dog
here, as F's 'loose' stands for both 'lose' and
'loose' = release.

47 **call** summon.

48 **call** Lance wilfully mistakes the word for
'call names'.

2.4 *Enter* VALENTINE, SILVIA, TURIO *and* SPEED

SILVIA   Servant!
VALENTINE   Mistress?
SPEED   Master, Sir Turio frowns on you.
VALENTINE   Ay, boy, it's for love.
SPEED   Not of you.   5
VALENTINE   Of my mistress then.
SPEED   'Twere good you knocked him.   [*Exit*]
SILVIA   Servant, you are sad.
VALENTINE   Indeed, madam, I seem so.
TURIO   Seem you that you are not?   10
VALENTINE   Haply I do.
TURIO   So do counterfeits.
VALENTINE   So do you.
TURIO   What seem I that I am not?
VALENTINE   Wise.   15
TURIO   What instance of the contrary?
VALENTINE   Your folly.
TURIO   And how quote you my folly?
VALENTINE   I quote it in your jerkin.
TURIO   My jerkin is a doublet.   20
VALENTINE   Well then I'll double your folly.
TURIO   How!

Act 2, Scene 4   2.4] *Scena Quarta* F   0 SD] *Rowe; Enter Valentine, Siluia, Thurio, Speed, Duke, Protheus.* F   1
Servant!] *Staunton;* Seruant. F; Servant, – *Theobald*   2 Mistress?] *Theobald;* Mistris. F   7 SD] *Cam.; not in* F   11
Haply] *Rowe;* Hap'ly F   22 How!] *Dyce;* How? F

Act 2, Scene 4

Location The manifold action of this scene would have required the full extent of the Elizabethan stage. Assuming that the stage house façade at the back represented the Duke's palace in Milan, the scene could be thought of as taking place in the palace grounds. Editors traditionally set it inside the palace, but Macready and Kean, for example, used an outdoor location.

1, 8 Servant See 2.1.87 n.

3 Bond felt the need to mitigate Speed's embarrassing interruption of the dialogue between his master and Silvia by introducing a stage direction *They converse apart* after 2.

7 SD Cam. editors have Speed exit here since he does not speak again in this scene. It certainly would be awkward to have the clown as a bystander for such a long time. Leech points out

that Speed is regarded as a page rather than a clown, but his lack of employment would still create difficulties in the theatre.

11 Haply Perhaps.

12 counterfeits deceivers.

18 quote detect. Also spelt and pronounced like 'coat'.

19 jerkin A short coat or long jacket worn over a doublet or in place of it.

20 doublet In Shakespeare the usual term for the male garment covering the upper part of the body (see illustration 2, p. 11 above). The variation from jerkin to doublet seems to have been chiefly invented to provide an occasion for the pat comment of the following line.

22 How! An expression of anger here. F's question mark could also indicate an exclamation.

SILVIA What, angry, Sir Turio? Do you change colour?

VALENTINE Give him leave, madam, he is a kind of chameleon.

TURIO That hath more mind to feed on your blood than live in your   25
    air.

VALENTINE You have said, sir.

TURIO Ay, sir, and done too for this time.

VALENTINE I know it well, sir, you always end ere you begin.

SILVIA A fine volley of words, gentlemen, and quickly shot off.   30

VALENTINE 'Tis indeed, madam; we thank the giver.

SILVIA Who is that, servant?

VALENTINE Yourself, sweet lady, for you gave the fire. Sir Turio
    borrows his wit from your ladyship's looks and spends what he
    borrows kindly in your company.   35

TURIO Sir, if you spend word for word with me, I shall make your
    wit bankrupt.

VALENTINE I know it well, sir; you have an exchequer of words and,
    I think, no other treasure to give your followers; for it appears
    by their bare liveries that they live by your bare words.   40

SILVIA No more, gentlemen, no more! Here comes my father.

[*Enter* DUKE]

DUKE Now, daughter Silvia, you are hard beset.
    Sir Valentine, your father is in good health.
    What say you to a letter from your friends
    Of much good news?

VALENTINE   My lord, I will be thankful   45
    To any happy messenger from thence.

DUKE Know ye Don Antonio, your countryman?

33–5] *As Pope; as verse,* F   38–40] *As Pope; as verse,* F   41] *As Pope;* No...more / ...father F   41 SD] *Rowe; not in*
F

25–6 live in your air Alluding again to the
supposed ability of the chameleon to exist on air
(see 2.1.159 n.) with a connotation of 'listen to
your words' according to the proverb 'Words are
but wind' (Tilley w833). In the following line
Valentine twists this meaning in ironic agreement
against Turio with the implication that the threat
just uttered can be disregarded as mere wind.

27–8 The development of the dialogue follows
the proverbial 'So said so done' (Tilley s117).
Turio indicates that for the time being he will not
pursue his threat. Valentine's answer (29) with its
reference to the proverbial 'Think on the end

before you begin' (Tilley E128) is spoken with
contempt for Turio's caution.

31 giver i.e. giver of the fire, as explained at
33.

35 kindly appropriately.

39–40 The poverty and the niggardliness of
which Turio is accused do not easily agree with
his 'huge possessions' (168) and the bountiful-
ness referred to at 3.1.65.

40 bare threadbare.

46 happy messenger bringer of good news.

47 Don Antonio For the title see 1.3.39 n.

VALENTINE Ay, my good lord, I know the gentleman
            To be of worth and worthy estimation,
            And not without desert so well reputed.   50
DUKE Hath he not a son?
VALENTINE Ay, my good lord, a son that well deserves
            The honour and regard of such a father.
DUKE You know him well?
VALENTINE I knew him as my self; for from our infancy   55
            We have conversed and spent our hours together;
            And though myself have been an idle truant,
            Omitting the sweet benefit of time
            To clothe mine age with angel-like perfection,
            Yet hath Sir Proteus, for that's his name,   60
            Made use and fair advantage of his days:
            His years but young, but his experience old;
            His head unmellowed, but his judgement ripe;
            And in a word – for far behind his worth
            Comes all the praises that I now bestow –   65
            He is complete in feature and in mind
            With all good grace to grace a gentleman.
DUKE Beshrew me, sir, but if he make this good,
            He is as worthy for an empress' love
            As meet to be an emperor's counsellor.   70
            Well, sir, this gentleman is come to me
            With commendation from great potentates,
            And here he means to spend his time awhile.
            I think 'tis no unwelcome news to you.
VALENTINE Should I have wished a thing, it had been he.   75
DUKE Welcome him then according to his worth.
            Silvia, I speak to you, and you, Sir Turio;

49 **worth** wealth. Don Antonio shows himself
very conscious of his superior means in comparison with Valentine's family (1.3.68–9).

55–67 For the relationship between the two
young gentlemen see pp. 5 and 11–12 above.

55 **knew** For Shakespeare's use of the past
tense in a similar context, compare *2H6* 2.1.2:
'I saw not better sport these seven years' day'
(Abbott 347; Franz 635).

58 i.e. not taking advantage of the precious gift
time offers.

59 **mine age** In view of 60–3, Valentine must
be referring to his present age.

62–3 An adaptation of the *puer senex* topos.

63 **unmellowed** i.e. without grey hair.

65 **Comes** Passages where a singular verb is
connected with a plural subject are frequent in
Shakespeare (Abbott 335).

66 **feature** shape or form of body.

68 **make this good** is equal to this.

69–70 **an empress' love…counsellor** The
Duke joins the ideal of the knightly courtly lover
of the Middle Ages with the ideal Renaissance
courtier as adviser to the ruler. Compare the
repetition of the first part at 5.4.137 and see pp.
4–5 above.

For Valentine, I need not cite him to it.
I will send him hither to you presently.   [*Exit*]

VALENTINE This is the gentleman I told your ladyship   80
    Had come along with me but that his mistress
    Did hold his eyes locked in her crystal looks.

SILVIA Belike that now she hath enfranchised them
    Upon some other pawn for fealty.

VALENTINE Nay, sure, I think she holds them prisoners still.   85

SILVIA Nay then he should be blind, and being blind
    How could he see his way to seek out you?

VALENTINE Why, lady, Love hath twenty pair of eyes.

TURIO They say that Love hath not an eye at all.

VALENTINE To see such lovers, Turio, as yourself;   90
    Upon a homely object Love can wink.

       [*Enter* PROTEUS]

SILVIA Have done, have done; here comes the gentleman.

VALENTINE Welcome, dear Proteus! Mistress, I beseech you
    Confirm his welcome with some special favour.

SILVIA His worth is warrant for his welcome hither,   95
    If this be he you oft have wished to hear from.

VALENTINE Mistress, it is. Sweet lady, entertain him
    To be my fellow servant to your ladyship.

SILVIA Too low a mistress for so high a servant.

PROTEUS Not so, sweet lady, but too mean a servant   100
    To have a look of such a worthy mistress.

VALENTINE Leave off discourse of disability.
    Sweet lady, entertain him for your servant.

PROTEUS My duty will I boast of, nothing else.

SILVIA And duty never yet did want his meed.   105
    Servant, you are welcome to a worthless mistress.

PROTEUS I'll die on him that says so but yourself.

79 SD] *Rowe; not in* F   91 SD] *Enter.* F2; *not in* F   92] F; gentleman. (*Exit* THURIO) *Collier*   101 worthy] F2; worthy a F

78 **cite** urge.
83 **Belike** Perhaps.
83 **enfranchised** set free.
83 **them** i.e. Proteus's eyes.
84 **pawn for fealty** pledge of loyalty and fidelity. In accordance with Elizabethan sonnet conventions, the phrase describes love as a form of vassalage.

89 **not an eye at all** Cupid is traditionally depicted as blind.
97 **entertain him** take him into your service.
101 **of...mistress** Subjective genitive rather than objective.
102 **disability** belittlement.
105 **meed** reward.
107 **die on him** fight him to death.

SILVIA That you are welcome?
PROTEUS   That you are worthless.

[*An attendant appears at the door to deliver a message to Turio*]

TURIO Madam, my lord your father would speak with you.
SILVIA I wait upon his pleasure. Come, Sir Turio,   110
   Go with me. Once more, new servant, welcome.
   I'll leave you to confer of home affairs;
   When you have done, we look to hear from you.
PROTEUS We'll both attend upon your ladyship.
                           [*Exeunt Silvia and Turio*]
VALENTINE Now tell me, how do all from whence you came?   115
PROTEUS Your friends are well and have them much commended.
VALENTINE And how do yours?
PROTEUS   I left them all in health.
VALENTINE How does your lady, and how thrives your love?
PROTEUS My tales of love were wont to weary you;
   I know you joy not in a love-discourse.   120
VALENTINE Ay, Proteus, but that life is altered now:
   I have done penance for contemning Love,
   Whose high imperious thoughts have punished me
   With bitter fasts, with penitential groans,
   With nightly tears and daily heart-sore sighs;   125
   For in revenge of my contempt of love
   Love hath chased sleep from my enthrallèd eyes
   And made them watchers of mine own heart's sorrow.
   O gentle Proteus, Love's a mighty lord
   And hath so humbled me as I confess   130
   There is no woe to his correction,
   Nor to his service no such joy on earth.

---

108 SD] *This edn; not in* F; *Enter* THURIO *Collier; Enter Servant / Theobald*   **109** SH] F; *Serv. / Theobald*   **114** SD] *Rowe; not in* F

108 SD Various other solutions have been suggested for giving Turio an opportunity to receive from the Duke the message he delivers at 109. Theobald gives the line to a servant, supposing the speech to have been wrongly attributed in the copy. Others, following Collier, have Turio leave the stage at 92 and re-enter at 108. The latter is less convincing because Turio would miss his meeting with Proteus, although the Duke had encouraged him to make his acquaintance (77). But given the unfinished state of the manuscript, even Theobald's emendation seems an unwarranted tampering with the text.
116 have...commended send their kind regards.
122 contemning disdaining, scorning.
123 imperious domineering. Implying the relationship of a liege lord to his vassal. See 'mighty lord' (129).
127 enthrallèd subjected. Continuing the image begun at 123.
131 to comparable to.

Now no discourse except it be of love.
Now can I break my fast, dine, sup and sleep
Upon the very naked name of Love.   135
PROTEUS Enough; I read your fortune in your eye.
       Was this the idol that you worship so?
VALENTINE Even she; and is she not a heavenly saint?
PROTEUS No, but she is an earthly paragon.
VALENTINE Call her divine.
PROTEUS   I will not flatter her.   140
VALENTINE O flatter me, for love delights in praises.
PROTEUS When I was sick, you gave me bitter pills,
       And I must minister the like to you.
VALENTINE Then speak the truth by her; if not divine,
       Yet let her be a principality,   145
       Sovereign to all the creatures on the earth.
PROTEUS Except my mistress.
VALENTINE   Sweet, except not any,
       Except thou wilt except against my love.
PROTEUS Have I not reason to prefer mine own?
VALENTINE And I will help thee to prefer her too: 150
       She shall be dignified with this high honour –
       To bear my lady's train, lest the base earth
       Should from her vesture chance to steal a kiss
       And, of so great a favour growing proud,
       Disdain to root the summer-swelling flower   155
       And make rough winter everlastingly.
PROTEUS Why, Valentine, what braggartism is this?
VALENTINE Pardon me, Proteus, all I can is nothing
       To her whose worth makes other worthies nothing;
       She is alone –
PROTEUS   Then let her alone.   160

159 makes] F2; make F

135 **very naked** mere.
144 **by her** about her.
145 **principality** A member of one of the orders of angels. Though archangels rank higher, this order seems to have been chosen for its verbal connection with prince, principal and principality which leads to the idea of sovereignty (146). The terms 'heavenly saint', 'divine' and 'principality' draw on a conception of love derived from Petrarchism. Proteus counters it with an alternative, namely that of sickness (142).
148 Unless you will object against my love.
150 **prefer** promote, advance. With a pun on 'prefer' = like better (149).
153 **vesture** garments.
158 **can** i.e. can say.
160 **alone** unique, without equal.

VALENTINE Not for the world! Why, man, she is mine own,
    And I as rich in having such a jewel
    As twenty seas, if all their sand were pearl,
    The water nectar and the rocks pure gold.
    Forgive me that I do not dream on thee,   165
    Because thou seest me dote upon my love.
    My foolish rival, that her father likes
    Only for his possessions are so huge,
    Is gone with her along, and I must after,
    For love, thou know'st, is full of jealousy.   170
PROTEUS But she loves you?
VALENTINE Ay, and we are betrothed; nay more, our marriage hour,
    With all the cunning manner of our flight,
    Determined of: how I must climb her window,
    The ladder made of cords, and all the means   175
    Plotted and 'greed on for my happiness.
    Good Proteus, go with me to my chamber,
    In these affairs to aid me with thy counsel.
PROTEUS Go on before; I shall enquire you forth.
    I must unto the road to disembark   180
    Some necessaries that I needs must use;
    And then I'll presently attend you.
VALENTINE Will you make haste?
PROTEUS I will.

Exit [Valentine]

    Even as one heat another heat expels,   185
    Or as one nail by strength drives out another,
    So the remembrance of my former love
    Is by a newer object quite forgotten.
    Is it mine eye or Valentine's praise,

---

184 SD] *Rowe; Exit* F (*after 183*)   189 Is it] F2; It is F   189 mine eye] *Theobald;* mine F; mine then F2; mine own
Capell; her mien *Var. 1821;* mine unstaid mind *Bond*

165 do not…thee do not think upon you,
i.e. disregard you and your concerns.

177 go…chamber The rapid change of
intention from 169 is probably due to the
unfinished state of the manuscript.

180 road anchoring-place. Compare 1.1.53.

185–8 The thought follows the proverb 'One
love drives out another' (Tilley L538) but, in
wording it, Shakespeare draws on the related
proverbs 'One fire drives out another' (F277) and
'One nail drives out another' (N17). The simile
was probably suggested by Arthur Brooke's

Romeus and Juliet (see p. 6 n. 1 above). This and
other parallels are listed in Allen, pp. 25–46.

189 *Is it mine eye Theobald's emendation
finds support from Sisson, who points to the loss
of the word 'eye' after 'mine' in *Sonnets* 113.14,
and Munro, who draws attention to Brooke's
Romeus, 203–8: 'he fixd on her his partiall perced
eye, / His former love, for which of late he ready
was to dye, / Is nowe as quite forgotte, as it had
never been' (Bullough, I, 291).

189 Valentine's Tetrasyllabic. There is no
need to change to 'Valentinus'.

Her true perfection or my false transgression   190
That makes me reasonless to reason thus?
She is fair; and so is Julia that I love –
That I did love, for now my love is thawed,
Which like a waxen image 'gainst a fire
Bears no impression of the thing it was.   195
Methinks my zeal to Valentine is cold
And that I love him not as I was wont.
O, but I love his lady too too much,
And that's the reason I love him so little.
How shall I dote on her with more advice   200
That thus without advice begin to love her?
'Tis but her picture I have yet beheld,
And that hath dazzlèd my reason's light;
But when I look on her perfections,
There is no reason but I shall be blind.   205
If I can check my erring love, I will;
If not, to compass her I'll use my skill.   *Exit*

2.5 *Enter* SPEED *and* LANCE [*with his dog*]

SPEED Lance, by mine honesty, welcome to Milan.
LANCE Forswear not thyself, sweet youth, for I am not welcome. I
  reckon this always, that a man is never undone till he be hanged,
  nor never welcome to a place till some certain shot be paid and
  the hostess say 'welcome'.   5
SPEED Come on, you madcap. I'll to the alehouse with you presently,

---

203 dazzlèd] dazel'd F; dazel'd so F2   207 SD] F2; *Exeunt* F   **Act 2, Scene 5**   2.5] *Scena Quinta.* F   0 SD] NS;
Enter Speed *and* Launce. F   1 Milan] *Pope;* Padua F

195 **impression** The sense seems to move
between the meanings 'mark produced by pressure' and 'effect on the senses or the mind' (*OED*
sv *sb* 2 and 6).
200 **advice** deliberation.
201 **advice** forethought.
202 **picture** Outward appearance as contrasted
with inner qualities: 'her perfections' (204). Some
editors take 'picture' in the sense of 'portrait' and
conjecture the loss of a scene in which Proteus
is supposed to have seen Silvia's picture before
meeting her in person.
203 **dazzlèd** Trisyllabic.
205 **no reason but** no doubt that.

207 **compass** obtain, win.

Act 2, Scene 5
Location As their masters are already in
Milan, this must also be the place of the servants'
first meeting. F's reference to 'Padua' (1) reflects
the unfinished state of the manuscript. The Elizabethan stage would have indicated the chance
nature of the meeting by simply having the two
actors enter from the doors on either side of the
stage.
4 **shot** tavern reckoning. As distinct from 'shot'
= dose (7).

where for one shot of five pence thou shalt have five thousand
welcomes. But, sirrah, how did thy master part with Madam
Julia?

LANCE Marry, after they closed in earnest, they parted very fairly   10
in jest.

SPEED But shall she marry him?

LANCE No.

SPEED How then? Shall he marry her?

LANCE No, neither.   15

SPEED What, are they broken?

LANCE No, they are both as whole as a fish.

SPEED Why then, how stands the matter with them?

LANCE Marry, thus: when it stands well with him, it stands well with
her.   20

SPEED What an ass art thou! I understand thee not.

LANCE What a block art thou that thou canst not! My staff
understands me.

SPEED What thou say'st?

LANCE Ay, and what I do too. Look thee, I'll but lean, and my staff   25
understands me.

SPEED It stands under thee indeed.

LANCE Why, stand under and understand is all one.

SPEED But tell me true, will't be a match?

LANCE Ask my dog. If he say 'ay', it will; if he say 'no', it will; if he   30
shake his tail and say nothing, it will.

SPEED The conclusion is then that it will.

LANCE Thou shalt never get such a secret from me but by a parable.

SPEED 'Tis well that I get it so. But, Lance, how say'st thou that my
master is become a notable lover?   35

LANCE I never knew him otherwise.

SPEED Than how?

LANCE A notable lubber, as thou reportest him to be.

34 that] F2; that that F

10 **closed** (1) agreed, came to terms, (2)
embraced.

16 **are they broken** have they quarrelled. But
Lance understands it as meaning 'in pieces' (17).

17 **whole** not broken. Lance modulates the
meaning to 'sound, hale, healthy' by referring to
the proverbial 'as whole as a fish' (Tilley F307).

19 **stands** Probably with a bawdy undertone.

22 **block** dull fellow.

33 **by a parable** indirectly.

34 **how say'st thou** what is your opinion
about the fact.

38 **lubber** clumsy, stupid fellow. With a pun
on 'lover'.

SPEED Why, thou whoreson ass, thou mistak'st me.

LANCE Why, fool, I meant not thee; I meant thy master.   40

SPEED I tell thee my master is become a hot lover.

LANCE Why, I tell thee I care not though he burn himself in love. If thou wilt go with me to the alehouse – [*Makes an inviting gesture*] if not, thou art an Hebrew, a Jew, and not worth the name of a Christian.   45

SPEED Why?

LANCE Because thou hast not so much charity in thee as to go to the ale with a Christian. Wilt thou go?

SPEED At thy service.

Exeunt

2.6 *Enter* PROTEUS

PROTEUS To leave my Julia, shall I be forsworn;
     To love fair Silvia, shall I be forsworn;
     To wrong my friend, I shall be much forsworn.
     And ev'n that power which gave me first my oath
     Provokes me to this threefold perjury.   5
     Love bade me swear, and Love bids me forswear.
     O sweet-suggesting Love, if thou hast sinned,
     Teach me, thy tempted subject, to excuse it.
     At first I did adore a twinkling star,
     But now I worship a celestial sun.   10

43 alehouse –] *This edn;* Alehouse: F; Alehouse, so F2   43 SD] *This edn; not in* F   **Act 2, Scene 6**   2.6] *Scœna Sexta.* F   0 SD] *Enter* Protheus *solus.* F   1 Julia,] *Theobald; Iulia;* F   1, 2 forsworn;] *Theobald;* forsworne? F   2 Silvia,] *Theobald; Silvia;* F

39 mistak'st wilfully misunderstand. Mistaking is one of Lance's tricks.

40 I meant not thee Lance mistakes again.

42–3 If…alehouse Editors have tried to make the sentence complete by inserting a comma after 'wilt', thus making the emendation in F2 unnecessary. But this can also be accomplished by a gesture.

48 ale The anti-Semitic joke of 44–5 rests upon a knowledge of the church-ale mentioned here, a festivity at which ale was sold to raise funds for the church.

Act 2, Scene 6
Location In the Elizabethan playhouse this like other soliloquies would be spoken at the front of the stage. The place requires no further specification.

1, 2, 3 forsworn At 2.2.8 Proteus promised true constancy to Julia, who later claims to hold him by 'a thousand oaths' (2.7.69). The text does not show the existence of a similar bond between Proteus and Valentine. See pp. 11–12 above.

7 sweet-suggesting The parallel with 'Two loves I have of comfort and despair, / Which like two spirits do suggest me still' (*Sonnets* 144.1–2) creates the impression that some sort of demonic influence is meant here.

7 if…sinned The impression of easy self-exoneration vanishes as soon as the idea of demonic influence is taken seriously.

Unheedful vows may heedfully be broken,
And he wants wit that wants resolvèd will
To learn his wit t'exchange the bad for better.
Fie, fie, unreverend tongue, to call her bad
Whose sovereignty so oft thou hast preferred   15
With twenty thousand soul-confirming oaths.
I cannot leave to love, and yet I do;
But there I leave to love where I should love.
Julia I lose, and Valentine I lose;
If I keep them, I needs must lose my self.   20
If I lose them, thus find I by their loss:
For Valentine my self, for Julia Silvia.
I to my self am dearer than a friend,
For love is still most precious in itself;
And Silvia – witness heaven that made her fair –   25
Shows Julia but a swarthy Ethiope.
I will forget that Julia is alive,
Rememb'ring that my love to her is dead;
And Valentine I'll hold an enemy,
Aiming at Silvia as a sweeter friend.   30
I cannot now prove constant to my self
Without some treachery used to Valentine.
This night he meaneth with a corded ladder
To climb celestial Silvia's chamber-window,
Myself in counsel, his competitor.   35
Now presently I'll give her father notice
Of their disguising and pretended flight,
Who, all enraged, will banish Valentine,
For Turio he intends shall wed his daughter.
But Valentine being gone, I'll quickly cross   40
By some sly trick blunt Turio's dull proceeding.

13 **learn** teach.
15 **preferred** recommended; or perhaps 'praised'.
16 **soul-confirming** The present participle has here the passive sense of 'soul-confirmed'. Compare 1.1.48.
17 **leave** cease.
19–24 The fear of loss of self in love, already expressed at 1.1.65, is now turned into a demonic fear of losing both love and self or of sacrificing his friend and Julia. Line 23 presents the inver-sion of the proverbial wisdom 'a friend is one's second self' (Tilley F696).
26 **Ethiope** Ethiopian; a dark-coloured person, the conventional antitype to the ideal white-skinned, blue-eyed, fair-haired woman.
35 **in counsel** i.e. taken into his confidence.
35 **competitor** (1) rival, (2) associate. Both meanings appear in Shakespeare, but the second would stress the irony of the situation.
37 **pretended** intended.

> Love, lend me wings to make my purpose swift,
> As thou hast lent me wit to plot this drift.   *Exit*

2.7 *Enter* JULIA *and* LUCETTA

JULIA Counsel, Lucetta; gentle girl, assist me;
      And even in kind love I do conjure thee,
      Who art the table wherein all my thoughts
      Are visibly charactered and engraved,
      To lesson me and tell me some good mean   5
      How with my honour I may undertake
      A journey to my loving Proteus.
LUCETTA Alas, the way is wearisome and long!
JULIA A true-devoted pilgrim is not weary
      To measure kingdoms with his feeble steps,   10
      Much less shall she that hath Love's wings to fly,
      And when the flight is made to one so dear,
      Of such divine perfection, as Sir Proteus.
LUCETTA Better forbear till Proteus make return.
JULIA O, know'st thou not his looks are my soul's food?   15
      Pity the dearth that I have pinèd in
      By longing for that food so long a time.
      Didst thou but know the inly touch of love,
      Thou wouldst as soon go kindle fire with snow
      As seek to quench the fire of love with words.   20
LUCETTA I do not seek to quench your love's hot fire

42 Love,] *Theobald; Loue* F   Act 2, Scene 7   2.7] *Scœna septima.* F

42 **to…swift** i.e. to facilitate quick execution of my plan.

43 **drift** plan.

Act 2, Scene 7

Location In the text the location is specified very little beyond the fact that it is not Julia's chamber (83). Staging-practice leads one to assume that the same properties would have been used here as in 1.2 and 2.2 to signalise the return of the action to Verona. It is interesting to note that even on the modern stage a garden setting is frequently provided, whereas editors have preferred an indoor setting.

2 **conjure** ask solemnly.

3 **table** A thick piece of heavily waxed cardboard, to be written on or engraved with a stylus. Such cardboard pieces could be bound together to make up a pocket-sized notebook.

4 **charactered** written. Accented on the second syllable.

6 **with my honour** i.e. without endangering my reputation.

15 There is irony in Julia's fascination with Proteus's good looks, as the mythological Proteus is characterised by his ability to take many different shapes, a quality that yields the adjective 'protean'.

18 **inly** inward.

But qualify the fire's extreme rage,
Lest it should burn above the bounds of reason.
JULIA The more thou damm'st it up, the more it burns.
    The current that with gentle murmur glides,   25
    Thou know'st, being stopped, impatiently doth rage;
    But when his fair course is not hinderèd,
    He makes sweet music with th'enamelled stones,
    Giving a gentle kiss to every sedge
    He overtaketh in his pilgrimage;   30
    And so by many winding nooks he strays
    With willing sport to the wild ocean.
    Then let me go and hinder not my course.
    I'll be as patient as a gentle stream
    And make a pastime of each weary step,   35
    Till the last step have brought me to my love;
    And there I'll rest, as after much turmoil
    A blessèd soul doth in Elysium.
LUCETTA But in what habit will you go along?
JULIA Not like a woman, for I would prevent   40
    The loose encounters of lascivious men.
    Gentle Lucetta, fit me with such weeds
    As may beseem some well-reputed page.
LUCETTA Why then your ladyship must cut your hair.
JULIA No, girl, I'll knit it up in silken strings   45
    With twenty odd-conceited true-love knots.
    To be fantastic may become a youth
    Of greater time than I shall show to be.
LUCETTA What fashion, madam, shall I make your breeches?
JULIA That fits as well as 'Tell me, good my lord,   50
    What compass will you wear your farthingale?'
    Why, ev'n what fashion thou best likes, Lucetta.
LUCETTA You must needs have them with a codpiece, madam.

22 fire's Disyllabic.
22 extreme Here stressed on the first syllable
(Kökeritz, pp. 333–4).
24 Julia is merely returning the proverbial
wisdom she has learned earlier from Lucetta
(1.2.30).
    32 wild ocean open sea.
    32 ocean Trisyllabic.
    40 prevent forestall.
    41 encounters accostings, addresses.

42 weeds garments.
46 odd-conceited strangely invented.
46 love knots A knot or bow of ribbon tied in a
peculiar way, supposed to be a love token (*OED*).
48 time age.
48 show to be appear.
51 compass circumference.
51 farthingale hooped petticoat.
53 codpiece Appendage like a small bag or
flap at the front of men's breeches.

JULIA Out, out, Lucetta, that will be ill-favoured.
LUCETTA A round hose, madam, now's not worth a pin   55
   Unless you have a codpiece to stick pins on.
JULIA Lucetta, as thou lov'st me, let me have
   What thou think'st meet and is most mannerly.
   But tell me, wench, how will the world repute me
   For undertaking so unstaid a journey?   60
   I fear me it will make me scandalised.
LUCETTA If you think so, then stay at home and go not.
JULIA Nay, that I will not.
LUCETTA Then never dream on infamy, but go.
   If Proteus like your journey when you come,   65
   No matter who's displeased when you are gone.
   I fear me he will scarce be pleased withal.
JULIA That is the least, Lucetta, of my fear.
   A thousand oaths, an ocean of his tears
   And instances of infinite of love   70
   Warrant me welcome to my Proteus.
LUCETTA All these are servants to deceitful men.
JULIA Base men that use them to so base effect!
   But truer stars did govern Proteus' birth.
   His words are bonds, his oaths are oracles,   75
   His love sincere, his thoughts immaculate,
   His tears pure messengers sent from his heart,
   His heart as far from fraud as heaven from earth.
LUCETTA Pray heaven he prove so when you come to him!
JULIA Now, as thou lov'st me, do him not that wrong   80
   To bear a hard opinion of his truth;
   Only deserve my love by loving him.
   And presently go with me to my chamber
   To take a note of what I stand in need of
   To furnish me upon my longing journey.   85
   All that is mine I leave at thy dispose:

67 withal] withall F2, with all F

55 **round hose** Breeches rounded by padding covering the upper part of the leg. See illustration 2, p. 11 above.
56 **stick pins on** A method sometimes used to decorate the codpiece.
60 **unstaid** unbecoming.
67 **withal** with it.
70 **infinite** an infinity.

81 **hard** unpleasant.
85 **longing** prompted by strong desire.
86 **at thy dispose** at your disposal, in your charge. That Julia entrusts Lucetta with the management of her possessions, although a father is mentioned at 1.2.129, is another sign of the unfinished state of F's copy-text.

My goods, my lands, my reputation;
Only in lieu thereof dispatch me hence.
Come, answer not, but to it presently!
I am impatient of my tarriance.   90

Exeunt

3.1 *Enter* DUKE, TURIO *and* PROTEUS

DUKE Sir Turio, give us leave, I pray, a while;
We have some secrets to confer about.

[*Exit Turio*]
Now tell me, Proteus, what's your will with me?
PROTEUS My gracious lord, that which I would discover
The law of friendship bids me to conceal,   5
But when I call to mind your gracious favours
Done to me, undeserving as I am,
My duty pricks me on to utter that
Which else no worldly good should draw from me.
Know, worthy prince, Sir Valentine, my friend,   10
This night intends to steal away your daughter;
Myself am one made privy to the plot.
I know you have determined to bestow her
On Turio, whom your gentle daughter hates;
And should she thus be stol'n away from you,   15
It would be much vexation to your age.
Thus, for my duty's sake, I rather chose
To cross my friend in his intended drift

Act 3, Scene 1   3.1] *Actus Tertius, Scena Prima.* F   o SD] *Rowe; Enter Duke, Thurio, Protheus; Valentine, Launce, Speed.* F   2 SD] *Rowe; not in* F

90 **tarriance** delay.

Act 3, Scene 1
Location This scene shows the great flexibility of the Elizabethan stage with respect to time and place. Its various groupings and bits of dialogue would follow each other naturally there. Theatres that have to rely on definite settings find it more difficult to accommodate all the events of the scene in one and the same location. Previous editors, following Capell, locate both the more public and the more private elements in a room inside the palace, though this would hardly be

the place for Valentine to show up with his ladder nor would he stay there after being banished. The search for him in the fashion of hare-coursing and the extended discussion of Lance's catalogue would be even more misplaced there. Victor and Kean in using the garden of the Duke's palace provide a less obviously inappropriate single location.

2 SD The entrance and immediate exit of Turio enhance the sinister atmosphere of Proteus's treachery.

4 **discover** reveal.

18 **drift** scheme.

Than, by concealing it, heap on your head
A pack of sorrows, which would press you down,   20
Being unprevented, to your timeless grave.
DUKE Proteus, I thank thee for thine honest care,
Which to requite command me while I live.
This love of theirs myself have often seen,
Haply when they have judged me fast asleep,   25
And oftentimes have purposed to forbid
Sir Valentine her company and my court;
But fearing lest my jealous aim might err
And so unworthily disgrace the man –
A rashness that I ever yet have shunned –   30
I gave him gentle looks, thereby to find
That which thyself hast now disclosed to me.
And that thou mayst perceive my fear of this,
Knowing that tender youth is soon suggested,
I nightly lodge her in an upper tower,   35
The key whereof myself have ever kept;
And thence she cannot be conveyed away.
PROTEUS Know, noble lord, they have devised a mean
How he her chamber-window will ascend
And with a corded ladder fetch her down;   40
For which the youthful lover now is gone,
And this way comes he with it presently,
Where, if it please you, you may intercept him.
But, good my lord, do it so cunningly
That my discovery be not aimèd at;   45
For love of you, not hate unto my friend,
Hath made me publisher of this pretence.
DUKE Upon mine honour, he shall never know
That I had any light from thee of this.

[Enter VALENTINE]

PROTEUS Adieu, my lord, Sir Valentine is coming.   *[Exit]*   50

49 SD] *Enter.* F2 *(at 50); not in* F   50 SD] *Rowe; not in* F

21 **timeless** premature.   45 **discovery** disclosure.
28 **jealous** apprehensive, fearful.   45 **aimèd** guessed.
28 **aim** conjecture, guess.   47 **pretence** intention.
34 **suggested** tempted, led astray.   49 **light** information.
40 **corded ladder** rope-ladder.

DUKE Sir Valentine, whither away so fast?
VALENTINE Please it your grace, there is a messenger
          That stays to bear my letters to my friends,
          And I am going to deliver them.
DUKE Be they of much import?   55
VALENTINE The tenor of them doth but signify
          My health and happy being at your court.
DUKE Nay, then no matter; stay with me a while;
          I am to break with thee of some affairs
          That touch me near, wherein thou must be secret.   60
          'Tis not unknown to thee that I have sought
          To match my friend Sir Turio to my daughter.
VALENTINE I know it well, my lord, and sure the match
          Were rich and honourable; besides, the gentleman
          Is full of virtue, bounty, worth, and qualities   65
          Beseeming such a wife as your fair daughter.
          Cannot your grace win her to fancy him?
DUKE No; trust me, she is peevish, sullen, froward,
          Proud, disobedient, stubborn, lacking duty,
          Neither regarding that she is my child   70
          Nor fearing me as if I were her father;
          And, may I say to thee, this pride of hers
          Upon advice hath drawn my love from her;
          And where I thought the remnant of mine age
          Should have been cherished by her childlike duty,   75
          I now am full resolved to take a wife
          And turn her out to who will take her in.
          Then let her beauty be her wedding-dower,
          For me and my possessions she esteems not.
VALENTINE What would your grace have me to do in this?   80
DUKE There is a lady of Verona here

56 tenor] *Steevens*, tenure F, Tenour *Theobald*   81 of Verona] *Young*; in Verona F; Sir, in *Milan* / *Pope*; in Milano *Collier²*

59 **break with thee of** disclose to you.
66 **Beseeming** Befitting.
68 **peevish** obstinate.
73 **advice** deliberation.
74 **where** whereas.
74 **age** lifetime.
77 **who** whoever.

81 ***of Verona here** Most modern editors try to make sense of the F text by changing to 'of Verona' or 'in Milan'. Shakespeare most likely wrote 'in Verona here' when the location of the main action had not been finally determined. See Textual Analysis, p. 151 below.

Whom I affect, but she is nice and coy
And nought esteems my aged eloquence.
Now therefore would I have thee to my tutor –
For long agone I have forgot to court,   85
Besides, the fashion of the time is changed –
How and which way I may bestow myself
To be regarded in her sun-bright eye.
VALENTINE Win her with gifts if she respect not words;
Dumb jewels often in their silent kind   90
More than quick words do move a woman's mind.
DUKE But she did scorn a present that I sent her.
VALENTINE A woman sometime scorns what best contents her.
Send her another; never give her o'er,
For scorn at first makes after-love the more.   95
If she do frown, 'tis not in hate of you
But rather to beget more love in you.
If she do chide, 'tis not to have you gone,
For why the fools are mad if left alone.
Take no repulse, whatever she doth say,   100
For 'get you gone' she doth not mean 'away'.
Flatter and praise, commend, extol their graces;
Though ne'er so black, say they have angels' faces.
That man that hath a tongue, I say, is no man
If with his tongue he cannot win a woman.   105
DUKE But she I mean is promised by her friends
Unto a youthful gentleman of worth,
And kept severely from resort of men,
That no man hath access by day to her.
VALENTINE Why then I would resort to her by night.   110
DUKE Ay, but the doors be locked and keys kept safe,
That no man hath recourse to her by night.

82 affect love.
82 nice shy, fastidious. It is not quite clear whether the lady is meant to be modestly shy or just difficult to please, as 'coy' is likewise open to both interpretations.
85 agone ago.
85 forgot forgotten how.
87 bestow conduct.
88 regarded i.e. approved of.
90–105 The use of rhyme is perhaps meant to suggest the artificiality and absurdity of Valentine's pose as an experienced and worldly-wise gallant. His more poetic expression of his love for Silvia (2.4.121–64), by contrast, does not rhyme.
90 kind nature.
91 quick lively. Quick words in antithesis to the dumb jewels.
99 For why Because.
99 fools Here used as a term of affection.
101 For By.
103 black See 2.6.26 n.
109 That So that. As at 112, 129.

VALENTINE What lets but one may enter at her window?

DUKE Her chamber is aloft, far from the ground,
  And built so shelving that one cannot climb it   115
  Without apparent hazard of his life.

VALENTINE Why then a ladder quaintly made of cords
  To cast up, with a pair of anchoring hooks,
  Would serve to scale another Hero's tower
  So bold Leander would adventure it.   120

DUKE Now, as thou art a gentleman of blood,
  Advise me where I may have such a ladder.

VALENTINE When would you use it? Pray, sir, tell me that.

DUKE This very night, for love is like a child
  That longs for every thing that he can come by.   125

VALENTINE By seven o'clock I'll get you such a ladder.

DUKE But hark thee: I will go to her alone;
  How shall I best convey the ladder thither?

VALENTINE It will be light, my lord, that you may bear it
  Under a cloak that is of any length.   130

DUKE A cloak as long as thine will serve the turn?

VALENTINE Ay, my good lord.

DUKE   Then let me see thy cloak;
  I'll get me one of such another length.

VALENTINE Why, any cloak will serve the turn, my lord.

DUKE How shall I fashion me to wear a cloak?   135
  I pray thee let me feel thy cloak upon me.
  [*Taking Valentine's cloak he finds a letter and a ladder*]
  What letter is this same? What's here? [*Reads*] 'To Silvia'!
  And here an engine fit for my proceeding.
  I'll be so bold to break the seal for once. [*Reads*]
  'My thoughts do harbour with my Silvia nightly,   140
  And slaves they are to me that send them flying.

---

136 SD] *NS subst.; not in* F; *Pulls off his cloak* / *Hanmer*   137 SD] *This edn; not in* F   139 SD] *Rowe subst.; not in* F

113 **What…enter** What hinders anyone from entering.
  115 **shelving** projecting.
  117 **quaintly** skilfully.
  120 **So** Provided that.
  121 **of blood** of good parentage. Perhaps with the connotation 'of high spirit'.
  133 **such another** i.e. the same.
  138 **engine** instrument. Refers to the rope-ladder.

140–9 The lines approach the form of the Shakespearean sonnet, shortened by one quatrain. For the conceit of the lover's thoughts going out to the beloved compare Sonnet 27. By reading aloud the clumsy hyperboles of the sonnet, the Duke mocks youthful pretension. Compare *LLL* 4.3, but there the young men read their sonnets themselves.
  140 **harbour** lodge.

O, could their master come and go as lightly,
   Himself would lodge where, senseless, they are lying.
My herald thoughts in thy pure bosom rest them,
   While I, their king, that thither them importune,   145
Do curse the grace that with such grace hath blessed them,
   Because myself do want my servants' fortune.
I curse myself for they are sent by me,
That they should harbour where their lord should be.'
What's here?   150
'Silvia, this night I will enfranchise thee!'
'Tis so; and here's the ladder for the purpose.
Why, Phaëton – for thou art Merops' son –
Wilt thou aspire to guide the heavenly car
And with thy daring folly burn the world?   155
Wilt thou reach stars because they shine on thee?
Go, base intruder, overweening slave,
Bestow thy fawning smiles on equal mates,
And think my patience, more than thy desert,
Is privilege for thy departure hence.   160
Thank me for this more than for all the favours
Which, all too much, I have bestowed on thee.
But if thou linger in my territories
Longer than swiftest expedition
Will give thee time to leave our royal court,   165
By heaven, my wrath shall far exceed the love
I ever bore my daughter or thyself.
Be gone! I will not hear thy vain excuse,
But as thou lov'st thy life, make speed from hence.   [*Exit*]
VALENTINE And why not death rather than living torment?   170

149 should be] F; would be F2   150–1] *As Var. 1803; as one line,* F   169 SD] F2; *not in* F

142 **lightly** nimbly, quickly.
143 **senseless** without feeling, insensible.
144 **My herald thoughts** i.e. my message-bearing thoughts.
144 **bosom** Also the name of a pocket in front of the bodice to keep love-letters or tokens in.
146 **grace...grace** fortune...favour.
147 **want** lack.
153–6 The Duke's diction takes its cue from Valentine's poetry and tops it in conscious burlesque.
153 **Phaëton** Figure of Greek legend, recalled here – by the Duke to decry Valentine – as a

flagrant example of presumptuous ambition. The illegitimate son of the sun-god aspired to drive his father's chariot and, in doing so, threatened to cause a global conflagration which was only stopped by the intervention of Zeus.
153 **for...son** Merops was married to Phaëton's mother. NS suggests that the phrase is meant to deny Phaëton the status of being fathered by the sun-god and that it possibly includes a pun on 'ropes', i.e. the rope-ladder.
160 **Is privilege for** Allows.
164 **expedition** motion.

To die is to be banished from my self,
And Silvia is my self; banished from her
Is self from self, a deadly banishment.
What light is light if Silvia be not seen?
What joy is joy if Silvia be not by?   175
Unless it be to think that she is by
And feed upon the shadow of perfection;
Except I be by Silvia in the night,
There is no music in the nightingale;
Unless I look on Silvia in the day,   180
There is no day for me to look upon:
She is my essence, and I leave to be
If I be not by her fair influence
Fostered, illumined, cherished, kept alive.
I fly not death to fly his deadly doom: 185
Tarry I here, I but attend on death;
But fly I hence, I fly away from life.

[Enter PROTEUS *and* LANCE]

PROTEUS Run, boy, run, run and seek him out.

171, 172 my self] my selfe F; myself *Johnson*   173 self, a deadly] *Pope subst.;* selfe. A deadly F; self...Ah! deadly *NS*   187 SD] F2; *not in* F

171–87 The lines take the form of a syllogism.
It applies the conception of ideal friendship – of
the friend as another self – to the relationship
between lovers. The truth conveyed by the syllogism is then tested in the examples that follow
(174–81). Towards the end of the monologue,
the idea of oneness is taken up again and tran-
scended in the phrase 'she is my essence' (182),
combining essential selfhood with the mysterious
quintessence which was thought to be the matter
from which stars were made. The Petrarchan
conception of the loved one as a star is then
extended into the astrological belief of heavenly
influence and determination (183–4). The dilemma that neither fleeing nor staying would save
Valentine from 'death' (185–7) serves as another
conclusion of what the speaker set out to prove by
means of the syllogism, a conclusion that perhaps
becomes clearer when F's punctuation is not
followed. Though the outburst is extremely close
to Romeo's in *Rom.* 3.3.29–51, which emphasises
the idea that lovers become one indissoluble self,
it is tested here more critically, as the following
confrontation with Lance and Proteus will show.
   177 **shadow** image.

182 **leave** cease.
185 **his** It seems best to take this as referring to
the Duke.
188 It has been suggested that a separate scene
should begin here, even that an intervening scene
has been lost. It is impossible that the banishment
should have been publicly proclaimed, that Silvia
should have tried to mitigate the sentence and
that Proteus should have set out to seek Valentine
within the time it takes to speak the foregoing
monologue. But the telescoping of time is justified
by the comic reduction of Valentine's pathos
immediately following his outburst. This is first
characterised as the over-emotional utterance of
a 'Valentine', the typical lover (191–2), then
deflated by Lance's offer to strike 'nothing', thus
palpably disproving that Valentine when losing
Silvia has also lost his life (199–203). The
sudden apprehension (209, 212) should make
everyone aware that there are things even worse
than banishment.
188 Proteus's instruction to Lance, coming
after the last line of Valentine's monologue, has a
burlesque ring.

LANCE So-ho, so-ho!

PROTEUS What seest thou?   190

LANCE Him we go to find. There's not a hair on's head but 'tis a
    Valentine.

PROTEUS Valentine?

VALENTINE No.

PROTEUS Who then? His spirit?   195

VALENTINE Neither.

PROTEUS What then?

VALENTINE Nothing.

LANCE Can nothing speak? Master, shall I strike?

PROTEUS Who wouldst thou strike?   200

LANCE Nothing.

PROTEUS Villain, forbear.

LANCE Why sir, I'll strike nothing. I pray you –

PROTEUS Sirrah, I say forbear. Friend Valentine, a word.

VALENTINE My ears are stopped and cannot hear good news,   205
    So much of bad already hath possessed them.

PROTEUS Then in dumb silence will I bury mine,
    For they are harsh, untunable and bad.

VALENTINE Is Silvia dead?

PROTEUS No, Valentine.   210

VALENTINE No Valentine, indeed, for sacred Silvia.
    Hath she forsworn me?

PROTEUS   No, Valentine.

VALENTINE No Valentine if Silvia have forsworn me.
    What is your news?

LANCE Sir, there is a proclamation that you are vanished.   215

PROTEUS That thou art banishèd – O, that's the news! –
    From hence, from Silvia and from me, thy friend.

VALENTINE O, I have fed upon this woe already,
    And now excess of it will make me surfeit.
    Doth Silvia know that I am banishèd?   220

PROTEUS Ay, ay; and she hath offered to the doom,

191–2] *As Capell; as verse,* F   203 you –] *Theobald subst.;* you. F

189 **So-ho** A hunting term used when a hare
was sighted. The use of this term is explained by
the quibble on 'hair' (191).

191–2 **There…Valentine** i.e. everything
about him, down to the last, suggests the lover.

208 **they** 'News' can be either singular or
plural in Shakespeare (Franz 186). See also 280.

215 **vanished** Lance's malapropism for 'banished' takes Valentine's pathetic talk of annihilation literally.

Which unreversed stands in effectual force,
A sea of melting pearl, which some call tears;
Those at her father's churlish feet she tendered,
With them, upon her knees, her humble self,   225
Wringing her hands, whose whiteness so became them
As if but now they waxèd pale for woe.
But neither bended knees, pure hands held up,
Sad sighs, deep groans, nor silver-shedding tears
Could penetrate her uncompassionate sire;   230
But Valentine, if he be ta'en, must die.
Besides, her intercession chafed him so,
When she for thy repeal was suppliant,
That to close prison he commanded her,
With many bitter threats of biding there.   235
VALENTINE No more, unless the next word that thou speak'st
Have some malignant power upon my life;
If so, I pray thee breathe it in mine ear
As ending anthem of my endless dolour.
PROTEUS Cease to lament for that thou canst not help,   240
And study help for that which thou lament'st.
Time is the nurse and breeder of all good.
Here, if thou stay, thou canst not see thy love;
Besides, thy staying will abridge thy life.
Hope is a lover's staff, walk hence with that   245
And manage it against despairing thoughts.
Thy letters may be here, though thou art hence,
Which, being writ to me, shall be delivered
Even in the milk-white bosom of thy love.
The time now serves not to expostulate.   250
Come, I'll convey thee through the city gate,
And, ere I part with thee, confer at large
Of all that may concern thy love-affairs.
As thou lov'st Silvia, though not for thyself,
Regard thy danger, and along with me!   255
VALENTINE I pray thee, Lance, and if thou seest my boy,
Bid him make haste and meet me at the North Gate.
PROTEUS Go, sirrah, find him out. Come, Valentine.

233 **repeal** recall.
239 **ending anthem** song of grief or mourning.
250 **expostulate** discuss.

VALENTINE O my dear Silvia! Hapless Valentine!

[*Exeunt Valentine and Proteus*]

LANCE I am but a fool, look you, and yet I have the wit to think my   260
master is a kind of a knave; but that's all one if he be but one
knave. He lives not now that knows me to be in love, yet I am in
love; but a team of horse shall not pluck that from me, nor who
'tis I love, and yet 'tis a woman; but what woman I will not tell
myself, and yet 'tis a milkmaid; yet 'tis not a maid, for she hath   265
had gossips; yet 'tis a maid, for she is her master's maid and
serves for wages. She hath more qualities than a water-spaniel,
which is much in a bare Christian. [*Pulls out a paper*] Here is the
cate-log of her condition. Inprimis, [*Reads*] 'She can fetch and
carry.' Why, a horse can do no more; nay, a horse cannot fetch,   270
but only carry, therefore is she better than a jade. Item, 'She
can milk.' Look you, a sweet virtue in a maid with clean hands.

[*Enter* SPEED]

SPEED How now, Signor Lance! What news with your mastership?

LANCE With my master's ship? Why, it is at sea.

SPEED Well, your old vice still: mistake the word. What news then   275
in your paper?

LANCE The black'st news that ever thou heard'st.

SPEED Why, man, how black?

259 SD] *Exeunt* F2; *not in* F 268 SD] *Rowe subst.; not in* F 269 condition] F; conditions F4 269–70
Inprimis,...'She...carry.'] *Collier; Inprimis,* Shee...carry: F; 'Imprimis, She...carry.' *Dyce* 269 SD] *Dyce (after
conditions.); not in* F 272 SD] F4; *not in* F 274 master's ship] *Theobald;* Mastership F

260–2 **I am...one knave** Lance's train of
thought from 'fool' to 'knave' may follow a
widespread association of these terms, perhaps
even more particularly the proverb 'Knaves and
fools divide the world' (Tilley K144). His condi-
tional acquiescence seems to allude to the proverb 'The more knaves the worse company'
(Tilley K146).

262–5 A parody of Valentine's enthusiastic
disclosure of his affairs to Proteus (2.4.121–35).

266 **gossips** Baptismal sponsors for a child, or
female friends attending a birth.

267 **water-spaniel** Spaniel used in hunting
waterfowl. Its manifold skills were praised in
contemporary books of hunting.

268–347 The form of the mock-blazon is also
used in *Err.* 3.2.90–147.

269 **cate-log** Regularly spelt 'catlog' at this
time. The F spelling may indicate Lance's pro-

nunciation of the word, providing a wordplay on
'cates' = dainties.

269 **Inprimis** Adapted from medieval Latin
imprimis, especially to indicate the beginning of a
list. Some editors understand it to be part of the
list that is being read by Lance; but Speed, when
he continues the reading (289), also begins the
enumeration with 'Inprimis', attaching this word
to an item that has been previously distinguished
as the second by Lance. The terms 'imprimis' (or
'inprimis') and 'item' appear on documents of
the time, and both Lance and Speed seem to have
their fun with the list in pretending it is official.
For the use of 'Inprimis' as introducing a merely
verbal report unsupported by any writing, see
Shr. 4.1.66.

274 ***master's ship** F's reading may have been
caused by the compositor's eye skipping to the
foregoing line.

LANCE Why, as black as ink.

SPEED Let me read them.   280

LANCE Fie on thee, jolthead, thou canst not read.

SPEED Thou liest, I can.

LANCE I will try thee. Tell me this: who begot thee?

SPEED Marry, the son of my grandfather.

LANCE O illiterate loiterer! It was the son of thy grandmother. This   285
proves that thou canst not read.

SPEED Come, fool, come; try me in thy paper.

LANCE [*Yields the paper*] There; and Saint Nicholas be thy speed!

SPEED Inprimis, 'She can milk.'

LANCE Ay, that she can.   290

SPEED Item, 'She brews good ale.'

LANCE And thereof comes the proverb, 'Blessing of your heart, you
brew good ale.'

SPEED Item, 'She can sew.'

LANCE That's as much as to say, 'Can she so?'   295

SPEED Item, 'She can knit.'

LANCE What need a man care for a stock with a wench when she can
knit him a stock?

SPEED Item, 'She can wash and scour.'

LANCE A special virtue, for then she need not be washed and   300
scoured.

SPEED Item, 'She can spin.'

LANCE Then may I set the world on wheels, when she can spin for
her living.

SPEED Item, 'She hath many nameless virtues.'   305

LANCE That's as much as to say 'bastard virtues', that indeed know
not their fathers and therefore have no names.

SPEED Here follow her vices.

288 SD] *NS; not in* F   294 sew] *Steevens;* sowe F   308 follow] F *corr.;* followes F *uncorr.*

281 **jolthead** blockhead.

288 **Saint Nicholas** Legendary patron saint of schoolboys.

288 **Saint...speed** may Saint Nicholas help you. With a pun on Speed's name.

292–3 **Blessing...ale** Proverb (Tilley B450).

297 **stock** dowry.

298 **knit him a stock** (1) knit him a stocking or netherstock, (2) knit (= conceive) a stock, which could mean both a 'stupid person' and a 'line of drunkards'.

300–1 **washed and scoured** A quibble has been suggested on the meaning 'knocked down and beaten', as 'wash' is a Shakespearean form of 'swash' (= strike violently), and 'scour' can mean 'beat' (NS, p. 110).

303 **set the world on wheels** pursue a course of ease and self-indulgence.

305 **nameless** too small to be worth detailed description.

308 **Here...vices** Some editors take this to be a quotation from Lance's catalogue.

LANCE Close at the heels of her virtues.

SPEED Item, 'She is not to be fasting in respect of her breath.'   310

LANCE Well, that fault may be mended with a breakfast. Read on.

SPEED Item, 'She hath a sweet mouth.'

LANCE That makes amends for her sour breath.

SPEED Item, 'She doth talk in her sleep.'

LANCE It's no matter for that, so she sleep not in her talk.   315

SPEED Item, 'She is slow in words.'

LANCE O villain, that set this down among her vices! To be slow in
words is a woman's only virtue. I pray thee, out with't and place
it for her chief virtue.

SPEED Item, 'She is proud.'   320

LANCE Out with that too; it was Eve's legacy and cannot be ta'en
from her.

SPEED Item, 'She hath no teeth.'

LANCE I care not for that neither, because I love crusts.

SPEED Item, 'She is curst.'   325

LANCE Well, the best is, she hath no teeth to bite.

SPEED Item, 'She will often praise her liquor.'

LANCE If her liquor be good, she shall; if she will not, I will; for good
things should be praised.

SPEED Item, 'She is too liberal.'   330

LANCE Of her tongue she cannot, for that's writ down she is slow
of; of her purse she shall not, for that I'll keep shut. Now, of
another thing she may, and that cannot I help. Well, proceed.

SPEED Item, 'She hath more hair than wit, and more faults than
hairs, and more wealth than faults.'   335

LANCE Stop there; I'll have her. She was mine and not mine twice or

---

310 fasting] F; kist fasting *Rowe*; – fasting *NS*   315 talk] F *corr.*; take F *uncorr.*   317 villain] villaine F *corr.*; villainie F
uncorr.   317–19] *As Pope; as verse*, F   321–2] *As Pope; as verse*, F   324 love] loue F *corr.*; lone F *uncorr.*   334 hair] F
corr.; haires F *uncorr.*

310 **to be fasting** i.e. to be kept fasting.
310 **in respect of** because of.
312 **hath a sweet mouth** i.e. likes sweets. The meaning 'a wanton and lecherous nature' has also been suggested.
315 **sleep not in her talk** With pun on 'slip' (Kökeritz, p. 146).
325 **curst** shrewish. But Lance in his answer (326) takes it in the sense of 'savage'.
327 **praise** appraise, test. Lance takes it as 'laud' at 328.

330 **liberal** unrestrained.
333 **another thing** i.e. her sexual favours.
334–5 **She hath...faults** Perhaps meant as a parody on Lily's *Euphues*: 'This gallant of more wit than wealth, and yet of more wealth than wisdom' (Bullough, I, 217).
334 **more hair than wit** Misogynistic proverbial expression, 'Long hair, short wit' (Tilley B736).

thrice in that last article. Rehearse that once more.

SPEED Item, 'She hath more hair than wit' –

LANCE More hair than wit? It may be; I'll prove it: the cover of the
salt hides the salt, and therefore it is more than the salt; the   340
hair that covers the wit is more than the wit, for the greater
hides the less. What's next?

SPEED 'and more faults than hairs' –

LANCE That's monstrous. O that that were out!

SPEED 'and more wealth than faults.'   345

LANCE Why, that word makes the faults gracious. Well, I'll have her;
and if it be a match, as nothing is impossible –

SPEED What then?

LANCE Why then will I tell thee that thy master stays for thee at the
North Gate.   350

SPEED For me?

LANCE For thee? Ay, who art thou? He hath stayed for a better man
than thee.

SPEED And must I go to him?

LANCE Thou must run to him, for thou hast stayed so long that going   355
will scarce serve the turn.

SPEED Why didst not tell me sooner?
                      [Returns the letter]
'Pox of your love-letters.   *[Exit]*

LANCE Now will he be swinged for reading my letter; an unmannerly slave, that will thrust himself into secrets! I'll after, to   360
rejoice in the boy's correction.   *Exit*

337 that last] F *corr.;* that F *uncorr.*   339 be;] *Theobald;* be F   347 impossible –] *Rowe;* impossible. F   357
SD] *Sanders (at 358); not in* F   358 SD] *Capell; not in* F   361 SD] *Capell; Exeunt.* F

339–42 the cover...less The syllogism is
supported by the allusion to the proverb 'The
greater embraces (includes, hides) the less' (Tilley G437).

339–40 cover of the salt lid of the salt-cellar.
With a quibble on 'salt' = wit. Often with the
implication of lewdness.

346 gracious attractive.

347 nothing...impossible The drift of the
conclusion of the sentence is indicated by the
proverb 'Nothing is impossible to a willing heart'
(Tilley N299).

349 stays waits.

358 'Pox of A vulgar curse.

358 'Pox of your love-letters A possible self-
parody by the author on the unusually frequent
use of letters which, in this play, almost never
function smoothly as an effective means of
communication.

359 swinged beaten.

359–60 unmannerly With a connotation of
'not an adult person'.

3.2 *Enter* DUKE *and* TURIO

DUKE Sir Turio, fear not but that she will love you
      Now Valentine is banished from her sight.
TURIO Since his exile she hath despised me most,
      Forsworn my company and railed at me,
      That I am desperate of obtaining her.   5
DUKE This weak impress of love is as a figure
      Trenchèd in ice, which with an hour's heat
      Dissolves to water and doth lose his form.
      A little time will melt her frozen thoughts,
      And worthless Valentine shall be forgot.   10

               [*Enter* PROTEUS]

      How now, Sir Proteus, is your countryman
      According to our proclamation gone?
PROTEUS Gone, my good lord.
DUKE My daughter takes his going grievously.
PROTEUS A little time, my lord, will kill that grief.   15
DUKE So I believe; but Turio thinks not so.
      Proteus, the good conceit I hold of thee –
      For thou hast shown some sign of good desert –
      Makes me the better to confer with thee.
PROTEUS Longer than I prove loyal to your grace   20
      Let me not live to look upon your grace.
DUKE Thou know'st how willingly I would effect
      The match between Sir Turio and my daughter?
PROTEUS I do, my lord.
DUKE And also, I think, thou art not ignorant   25

Act 3, Scene 2   3.2] *Scena Secunda.* F   0 SD] *Rowe; Enter Duke, Thurio, Protheus.* F   10 SD] *Rowe; not in* F   13 SH] F *corr.; not in* F *uncorr.*   14 grievously.] *Capell; grieuously?* F *corr.; heauily?* F *uncorr.,* heavily. F4   25 I] F; I doe F2

Act 3, Scene 2
  Location Since the location of this scene is not given in the text, the presence of the Duke has been taken by some earlier editors to indicate a location inside the palace, though a garden is equally possible.
  1 but that she will that she will not.
  3 Since his exile The time-lapse between 3.1 and 3.2 cannot be very long because the Duke has had no information of Valentine's departure yet (11–15).

3 exile Accented on the second syllable.
5 That So that.
6 impress impression. Accented on the second syllable.
7 Trenchèd Cut.
7 hour's Disyllabic.
8 his i.e. the figure's.
17 conceit opinion.
19 the better i.e. more willing.

How she opposes her against my will?
PROTEUS She did, my lord, when Valentine was here.
DUKE Ay, and perversely she persevers so.
      What might we do to make the girl forget
      The love of Valentine and love Sir Turio?   30
PROTEUS The best way is to slander Valentine
      With falsehood, cowardice and poor descent,
      Three things that women highly hold in hate.
DUKE Ay, but she'll think that it is spoke in hate.
PROTEUS Ay, if his enemy deliver it.   35
      Therefore it must with circumstance be spoken
      By one whom she esteemeth as his friend.
DUKE Then you must undertake to slander him.
PROTEUS And that, my lord, I shall be loath to do;
      'Tis an ill office for a gentleman,   40
      Especially against his very friend.
DUKE Where your good word cannot advantage him,
      Your slander never can endamage him;
      Therefore the office is indifferent,
      Being entreated to it by your friend.   45
PROTEUS You have prevailed, my lord; if I can do it
      By aught that I can speak in his dispraise,
      She shall not long continue love to him.
      But say this weed her love from Valentine,
      It follows not that she will love Sir Turio.   50
TURIO Therefore, as you unwind her love from him,
      Lest it should ravel and be good to none,
      You must provide to bottom it on me;
      Which must be done by praising me as much
      As you in worth dispraise Sir Valentine.   55
DUKE And, Proteus, we dare trust you in this kind,

---

49 weed] weede F; wean *Rowe;* woo *Sisson;* wind *Leech*

28 **persevers** perseveres. Accented on the second syllable.
34 **spoke** Past participle (Franz 169).
35 **deliver** declare, report.
36 **circumstance** incidental detail.
41 **very** veritable.
45 **your friend** i.e. the Duke. This diplomatic ruse disregards the doctrine that friendship can only exist between equals.
49 **weed** Figuratively, 'uproot, eradicate'.

There is no need for an emendation, though Leech's 'wind', suggested by the reappearance of the word in the next speech as 'unwind' (51), is noteworthy.
   51 **unwind** The image, continued in 'ravel' (52) and 'bottom' (53), suggests a skein of thread transferred by winding from one spool or 'bottom' to another.
   56 **kind** i.e. kind of business.

Because we know, on Valentine's report,
You are already Love's firm votary
And cannot soon revolt and change your mind.
Upon this warrant shall you have access   60
Where you with Silvia may confer at large –
For she is lumpish, heavy, melancholy
And, for your friend's sake, will be glad of you –
Where you may temper her by your persuasion
To hate young Valentine and love my friend.   65

PROTEUS As much as I can do I will effect.
But you, Sir Turio, are not sharp enough;
You must lay lime to tangle her desires
By wailful sonnets, whose composèd rhymes
Should be full fraught with serviceable vows.   70

DUKE Ay, much is the force of heaven-bred poesy.

PROTEUS Say that upon the altar of her beauty
You sacrifice your tears, your sighs, your heart;
Write till your ink be dry, and with your tears
Moist it again, and frame some feeling line   75
That may discover such integrity;
For Orpheus' lute was strung with poets' sinews,
Whose golden touch could soften steel and stones,
Make tigers tame and huge leviathans
Forsake unsounded deeps to dance on sands.   80
After your dire-lamenting elegies,
Visit by night your lady's chamber-window
With some sweet consort; to their instruments
Tune a deploring dump. The night's dead silence

60 warrant pledge.
60 access Accented on the second syllable.
62 lumpish low-spirited.
68 lime birdlime. The idea of ensnaring the lover is more typical of Shakespeare's later comedies. Compare *Ado* 3.1.104 and Malvolio's triumphant cry 'I have lim'd her' (*TN* 3.4.74). There is a difference in the quality of love depending on whether the lovers are depicted as having been wounded by Cupid's arrow or as having been limed.
70 serviceable expressing readiness to serve.
71 The Duke's remark is rather heavily ironic in the light of 3.1.140–56.

76 discover such integrity show such loyal devotion. 'Such' refers to the sacrifice of 'tears…sighs…heart' (73).
77 Orpheus Legendary Greek figure, mentioned here as the prototype of the poet endowed with magical powers.
81 elegies Love poems rather than laments for the dead.
83 consort harmonious music. But the following sentence modulates the meaning to the 'group of musicians' who produce it.
84 Tune Sing.
84 dump mournful melody.

Will well become such sweet-complaining grievance.   85
This, or else nothing, will inherit her.
DUKE This discipline shows thou hast been in love.
TURIO And thy advice this night I'll put in practice.
Therefore, sweet Proteus, my direction-giver,
Let us into the city presently   90
To sort some gentlemen well skilled in music.
I have a sonnet that will serve the turn
To give the onset to thy good advice.
DUKE About it, gentlemen!
PROTEUS We'll wait upon your grace till after supper   95
And afterward determine our proceedings.
DUKE Even now about it! I will pardon you.

Exeunt

4.1 *Enter certain* OUTLAWS

1 OUTLAW Fellows, stand fast. I see a passenger.
2 OUTLAW If there be ten, shrink not, but down with 'em.

[*Enter* VALENTINE *and* SPEED]

3 OUTLAW Stand, sir, and throw us that you have about ye.
If not, we'll make you sit, and rifle you.
SPEED Sir, we are undone. These are the villains   5
That all the travellers do fear so much.
VALENTINE My friends –
1 OUTLAW That's not so, sir; we are your enemies.

85 sweet-complaining] *Capell;* sweet complaining F   **Act 4, Scene 1**   4.1] *Actus Quartus. Scæna Prima.* F   0
SD] *Rowe; Enter Valentine, Speed, and certaine Out-lawes.* F   2 SD] *Rowe; not in* F   4 you sit] F; you sir F3, you, Sir
Rowe   7 friends –] *Theobald subst.;* friends. F

86 **inherit** win.
87 **discipline** instruction.
91 **sort** select.
93 i.e. to begin with the execution of your advice.
93 **onset** start.

Act 4, Scene 1
Location References in the text indicate a forest scene. It is understood to be between Milan and Verona (17–19), though later it is in the vicinity of Mantua (4.3.23 and 5.2.45). On the Elizabethan stage, property trees may have been used to suggest the forest scenes, but it is quite possible that actors made do with the stage columns as trees for the purpose of hiding.
1 **passenger** traveller.
3 **that** that which; elliptically uniting the functions of a demonstrative and a relative pronoun.
4 **rifle** body-search.

2 OUTLAW Peace! We'll hear him.

3 OUTLAW Ay, by my beard will we; for he is a proper man.   10

VALENTINE Then know that I have little wealth to lose;
  A man I am crossed with adversity.
  My riches are these poor habiliments,
  Of which if you should here disfurnish me,
  You take the sum and substance that I have.   15

2 OUTLAW Whither travel you?

VALENTINE To Verona.

1 OUTLAW Whence came you?

VALENTINE From Milan.

3 OUTLAW Have you long sojourned there?   20

VALENTINE Some sixteen months, and longer might have stayed
  If crooked fortune had not thwarted me.

1 OUTLAW What, were you banished thence?

VALENTINE I was.

2 OUTLAW For what offence?   25

VALENTINE For that which now torments me to rehearse:
  I killed a man, whose death I much repent;
  But yet I slew him manfully in fight,
  Without false vantage or base treachery.

1 OUTLAW Why, ne'er repent it if it were done so;   30
  But were you banished for so small a fault?

VALENTINE I was, and held me glad of such a doom.

2 OUTLAW Have you the tongues?

VALENTINE My youthful travail therein made me happy,
  Or else I often had been miserable.   35

3 OUTLAW By the bare scalp of Robin Hood's fat friar,
  This fellow were a king for our wild faction!

34 travail] travaile F; *travel* F3 35 often had been] F2; often had beene often F; had been often *Collier*

10 proper good-looking.

12 crossed with thwarted by.

22 crooked malignant.

27–9 I killed...treachery Various reasons have been adduced for the lie with which Valentine covers up the real cause for his banishment: (1) the courtly-love code, (2) the wish to appear as a formidable opponent, (3) simple reproduction of a source: Brooke's *Romeus* (Allen, p. 40).

29 vantage advantage.

32 held...doom i.e. thought myself lucky to escape a death sentence.

33 Do you speak foreign languages?

34 youthful travail Some editors explain this as 'travels in my youth', as the F spelling 'travaile' could stand for either 'work' or 'travel'. But when Valentine sets out 'to see the wonders of the world' in 1.1, no earlier travel is mentioned.

34 happy skilful.

36 fat friar Friar Tuck of Robin Hood's band. This reference marks the Outlaws as belonging to the pastoral tradition. For a discussion of this aspect, see pp. 15–17 above.

1 OUTLAW We'll have him. Sirs, a word.
                    [*The Outlaws deliberate*]
SPEED Master, be one of them;
             It's an honourable kind of thievery.   40
VALENTINE Peace, villain!
2 OUTLAW Tell us this: have you anything to take to?
VALENTINE Nothing but my fortune.
3 OUTLAW Know then that some of us are gentlemen,
             Such as the fury of ungoverned youth   45
             Thrust from the company of awful men.
             Myself was from Verona banishèd
             For practising to steal away a lady,
             An heir, and near allied unto the duke.
2 OUTLAW And I from Mantua, for a gentleman   50
             Who, in my mood, I stabbed unto the heart.
1 OUTLAW And I for suchlike petty crimes as these.
             But to the purpose, for we cite our faults
             That they may hold excused our lawless lives;
             And partly, seeing you are beautified   55
             With goodly shape, and by your own report
             A linguist, and a man of such perfection
             As we do in our quality much want –
2 OUTLAW Indeed because you are a banished man,
             Therefore, above the rest, we parley to you.   60
             Are you content to be our general,
             To make a virtue of necessity
             And live as we do in this wilderness?
3 OUTLAW What say'st thou? Wilt thou be of our consort?

38 SD] *Capell subst.; not in* F   49 An] F3; *And* F   49 and near] *Theobald;* and Neece, F   52 suchlike] *Riverside;* such
like F; such-like *Dyce*   58 want –] *Theobald subst.;* want. F

41 **villain** Conventional address to a servant,
with no implication of dishonesty.
42 **take to** have recourse to.
46 **awful** commanding respect.
49 **An heir** i.e. heiress.
49 ***near** Theobald's generally followed emendation achieves the maximum improvement of the
sense by a minimal change of the copy-text. But
Bond accepts 'niece allied', taking this to mean
'niece by marriage'.
49 **duke** This Duke of Verona is probably
lifted from Brooke's *Romeus.* If one relates the
time of the action to the rule of the Emperor

Charles V and his son Philip (compare 1.3.27 n.),
the existence of a Duke of Verona is an
anachronism, since the territory became Venetian
after the death of the last Scaliger. In *Rom.* the
ruler of Verona is called 'prince'.
57 **linguist** speaker of foreign languages.
58 **quality** profession, occupation.
62 **make...necessity** Proverb (Tilley v73).
The quotation of this admirable piece of advice in
this context is probably meant to heighten the
fun.
64 **consort** fellowship, company. Accented on
the second syllable.

> Say 'ay', and be the captain of us all.   65
> We'll do thee homage and be ruled by thee,
> Love thee as our commander and our king.
> 1 OUTLAW But if thou scorn our courtesy, thou diest.
> 2 OUTLAW Thou shalt not live to brag what we have offered.
> VALENTINE I take your offer and will live with you,   70
> Provided that you do no outrages
> On silly women or poor passengers.
> 3 OUTLAW No, we detest such vile base practices.
> Come, go with us, we'll bring thee to our crews
> And show thee all the treasure we have got,   75
> Which, with ourselves, all rest at thy dispose.

>   *Exeunt*

4.2 *Enter* PROTEUS

> PROTEUS Already have I been false to Valentine,
> And now I must be as unjust to Turio:
> Under the colour of commending him,
> I have access my own love to prefer.
> But Silvia is too fair, too true, too holy   5
> To be corrupted with my worthless gifts.
> When I protest true loyalty to her,
> She twits me with my falsehood to my friend;
> When to her beauty I commend my vows,

Act 4, Scene 2   4.2] *Scœna Secunda.* F   0 SD] *Rowe; Enter Protheus, Thurio, Iulia, Host, Musitian, Siluia.* F

72 silly helpless.
74 crews This has been interpreted as a misprint for 'caves', possibly because the plural of 'crews' seems unnecessary. But the plural may have been intended to indicate large groups of Outlaws, justifying them in talking of their prospective leader not only as 'captain' (65) but also as 'general' (61) and 'king' (67).
76 dispose disposal.

Act 4, Scene 2
Location The text locates this scene in a place with a view of Silvia's window (16), which is 'aloft' (3.1.114). 3.2.88 has led us to expect a night scene, which is corroborated by 87, 130–2 and Silvia's reference to the moon (93). Elizabethan theatres usually played by daylight,

without artificial lighting, but torch-bearers could indicate night-time and the Host could have been fitted out with a lantern. On the Elizabethan stage, Silvia presumably entered at a window or gallery above. (For the frequency of such scenes 'aloft' in Shakespeare's early plays and their possible staging see the discussion in Ann Thompson (ed.), *Shr.*, 1984, pp. 181–5.) There could have been some properties such as a tree or a movable arbour for Julia/Sebastian and the Host to hide behind and a seat on which the Host sits down and falls asleep.
3 colour pretence.
4 access Accented on the second syllable.
4 prefer put forward, advance.
5 holy For the significance of this attribute, see p. 5 above.

She bids me think how I have been forsworn   10
In breaking faith with Julia, whom I loved.
And notwithstanding all her sudden quips,
The least whereof would quell a lover's hope,
Yet, spaniel-like, the more she spurns my love,
The more it grows and fawneth on her still.   15

[Enter TURIO *and Musicians]*

But here comes Turio. Now must we to her window
And give some evening music to her ear.
TURIO How now, Sir Proteus, are you crept before us?
PROTEUS Ay, gentle Turio, for you know that love
  Will creep in service where it cannot go.   20
TURIO Ay, but I hope, sir, that you love not here.
PROTEUS Sir, but I do; or else I would be hence.
TURIO Who? Silvia?
PROTEUS   Ay, Silvia, for your sake.
TURIO I thank you for your own. Now, gentlemen,
  Let's tune, and to it lustily awhile.   25

[Enter HOST *and* JULIA *disguised as page]*

HOST Now, my young guest, methinks you're allycholly. I pray you,
  why is it?
JULIA Marry, mine host, because I cannot be merry.
HOST Come, we'll have you merry; I'll bring you where you shall
  hear music and see the gentleman that you asked for.   30
JULIA But shall I hear him speak?
HOST Ay, that you shall.
JULIA That will be music!
[Prelude to the song begins]

---

15 SD] *Rowe (after 17); not in* F   25 SD] *Rowe subst.; not in* F   33 SD] *Capell subst. (after 34); not in* F

12 sudden quips sharp or sarcastic remarks. As the audience has not as yet witnessed Proteus courting Silvia, this side of her character has not been shown, but it is plentifully illustrated at 86–7, 106–7, 109–10, 122–3. There is also an undiplomatic sharpness in her rejection of Proteus at 5.4.33–5.
14 spaniel-like The spaniel was proverbially an example of servile flattery (Tilley S704).
14–15 A rewriting of the proverb 'The spaniel that fawns when he is beaten will never forsake his master' (Tilley S705).
15 still continually.

18 crept Turio expresses suspicion by using 'creep' in the sense 'advance stealthily'.
20 creep Proteus turns to the meaning 'crawl' as opposed to 'go upright'. His allusion to the proverb 'Love will creep in service where it cannot go' (Tilley K49) half reveals his own interest in Silvia.
26 allycholly Corruption of 'malycholy', an old form of 'melancholy'.
28 because...merry Julia evades the Host's question by recourse to the proverb 'I am sad because I cannot be glad' (Tilley S14).

HOST Hark! Hark!
JULIA Is he among these?   35
HOST Ay; but peace, let's hear 'em.

Song

Who is Silvia? What is she,
  That all our swains commend her?
Holy, fair and wise is she;
  The heaven such grace did lend her   40
That she might admirèd be.

Is she kind as she is fair?
  For Beauty lives with Kindness.
Love doth to her eyes repair
  To help him of his blindness,   45
And, being helped, inhabits there.

Then to Silvia let us sing
  That Silvia is excelling;
She excels each mortal thing
  Upon the dull earth dwelling.   50
To her let us garlands bring.

HOST How now, are you sadder than you were before? How do you,
    man? The music likes you not.
JULIA You mistake; the musician likes me not.
HOST Why, my pretty youth?   55

37–51 In view of 29–32, 54 and 56, it seems likely that this song was intended to be performed by the actor playing Proteus. In Montemayor's *Diana*, where the serenading extends to a more elaborate performance, Don Felix at least takes part in it, contributing a solo sonnet. But the problem is more complicated here since it is Turio who brings Silvia the serenade and it is almost certainly his 'sonnet' that is performed (3.2.92–3). But in the theatre the song is usually sung by Proteus, accompanied by musicians, with Turio sometimes among them, or by a professional singer. Hall has Turio throw a 'purse to the singers' before they exit. Though the original tune for the song is unknown, it has been frequently set to music. Perhaps the best known is the one by Franz Schubert, but modern productions have often used musical versions closer in style to that of the period in which the

story is set. For a list of compositions ranging from 1727 to 1883 see J. Greenhill *et al., A List of All the Songs and Passages in Shakespeare which Have Been Set to Music*, 1884.
38 swains young lovers, country youth. Here a pointer to the frequent pastoral ambience of love poetry.
41 admirèd wondered at. For the strong sense of this word, compare 'so much admire/That they devour their reason' (*Temp.* 5.1.154–5).
44 Love Cupid, the blind god of love.
52–66 The discussion of the music brings back to mind the use of musical terms and their double meanings in 1.2.76–95, where the musical conceits were used to induce Julia to fall in love. Here, the ambiguities reveal Julia's unhappiness to the audience while hiding it from the Host.
53 likes pleases.

JULIA   He plays false, father.

HOST   How, out of tune on the strings?

JULIA   Not so; but yet so false that he grieves my very heart-strings.

HOST   You have a quick ear.

JULIA   Ay, I would I were deaf; it makes me have a slow heart.   60

HOST   I perceive you delight not in music.

JULIA   Not a whit when it jars so.

HOST   Hark, what fine change is in the music!

JULIA   Ay, that change is the spite.

HOST   You would have them always play but one thing?   65

JULIA   I would always have one play but one thing.
    But host, doth this Sir Proteus that we talk on
    Often resort unto this gentlewoman?

HOST   I tell you what Lance, his man, told me: he loved her out of all
  nick.   70

JULIA   Where is Lance?

HOST   Gone to seek his dog, which tomorrow, by his master's command, he must carry for a present to his lady.
      [Music ceases]

JULIA   Peace, stand aside, the company parts.
    [They retire and Host sits down]

PROTEUS   Sir Turio, fear not you; I will so plead   75
    That you shall say my cunning drift excels.

TURIO   Where meet we?

PROTEUS   At Saint Gregory's Well.

TURIO   Farewell.
    [Exeunt Turio and Musicians]

  [Enter SILVIA above]

58] *As Pope; as verse,* F 65 thing?] *Pope; thing.* F 69–70] *As Pope; as verse,* F 73 SD] *Capell; not in* F 74 SD] *This edn (after Kittredge); not in* F 77 SD.1 *Exeunt Turio and Musicians*] *Rowe subst.; not in* F 77 SD.2 *Enter* SILVIA *above*] *Rowe; not in* F

56 plays false Julia means 'is unfaithful', but the Host refers it to the music (57).

59 quick readily perceptive, discriminating.

60 slow heavy. With an obvious antithesis to 'quick' (59).

63 change variation or modulation (in music). Julia takes this up in the next line as referring to Proteus's change of allegiance.

66 thing Audiences may hear an innuendo ('thing' meaning 'vagina'), but it can hardly be assumed that this is the speaker's intention as it was at 3.1.333.

69–70 out of all nick beyond all reckoning, exceedingly. The Host uses a phrase derived from his trade – that is, to keep an account by carving 'nicks' into a stick.

72–3 Gone...lady Proteus had actually commanded Lance to deliver not Crab but another small dog to Silvia. However, the dog was stolen and Lance therefore substituted his own (4.4.39–50). In 4.4.5–32, he tells the audience of the disastrous consequences of this attempt.

77 Saint Gregory's Well This refers to an actual well near Milan.

PROTEUS Madam, good even to your ladyship.
SILVIA I thank you for your music, gentlemen.
         Who is that that spake?   80
PROTEUS One, lady, if you knew his pure heart's truth,
         You would quickly learn to know him by his voice.
SILVIA Sir Proteus, as I take it.
PROTEUS Sir Proteus, gentle lady, and your servant.
SILVIA What's your will?
PROTEUS   That I may compass yours.   85
SILVIA You have your wish; my will is even this,
         That presently you hie you home to bed.
         Thou subtle, perjured, false, disloyal man,
         Think'st thou I am so shallow, so conceitless,
         To be seducèd by thy flattery,   90
         That hast deceived so many with thy vows?
         Return, return, and make thy love amends.
         For me – by this pale queen of night I swear –
         I am so far from granting thy request
         That I despise thee for thy wrongful suit   95
         And by and by intend to chide myself
         Even for this time I spend in talking to thee.
PROTEUS I grant, sweet love, that I did love a lady,
         But she is dead.
JULIA [*Aside*]   'Twere false if I should speak it,
         For I am sure she is not burièd.   100
SILVIA Say that she be; yet Valentine, thy friend,

99, 111, 119 SD] *Pope; not in* F

85 **will** wish, request. Proteus, in his answer, applies to it the sense of 'good will, consent', the more common Shakespearean meaning, perhaps with the underlying meaning of 'sexual desire'.
85 **compass** obtain.
87–8 **you...Thou** Leech draws attention to the change from 'you' to 'thou' in Silvia's speech as an expression of ill humour or anger which, as here, is often accompanied by disparaging words. Although rather archaic in Shakespeare's time, 'thou' was still used in higher poetic style among friends (Valentine and Proteus) and persons of lower rank (Lance and Speed) as well as by persons of higher rank towards their inferiors (Proteus to Speed and Lance, Julia to Lucetta, even Lance when speaking to his dog), while those so addressed used 'you' in return. But

Valentine addresses his page Speed as 'you', which characterises their relationship as friendly companions rather than master and servant. Speaking to Valentine, the Outlaws change to the familiar 'thou' when they finally ask him to be one of them and offer him the leadership (4.1.64). For euphonic and other reasons, these rules are often modified (Franz 289, Abbott 231–2).
88 **subtle** treacherously cunning.
89 **conceitless** witless.
90 **To be** As to be.
93 **pale queen of night** The moon as Diana, goddess of chastity. Swearing by her renders Proteus's suit hopeless.
99 **if** even if. Julia, though now Sebastian, is not 'dead'.

Survives, to whom, thyself art witness,
I am betrothed; and art thou not ashamed
To wrong him with thy importunacy?
PROTEUS I likewise hear that Valentine is dead.   105
SILVIA And so suppose am I; for in his grave,
Assure thyself, my love is burièd.
PROTEUS Sweet lady, let me rake it from the earth.
SILVIA Go to thy lady's grave and call hers thence,
Or, at the least, in hers sepulchre thine.   110
JULIA [*Aside*] He heard not that.
PROTEUS Madam, if your heart be so obdurate,
Vouchsafe me yet your picture for my love,
The picture that is hanging in your chamber.
To that I'll speak, to that I'll sigh and weep;   115
For since the substance of your perfect self
Is else devoted, I am but a shadow,
And to your shadow will I make true love.
JULIA [*Aside*] If 'twere a substance, you would sure deceive it
And make it but a shadow, as I am.   120
SILVIA I am very loath to be your idol, sir;
But since your falsehood shall become you well
To worship shadows and adore false shapes,
Send to me in the morning, and I'll send it.
And so, good rest.   [*Exit*]
PROTEUS   As wretches have o'ernight   125
That wait for execution in the morn.   [*Exit*]
JULIA Host, will you go?
HOST By my halidom, I was fast asleep.

106 his] F2; her F   125 SD] NS subst.; not in F   126 SD] NS subst.; not in F; Exeunt F2; Exeunt Pro. and Sil. Rowe

106 *his F2 corrects F's 'her', which is most likely a compositor's misreading.
109–10 Go...thine Silvia recommends a kind of conduct here which she finds laudable in Eglamour. Compare 4.3.18–21.
110 sepulchre Accented on the second syllable.
112 obdurate Accented on the second syllable.
116–18 since...love Proteus acknowledges the defeat of his suit in suggesting the division of Silvia's self into its substance (a synonym of 'essence' – compare 3.1.182) and its shadow. In clinging to this shadow, he is hopelessly lost and incapable of reorientating himself to a rational

course of action. When Silvia grants him his request for her picture, she is merely ratifying his defeat (121–4).
117 else elsewhere, to another person.
118 shadow i.e. the portrait as referred to at 113–14.
120 shadow, as I am i.e. a person robbed of her substance, with an allusion to her disguise.
122–3 since...shapes i.e. since you are false and deserve to direct your devotion to mere pictures and images of deceptive idols.
128 By my halidom A conventional oath; originally a reference to the relics on which oaths were sworn.

JULIA Pray you, where lies Sir Proteus?
HOST Marry, at my house. Trust me, I think 'tis almost day.   130
JULIA Not so; but it hath been the longest night
            That e'er I watched, and the most heaviest.

                                                        [*Exeunt*]

4.3 *Enter* EGLAMOUR

EGLAMOUR This is the hour that Madam Silvia
            Entreated me to call and know her mind;
            There's some great matter she'd employ me in.
            Madam, madam!

                        [*Enter* SILVIA *above*]

SILVIA   Who calls?
EGLAMOUR   Your servant and your friend;
            One that attends your ladyship's command.   5
SILVIA Sir Eglamour, a thousand times good morrow.
EGLAMOUR As many, worthy lady, to yourself.
            According to your ladyship's impose,
            I am thus early come to know what service
            It is your pleasure to command me in.   10
SILVIA O Eglamour, thou art a gentleman –
            Think not I flatter, for I swear I do not –
            Valiant, wise, remorseful, well accomplished.
            Thou art not ignorant what dear good will
            I bear unto the banished Valentine,   15
            Nor how my father would enforce me marry
            Vain Turio, whom my very soul abhorred.

130] *As Pope; as verse,* F   132 SD] F2; *not in* F   Act 4, Scene 3   4.3] *Scœna Tertia.* F   o SD] *Rowe; Enter Eglamore, Siluia.* F   4 SD] *Rowe; not in* F   17 abhorred] abhor'd F; abhors *Hanmer*

129 **lies** lodges.
132 **most heaviest** A deliberate use of a double superlative for emphasis.

Act 4, Scene 3
Location The text demands the same location under Silvia's window as 4.2, since Eglamour has to call out for her (4). The repeated references to the early morning (1, 6, 9) ensure the privacy of the meeting in such a public place.
1 EGLAMOUR On the identity of the character,

see the note on p. 53 above.
4 **Madam, madam** Monosyllabic, like modern 'ma'am' (Kökeritz, pp. 300–1).
8 **impose** command.
13 **remorseful** compassionate.
17 **abhorred** Some editors explain the past tense in F as a compositor's error. This seems unnecessary if we see it as dependent on the past form 'would' in the previous line, with the meaning that Silvia abhors the idea of Turio as her husband but could otherwise tolerate him.

Thyself hast loved, and I have heard thee say
No grief did ever come so near thy heart
As when thy lady and thy true love died,   20
Upon whose grave thou vow'dst pure chastity.
Sir Eglamour, I would to Valentine,
To Mantua, where I hear he makes abode;
And, for the ways are dangerous to pass,
I do desire thy worthy company,   25
Upon whose faith and honour I repose.
Urge not my father's anger, Eglamour,
But think upon my grief, a lady's grief,
And on the justice of my flying hence
To keep me from a most unholy match,   30
Which heaven and fortune still rewards with plagues.
I do desire thee, even from a heart
As full of sorrows as the sea of sands,
To bear me company and go with me;
If not, to hide what I have said to thee,   35
That I may venture to depart alone.

EGLAMOUR Madam, I pity much your grievances,
Which since I know they virtuously are placed,
I give consent to go along with you,
Recking as little what betideth me   40
As much I wish all good befortune you.
When will you go?

SILVIA This evening coming.

EGLAMOUR Where shall I meet you?

SILVIA   At Friar Patrick's cell,

---

40 Recking] *Pope;* Wreaking F; Reaking *Riverside*

---

23 **Mantua** As a place of refuge it was probably
suggested by Brooke's *Romeus*.

24 **for** because.

26 **repose** rely.

29–31 Silvia's argument corresponds with
English church law in Shakespeare's time. In
contrast with continental practice, all that was
needed to make a marriage valid was the free and
mutual agreement of the partners, though they
were advised to seek their parents' consent (Alan
Macfarlane, *Marriage and Love in England: Modes
of Reproduction 1300–1840*, 1986, pp. 124–45).
On the other hand, Silvia is the daughter of an
Italian duke, whose prerogative to decide about
her future husband is not to be questioned. The
ensuing conflict was also a feature of those Italian
comedies that influenced Shakespeare in this
play.

31 **rewards** In Shakespearean grammar, two
singular subjects are frequently followed by the
singular form of the verb (Abbott 336, Franz
673).

37 **grievances** sufferings, distress.

37–8 **grievances...placed** Although the
construction is vague, the general sense that
Silvia has not caused her distress by her own
failings is clear.

40 **Recking** Heeding. F's 'Wreaking' is a
variant spelling.

Where I intend holy confession.   45
EGLAMOUR I will not fail your ladyship.
        Good morrow, gentle lady.
SILVIA Good morrow, kind Sir Eglamour.

                                                            Exeunt

4.4 *Enter* LANCE [*with his dog*]

LANCE [*Pointing at his dog*] When a man's servant shall play the cur
    with him, look you, it goes hard – one that I brought up of a
    puppy, one that I saved from drowning when three or four of his
    blind brothers and sisters went to it. I have taught him, even as
    one would say precisely, 'Thus I would teach a dog.' I was sent   5
    to deliver him as a present to Mistress Silvia from my master;
    and I came no sooner into the dining-chamber but he steps me
    to her trencher and steals her capon's leg. O, 'tis a foul thing
    when a cur cannot keep himself in all companies. I would have,
    as one should say, one that takes upon him to be a dog indeed,   10
    to be, as it were, a dog at all things. If I had not had more wit

---

Act 4, Scene 4   4.4] *Scena Quarta.* F   0 SD] *Pope; Enter Launce, Protheus, Iulia, Siluia.* F   1 SD] *This edn; not in*
F   5 say precisely, 'Thus] say precisely, thus F; say, 'precisely thus *Bond*

---

45 confession Tetrasyllabic here.

Act 4, Scene 4
  Location F's scene division creates problems
here by the stitching together of various sections
that fit each other uneasily in time and place. 4.2
has determined the time to be morning (72 and
124) so that some producers have found it necessary to replace 'dining-chamber' (7) by 'breakfast table' on the assumption that Lance has just
left Silvia when he enters to speak his monologue.
The localisation of this scene then involves a
further problem. When instructing his newly-
engaged page Julia/Sebastian, Proteus points
towards Silvia's chamber (77). If we assume a
location outside the palace as in 4.2 and 4.3, there
is then the problem of the stage level, since
Silvia's chamber is 'aloft', but the called-for
picture is handed over to the page without delay
(108–9). If we assume a location inside the
palace on the floor that leads to the chamber, the
immediate handing out of the portrait would be
possible, but such a location would not seem to
be the appropriate place either for Lance's mon-

ologue or for the engagement of a new page.
On the Elizabethan stage, each of these scene-
sections would probably be performed on the
main stage and the fluidity of space supported by
Julia's monologue, wedged in between the two
locations (see illustration 1, p. 8 above).
  2 of from.
  4–5 even…dog i.e. as a dog should be
taught.
  5 precisely This expression mimics the speech
of the pedagogue and his pride in his craft.
Compare the later reference to the admirable but,
in this case, totally misapplied method of teaching
manners by the observation of example (30–2),
and see p. 15 above. Bond changes F's punctuation to gain the meaning 'I have taught him the
most precise manners.'
  7 steps me Lance's frequent use of the so-
called ethical dative indicates his concern about
the behaviour of the dog. Compare 'thrusts me'
(14) and 'goes me' (20).
  9 keep restrain.
  11 be…a dog at be adept at. Allusion to the
proverbial 'be old dog at' (Tilley D506).

than he, to take a fault upon me that he did, I think verily he had
been hanged for't; sure as I live, he had suffered for't. You shall
judge. He thrusts me himself into the company of three or four
gentlemanlike dogs under the duke's table. He had not been   15
there, bless the mark, a pissing while but all the chamber smelt
him. 'Out with the dog', says one; 'What cur is that?', says
another; 'Whip him out', says the third; 'Hang him up', says the
duke. I, having been acquainted with the smell before, knew
it was Crab, and goes me to the fellow that whips the dogs.   20
'Friend', quoth I, 'you mean to whip the dog?' 'Ay, marry, do I',
quoth he. 'You do him the more wrong', quoth I, ''twas I did the
thing you wot of.' He makes me no more ado but whips me out
of the chamber. How many masters would do this for his servant? Nay, I'll be sworn I have sat in the stocks for puddings   25
he hath stolen, otherwise he had been executed. I have stood on
the pillory for geese he hath killed, otherwise he had suffered
for't. [*To his dog*] Thou think'st not of this now. Nay, I remember
the trick you served me when I took my leave of Madam Silvia.
Did not I bid thee still mark me and do as I do? When didst thou   30
see me heave up my leg and make water against a gentlewoman's
farthingale? Didst thou ever see me do such a trick?

[*Enter* PROTEUS *and* JULIA *disguised as Sebastian*]

PROTEUS Sebastian is thy name? I like thee well
          And will employ thee in some service presently.
JULIA   In what you please; I'll do what I can.   35
PROTEUS I hope thou wilt. [*To Lance*] How now, you whoreson
          peasant,

---

21 dog?] *Rowe;* dog: F   28 SD] *This edn; not in* F   32 SD] *Rowe subst.; not in* F   33 name?] *Rowe;* name: F   35 I'll
do] ile doe F; ile doe Sir F2; I will do *Var. 1803*   36] *As Pope;* I...wilt / ...pezant F   36 SD] *Johnson; not in* F

---

13 sure...live Proverbial (Tilley L374).

16 bless the mark An apology for using a
coarse expression.

16 a pissing while Proverbial for 'a very short
time' (Tilley P355) but here, as it turns out, with
literal meaning.

18 Hang him up In Elizabethan times dogs
were actually punished in this way.

24–5 How...servant Leech points to the
parallel with Julia's exclamation at 81.

25 stocks Instrument of punishment for petty
offenders in which the prisoner was clamped by

his legs (and sometimes hands). To be distinguished from the pillory (27), which held the
prisoner by his head and hands.

25 puddings A dish made of animals' stomachs
or intestines stuffed with meat, etc., and boiled. A
variety of such meat puddings is still eaten in the
north of England, known as 'black pudding'; in
Scotland there is another, the haggis.

36 whoreson Not necessarily an expression of
anger here. The word seems to have been
frequently used in coarse playfulness.

Where have you been these two days loitering?

LANCE Marry, sir, I carried Mistress Silvia the dog you bade me.

PROTEUS And what says she to my little jewel?

LANCE Marry, she says your dog was a cur, and tells you currish   40
thanks is good enough for such a present.

PROTEUS But she received my dog?

LANCE No, indeed, did she not. Here have I brought him back again.

PROTEUS What, didst thou offer her this from me? [*Points to Crab*]

LANCE Ay, sir; the other squirrel was stolen from me by the   45
hangman's boys in the market-place; and then I offered her
mine own, who is a dog as big as ten of yours, and therefore the
gift the greater.

PROTEUS Go, get thee hence and find my dog again,
Or ne'er return again into my sight.   50
Away, I say! Stayest thou to vex me here?

                                        [*Exit Lance*]

A slave that still an end turns me to shame!
Sebastian, I have entertainèd thee
Partly that I have need of such a youth
That can with some discretion do my business,   55
For 'tis no trusting to yond foolish lout,
But chiefly for thy face and thy behaviour,
Which, if my augury deceive me not,
Witness good bringing up, fortune and truth.

39 jewel] *Pope;* Iewell F; *Jewel* F4, *followed by NS*   43] *As Pope; as verse,* F   44 this] F; this cur *Collier²*   44 SD] *This edn; not in* F   45–8] *As Pope; as verse,* F   45 other squirrel] *Pope;* other Squirrill F; other, *Squirrel, / Hanmer*   46 hangman's boys] *Var. 1803;* Hangmans boyes F; hangmans boy F2; a hangman boy *Collier²;* the hangman boys *Dyce*   51 SD] *Exit* F2 *(after 52); not in* F

39 jewel i.e. the dog. Since F writes the word with a capital, some editors have taken it to be the dog's name, disregarding F's lavish use of capitals.

40 currish snappish.

45 squirrel Lance's expression of contempt for the small size of the dog. Again, the suggestion that this is to be understood as the dog's name is far less convincing.

46 hangman's boys boys fit for the hangman. Some editors write 'hangman boys' to exclude the meaning 'the hangman's own boys', but this seems unnecessary.

46–7 Judging from the profuse descriptions and evaluations of Crab's acting abilities in theatre critics' reviews, small dogs have been chosen more often than others, probably for their convenience. But Gordon Crosse is right in pointing out that 'Crab should be a good-sized cur, not a tiny lapdog' (*Shakespearean Playgoing*, 1953, p. 74).

51 SD Lance possibly goes off with reluctance, so that he is still in sight when Proteus speaks of 'yond foolish lout' (56).

52 still an end continually.

53 entertainèd taken into service. As at 2.4.103.

57 chiefly...face Proteus's habit of judging by appearances is noteworthy.

> Therefore, know thee, for this I entertain thee: 60
> Go presently, and take this ring with thee,
> Deliver it to Madam Silvia –
> She loved me well delivered it to me.

JULIA It seems you loved not her, to leave her token;
> She is dead belike?

PROTEUS   Not so; I think she lives.   65

JULIA Alas!

PROTEUS Why dost thou cry 'alas'?

JULIA I cannot choose but pity her.

PROTEUS Wherefore shouldst thou pity her?

JULIA Because methinks that she loved you as well   70
> As you do love your lady Silvia:
> She dreams on him that has forgot her love,
> You dote on her that cares not for your love.
> 'Tis pity love should be so contrary;
> And thinking on it makes me cry 'alas'.   75

PROTEUS Well, give her that ring and therewithal
> This letter. That's her chamber. [*Points upward*] Tell my
> lady
> I claim the promise for her heavenly picture.
> Your message done, hie home unto my chamber,
> Where thou shalt find me sad and solitary.   [*Exit*]   80

JULIA How many women would do such a message?
> Alas, poor Proteus, thou hast entertained
> A fox to be the shepherd of thy lambs.
> Alas, poor fool, why do I pity him
> That with his very heart despiseth me?   85
> Because he loves her, he despiseth me;
> Because I love him, I must pity him.
> This ring I gave him when he parted from me,
> To bind him to remember my good will;

60 know thee] F; know thou F2   64 to leave] F2; not leaue F   77 SD] NS subst.; not in F   80 SD] F2; not in F

60 know thee Abbott points out that, in Shakespeare's usage, 'thee' particularly appears after imperatives as an unaffected 'thou' (212). F2's substitution certainly reflects a change of taste. Modern editors leave it open whether their adoption of 'thou' is based on the assumption of a compositor's or copyist's error or whether it is merely a product of their own modernisation.

63 delivered who delivered. For the loss of the relative pronoun, see Franz 348, Abbott 244.

64 *to leave F's 'not leave' is probably a compositor's memory error, caused by the 'loved not her' of the same line.

76 therewithal with it.

84 poor fool Said pityingly to herself.

And now am I, unhappy messenger,   90
To plead for that which I would not obtain,
To carry that which I would have refused,
To praise his faith which I would have dispraised.
I am my master's true confirmèd love,
But cannot be true servant to my master   95
Unless I prove false traitor to myself.
Yet will I woo for him, but yet so coldly
As, heaven it knows, I would not have him speed.

[Enter SILVIA *attended]*

Gentlewoman, good day. I pray you be my mean
To bring me where to speak with Madam Silvia.   100
SILVIA What would you with her, if that I be she?
JULIA If you be she, I do entreat your patience
To hear me speak the message I am sent on.
SILVIA From whom?
JULIA From my master, Sir Proteus, madam.   105
SILVIA O, he sends you for a picture?
JULIA Ay, madam.
SILVIA Ursula, bring my picture there.
[One of the attendants fetches the portrait]
Go, give your master this. Tell him from me,
One Julia, that his changing thoughts forget,   110
Would better fit his chamber than this shadow.
JULIA Madam, please you peruse this letter –
[Gives a letter]

98 SD] *Var. 1803; not in* F*; Enter Silvia.* F2   99 Gentlewoman] F*; Lady* Pope   108 SD] *Capell subst.; not in* F   112
SD] *Dyce; not in* F

98 speed succeed.
99 mean agent, means.
111 shadow portrait. For the full range of
meanings in this play, compare notes to 3.1.177,
4.2.116–20 and 4.4.188.
112–22 The question how and when the two
letters pass between the two ladies presents some
difficulties, though 112 must be read as an
internal stage direction; that the letter is not only
offered here but also given may be derived from
the following two lines. This edition suggests that
Silvia offers to return the letter at 118, but Julia
refuses to accept it then. The question has been
raised why two letters are introduced here at all.

Editors have offered the explanation that the first
letter is one from Proteus to Julia herself.
Macready clarified this in his prompt-book by
having her take it out of her bosom pocket while
she keeps the other in her girdle. Whether Julia
offers the first one inadvertently or intentionally
remains open to interpretation, but this is perhaps
another example of the difficulties that Shakespeare's disguised young ladies have in keeping
their adopted roles when under emotional strain
(compare Rosalind in *AYLI* and Viola in *TN*).
The pressure Julia feels to reveal her identity
is again reflected in her invented tale of her
performance as Ariadne (149–63).

Pardon me, madam, I have unadvised
Delivered you a paper that I should not.
[Takes the first letter back and gives another one]
This is the letter to your ladyship.   115
SILVIA I pray thee let me look on that again.
JULIA It may not be; good madam, pardon me.
SILVIA There, hold!
[Offers to return the second letter which Julia refuses to take]
I will not look upon your master's lines.
I know they are stuffed with protestations   120
And full of new-found oaths, which he will break –
[Tears the letter]
As easily as I do tear his paper.
JULIA Madam, he sends your ladyship this ring.
SILVIA The more shame for him that he sends it me;
For I have heard him say a thousand times   125
His Julia gave it him at his departure.
Though his false finger have profaned the ring,
Mine shall not do his Julia so much wrong.
JULIA She thanks you.
SILVIA What say'st thou?
JULIA I thank you, madam, that you tender her.   130
Poor gentlewoman, my master wrongs her much.
SILVIA Dost thou know her?
JULIA Almost as well as I do know myself.
To think upon her woes, I do protest
That I have wept a hundred several times.   135
SILVIA Belike she thinks that Proteus hath forsook her?
JULIA I think she doth, and that's her cause of sorrow.
SILVIA Is she not passing fair?
JULIA She hath been fairer, madam, than she is.   140
When she did think my master loved her well,
She, in my judgement, was as fair as you.

---

114 SD] *NS subst.; not in* F   118 SD] *This edn; not in* F   121 SD] *Dyce (after 122); not in* F   140 is.] *Collier;* is, F; is;
Rowe   141 well,] *Rowe;* well; F

113 **unadvised** inadvertently.
118 On the problem of how to play this line, see pp. 153–4 below.
125 **a thousand times** An overstatement expressive of Silvia's vexation. Compare also 4.2.91 and Julia's exaggerations at 2.7.69–70.

129 **She thanks you** Whenever Silvia shows concern for the wrongs done by Proteus to his former love, Julia finds it difficult to keep up her role as Sebastian.
131 **tender** feel compassion for.
139 **passing** exceedingly.

> But since she did neglect her looking-glass
> And threw her sun-expelling mask away,
> The air hath starved the roses in her cheeks   145
> And pinched the lily-tincture of her face,
> That now she is become as black as I.

SILVIA How tall was she?

JULIA About my stature; for at Pentecost,
> When all our pageants of delight were played,   150
> Our youth got me to play the woman's part,
> And I was trimmed in Madam Julia's gown,
> Which servèd me as fit, by all men's judgements,
> As if the garment had been made for me;
> Therefore I know she is about my height.   155
> And at that time I made her weep agood,
> For I did play a lamentable part.
> Madam, 'twas Ariadne passioning
> For Theseus' perjury and unjust flight,
> Which I so lively acted with my tears   160
> That my poor mistress, movèd therewithal,
> Wept bitterly; and would I might be dead
> If I in thought felt not her very sorrow.

SILVIA She is beholding to thee, gentle youth.
> Alas, poor lady, desolate and left!   165
> I weep myself to think upon thy words.

156 agood] F2; a good F

144 **sun-expelling mask** Masks were worn to preserve the whiteness ('lily-tincture', 146) of the skin. The coveted modern sun-tan would have been considered ugly. But the facial skin also needed protection against the influence of cold and rough weather (145–6). For the custom of wearing masks, see also 5.2.38.

145 **starved** nipped with cold.

147 **That** So that.

147 **black** i.e. ugly.

149 **Pentecost** Whitsuntide was a time for theatrical entertainment. Compare the reference to Whitsun pastorals in *WT* 4.4.133–4.

151 **the woman's part** Played by boys in the Elizabethan theatre.

152 **trimmed** dressed.

156 **agood** plentifully.

158 **Ariadne** Legendary heroine of Greek mythology, mentioned here as a prototype of the woman undeservedly abandoned by her lover.

Sebastian's invented tale of having played a role in a non-existent play based on a mythological fiction leads up to the revelation of her suffering as Julia. Her identification with the mythological prototype allows her to reidentify herself as a woman. The effect of compassion this elicits from Silvia is not undercut by irony but corroborated by her response.

158 **passioning** passionately grieving. Perhaps = enacting a speech representing such a state. Compare 'her passion ends the play' (*MND* 5.1.315).

161 **my poor mistress** i.e. Julia herself as the beloved of Proteus. Julia's alienation from herself is underlined by the double representation, first in the invented role of Ariadne and second as a member of the audience watching the performance, whose reaction is watched and reacted to by the actress (160–3).

164 **beholding** beholden.

Here, youth, there is my purse; I give thee this
For thy sweet mistress' sake, because thou lov'st her.
Farewell.

                                      [*Exit with attendants*]

JULIA And she shall thank you for't, if e'er you know her.   170
A virtuous gentlewoman, mild and beautiful!
I hope my master's suit will be but cold,
Since she respects my mistress' love so much.
Alas, how love can trifle with itself!
Here is her picture; let me see; I think,   175
If I had such a tire, this face of mine
Were full as lovely as is this of hers.
And yet the painter flattered her a little,
Unless I flatter with myself too much.
Her hair is auburn, mine is perfect yellow;   180
If that be all the difference in his love,
I'll get me such a coloured periwig.
Her eyes are grey as glass, and so are mine;
Ay, but her forehead's low, and mine's as high.
What should it be that he respects in her   185
But I can make respective in myself,
If this fond Love were not a blinded god?
Come, shadow, come, and take this shadow up,

                    [*Looking at the portrait*]

168–9] *As* F2; *as one line,* F   169 SD] F2 *subst.; not in* F   188 SD] *This edn; not in* F

172 **cold** i.e. without power to move.

173 **my mistress'** Julia's self-division is continued even in her monologue where there is no need to keep up the fiction. See 161 n. above.

176–87 Although beauty is in the eye of the beholder, casting-directors, costumiers and make-up artists should note that the two female leads approach in equal measure the contemporary standards of ideal feminine beauty, whereas Felismena, Julia's counterpart in Montemayor's *Diana*, is depicted as being clearly superior to her rival. A considerable difference in their attractiveness, however, would change the meaning of this passage and 5.4.111–12.

176 **tire** head-dress.

180 **auburn** In Elizabethan English = 'nearly white, whitish'; refers here to a variant of blond-

ness. The prevalence of the modern meaning 'amber-coloured' developed later.

183 **grey** Probably a bluish or pearl grey, like 'griseous', a term still used in botany and zoology, related to Latin *griseus*.

184 **her...as high** 'as' is used as a correlative. The point is that both meet the highest standards of beauty with respect to colour of hair and eyes (180–3), but both fall below it with respect to the height of the forehead.

186 **But I can** That I cannot.

186 **make** (1) bring about, (2) consider to be.

186 **respective** worthy of respect.

188 **shadow** Julia first refers to herself in her disguise and then to the portrait of Silvia.

188 **take this shadow up** With the connotation 'accept the challenge'.

For 'tis thy rival. O thou senseless form,
Thou shalt be worshipped, kissed, loved and adored!   190
And were there sense in his idolatry,
My substance should be statue in thy stead.
I'll use thee kindly for thy mistress' sake
That used me so; or else, by Jove I vow,
I should have scratched out your unseeing eyes,   195
To make my master out of love with thee.   *Exit*

5.1 *Enter* EGLAMOUR

EGLAMOUR The sun begins to gild the western sky,
And now it is about the very hour
That Silvia at Friar Patrick's cell should meet me.
She will not fail; for lovers break not hours,
Unless it be to come before their time,   5
So much they spur their expedition.

                    [*Enter* SILVIA]

See where she comes. Lady, a happy evening.
SILVIA Amen, amen; go on, good Eglamour,
Out at the postern by the abbey wall;
I fear I am attended by some spies.   10
EGLAMOUR Fear not; the forest is not three leagues off.
If we recover that, we are sure enough.

                         Exeunt

196 SD] F2; *Exeunt* F   Act 5, Scene 1   5.1] *Actus Quintus. Scœna Prima.* F   o SD] *Rowe; Enter Eglamoure, Siluia.*
F   6 SD] *Rowe (after 7); not in* F

189 **senseless** incapable of feeling.
191 **idolatry** This word may express both the intensity of Proteus's feelings and the wrongness of their direction.
192 **statue** The opposition between form and substance is paralleled by that of the picture and the sculpture.

Act 5, Scene 1
Location References to sunset and the time of evening (1–2, 7) as well as the location of Friar Patrick's cell (3), take up 4.3.42–4. The text indicates a place within walls (9), but the Elizabethan stage would not have bothered about representing any of these points physically.
4 **lovers…hours** This expression is not catalogued as a proverb, but the explanation that follows (5–6) alludes to proverbs listed in Tilley (L568 and L481).
6 **expedition** motion, progress. Here read as five syllables.
9 **postern** small back- or side-door.
10 **attended** watched.
12 **recover** reach.
12 **sure** safe.

5.2 *Enter* TURIO, PROTEUS *and* JULIA [*disguised as Sebastian*]

TURIO Sir Proteus, what says Silvia to my suit?
PROTEUS O sir, I find her milder than she was,
    And yet she takes exceptions at your person.
TURIO What? That my leg is too long?
PROTEUS No, that it is too little. 5
TURIO I'll wear a boot to make it somewhat rounder.
[JULIA] [*Aside*] But love will not be spurred to what it loathes.
TURIO What says she to my face?
PROTEUS She says it is a fair one.
TURIO Nay then the wanton lies; my face is black. 10
PROTEUS But pearls are fair; and the old saying is:
    Black men are pearls in beauteous ladies' eyes.
[JULIA] [*Aside*] 'Tis true, such pearls as put out ladies' eyes,
    For I had rather wink than look on them.
TURIO How likes she my discourse? 15
PROTEUS Ill, when you talk of war.
TURIO But well when I discourse of love and peace.
JULIA [*Aside*] But better, indeed, when you hold your peace.
TURIO What says she to my valour?
PROTEUS O sir, she makes no doubt of that. 20
JULIA [*Aside*] She needs not, when she knows it cowardice.

Act 5, Scene 2   **5.2**] *Scœna Secunda.* F   0 SD] *NS, after Rowe; Enter Thurio, Protheus, Iulia, Duke.* F   **7** SH
JULIA] *Collier; Pro.* F   **7** SD] *Collier; not in* F   **13** SH JULIA] *Rowe; Thu.* F   **13** SD] *Rowe (at 14); not in* F   **18, 21, 24,**
28 SD] *Johnson; not in* F   **18** your peace] F4; *you peace* F

Act 5, Scene 2

Location The text yields no direct hint as to the location. The traditional 'inside the Duke's palace' is deduced from the appearance of the Duke during the scene, but see note on the location of 3.2.

1–29 For similar devices poking fun at a fool, compare *Cym.* 1.2 and 2.1.

3 takes exceptions at disapproves of, finds fault with.

5 too little The following line suggests that the meaning here is 'too thin'.

6 boot Julia's aside (7) takes this to be a riding-boot.

7 SH* In view of Julia's asides at 18, 21, 24 and 28, Collier's emendation, which attributes 7 and 13–14 to her, seems right. The confusion of the speech headings was probably already in the compositor's copy (see p. 148 below). The inclination to write the text first and supply the speech headings later, which Howard-Hill attributes to Crane, would explain the occasional error.

9 fair beautiful. But Turio understands it in the sense of 'pale-complexioned' (10).

10 black dark-complexioned.

12 This proverb (Tilley M79) is a conventional piece of flattery to a man who has not the advantage of a fair complexion.

13 pearls Grey cataract in the eye, a condition in which the lens becomes more and more opaque.

14 wink shut my eyes.

TURIO What says she to my birth?
PROTEUS That you are well derived.
JULIA [*Aside*] True, from a gentleman to a fool.
TURIO Considers she my possessions?   25
PROTEUS O, ay; and pities them.
TURIO Wherefore?
JULIA [*Aside*] That such an ass should owe them.
PROTEUS That they are out by lease.

[*Enter* DUKE]

JULIA   Here comes the duke.
DUKE How now, Sir Proteus, how now, Turio,   30
      Which of you saw Sir Eglamour of late?
TURIO Not I.
PROTEUS   Nor I.
DUKE   Saw you my daughter?
PROTEUS   Neither.
DUKE Why then she's fled unto that peasant Valentine,
      And Eglamour is in her company.
      'Tis true, for Friar Laurence met them both   35
      As he in penance wandered through the forest;
      Him he knew well and guessed that it was she,
      But, being masked, he was not sure of it.
      Besides, she did intend confession
      At Patrick's cell this even, and there she was not.   40
      These likelihoods confirm her flight from hence;
      Therefore, I pray you, stand not to discourse,
      But mount you presently and meet with me
      Upon the rising of the mountain foot
      That leads toward Mantua, whither they are fled.   45
      Dispatch, sweet gentlemen, and follow me.   [*Exit*]

29 SD] *Rowe; not in* F   33] *As Capell;* Why then / ...Valentine F   46 SD] *Rowe; not in* F

23 **derived** descended.
24 **from... fool** Julia takes descent literally as 'coming down'.
25–9 The obvious meaning is that the term 'possessions' refers to Turio's properties, which are in a pitiful state. Editors have tried to enrich the dialogue by attributing to it the sense 'being possessed by evil spirits' or, alternatively, 'mental endowments'.
28 **owe** own.
33 **peasant** low fellow.
41 **likelihoods** indications.
46 **Dispatch** Make haste.

TURIO Why, this it is to be a peevish girl,
  That flies her fortune when it follows her.
  I'll after, more to be revenged on Eglamour
  Than for the love of reckless Silvia.   *[Exit]* 50
PROTEUS And I will follow, more for Silvia's love
  Than hate of Eglamour that goes with her. *[Exit]*
JULIA And I will follow, more to cross that love
  Than hate for Silvia that is gone for love. *Exit*

5.3 *Enter* SILVIA *and* OUTLAWS

1 OUTLAW Come, come,
  Be patient, we must bring you to our captain.
SILVIA A thousand more mischances than this one
  Have learned me how to brook this patiently.
2 OUTLAW Come, bring her away.   5
1 OUTLAW Where is the gentleman that was with her?
3 OUTLAW Being nimble-footed, he hath outrun us.
  But Moses and Valerius follow him.
  Go thou with her to the west end of the wood;
  There is our captain. We'll follow him that's fled. 10
  The thicket is beset, he cannot 'scape.
     [Exeunt all except First Outlaw and Silvia]
1 OUTLAW Come, I must bring you to our captain's cave.
  Fear not; he bears an honourable mind
  And will not use a woman lawlessly.
SILVIA O Valentine, this I endure for thee!   15
          Exeunt

50 SD] *Capell; not in* F 52 SD] *Capell; not in* F 54 SD] *Capell; Exeunt.* F Act 5, Scene 3 5.3] *Scena Tertia.* F 0
SD] *Rowe; Siluia, Out-lawes.* F 1–2 *As Capell;* Come...patient / ...Captaine. F; *as one line, Pope* 11 SD] *Dyce; not
in* F; *Exeunt. / Capell*

47 **peevish** perverse, obstinate.
47–8 **girl...her** 'Love (Woman) like a
shadow flies one following and pursues one
fleeing' (Tilley L518).

Act 5, Scene 3
Location The text calls for a forest scene (9,
11). For the presentation of such scenes on the
Elizabethan stage, see note on the location of 4.1.
3 **thousand...mischances** A brave overstatement.

3 **more** greater.
4 **learned** taught.
4 **brook** endure.
6–7 **gentleman...us** i.e. Sir Eglamour.
Shakespeare shows him to be another paragon
who disappoints. Compare his characterisation as
'valiant' at 4.3.13.
11 **'scape** escape; really one of the many
aphetic forms so typical of Shakespeare's English.

5.4 *Enter* VALENTINE

VALENTINE How use doth breed a habit in a man!
This shadowy desert, unfrequented woods
I better brook than flourishing peopled towns.
Here can I sit alone, unseen of any,
And to the nightingale's complaining notes   5
Tune my distresses and record my woes.
O thou that dost inhabit in my breast,
Leave not the mansion so long tenantless,
Lest, growing ruinous, the building fall
And leave no memory of what it was!   10
Repair me with thy presence, Silvia;
Thou gentle nymph, cherish thy forlorn swain.
    [Shouts and sounds of fighting within]
What halloing and what stir is this today?
These are my mates, that make their wills their law,
Have some unhappy passenger in chase.   15
They love me well; yet I have much to do
To keep them from uncivil outrages.
Withdraw thee, Valentine; who's this comes here?
    [Steps aside]

    [Enter PROTEUS, SILVIA *and* JULIA *as Sebastian]*

PROTEUS Madam, this service I have done for you,
Though you respect not aught your servant doth,   20
To hazard life and rescue you from him
That would have forced your honour and your love.
Vouchsafe me for my meed but one fair look;

Act 5, Scene 4   5.4] *Scæna Quarta* F   0 SD] *Rowe; Enter Valentine, Protheus, Siluia, Iulia, Duke, Thurio, Out-lawes.*
F   6 distresses] F3; distrestes F   12 SD] *Collier² subst. (at 13); not in* F   18 SD.1 *Steps aside*] *Johnson; not in* F   18
SD.2 *Enter* PROTEUS...*Sebastian*] *Rowe subst.; not in* F

Act 5, Scene 4
  Location One function of Valentine's introductory monologue is to paint the scene (2, 5). As
referred to at 5.3.9 and 12, this must be the west
end of the forest near Valentine's cave. The inner
recess of the Elizabethan stage might have served
to indicate the cave, from where Valentine could
enter to deliver his monologue at the front of the
stage. The eighteenth-century stage provided a
stock setting for scenery involving caves.
  2 desert uninhabited place.

6 record sing.
  8 mansion Refers to himself or, more specifically, to his body.
  12 nymph...swain Appellations that point
to the pastoral context in which the bandits in the
wood have to be seen. Compare 4.1.36 n.
  12 forlorn Accented on the first syllable.
  15 Have Who have.
  21 him i.e. the First Outlaw.
  23 meed reward.

A smaller boon than this I cannot beg,
And less than this, I am sure, you cannot give.   25
VALENTINE [*Aside*] How like a dream is this I see and hear!
Love, lend me patience to forbear a while!
SILVIA O miserable, unhappy that I am!
PROTEUS Unhappy were you, madam, ere I came;
But by my coming I have made you happy.   30
SILVIA By thy approach thou mak'st me most unhappy.
JULIA [*Aside*] And me, when he approacheth to your presence.
SILVIA Had I been seizèd by a hungry lion,
I would have been a breakfast to the beast
Rather than have false Proteus rescue me.   35
O heaven be judge how I love Valentine,
Whose life's as tender to me as my soul!
And full as much, for more there cannot be,
I do detest false, perjured Proteus.
Therefore be gone, solicit me no more.   40
PROTEUS What dangerous action, stood it next to death,
Would I not undergo for one calm look!
O 'tis the curse in love, and still approved,
When women cannot love where they're beloved!
SILVIA When Proteus cannot love where he's beloved.   45
Read over Julia's heart, thy first best love,
For whose dear sake thou didst then rend thy faith
Into a thousand oaths, and all those oaths
Descended into perjury to love me.
Thou hast no faith left now, unless thou'dst two,   50
And that's far worse than none; better have none
Than plural faith, which is too much by one.
Thou counterfeit to thy true friend!
PROTEUS   In love
Who respects friend?
SILVIA   All men but Proteus.

26 SD] *Theobald (at 27); not in* F   26 this I see and hear!] *Hanmer;* this? I see, and heare: F; this, I see, and hear? *Theobald*   28 am!] F4; am, F   32 SD] *Rowe; not in* F   49 love] F; deceive F2

31 **approach** With an underlying meaning of 'amorous advance'.
37 **tender** dear, precious.
42 **calm** i.e. gentle.
43 **still approved** always confirmed.
46–7 The words 'Read' and 'rend' point

towards a submerged image of a contract, where Proteus's multiple affirmations already indicate the beginning of faithlessness, which turns into full perjury with his offer of love to Silvia.
54 **respects** takes into account, considers.

PROTEUS Nay, if the gentle spirit of moving words   55
         Can no way change you to a milder form,
         I'll woo you like a soldier, at arm's end,
         And love you 'gainst the nature of love – force ye.

SILVIA O heaven!

PROTEUS   I'll force thee yield to my desire.
                    [*He lays hands on her*]

VALENTINE [*Comes forward*]
           Ruffian, let go that rude uncivil touch,   60
           Thou friend of an ill fashion!

PROTEUS   Valentine!

VALENTINE Thou common friend, that's without faith or love,
           For such is a friend now! Treacherous man,
           Thou hast beguiled my hopes! Nought but mine eye
           Could have persuaded me. Now I dare not say   65
           I have one friend alive; thou wouldst disprove me.
           Who should be trusted when one's right hand
           Is perjured to the bosom? Proteus,
           I am sorry I must never trust thee more
           But count the world a stranger for thy sake.   70
           The private wound is deepest. O time most accurst!
           'Mongst all foes that a friend should be the worst!

PROTEUS My shame and guilt confounds me.
         Forgive me, Valentine; if hearty sorrow

57 woo] wooe F; move F2 57 arm's] *Capell;* armes F; arms' *Var. 1803* 59 SD] *This edn;* not in F 60 SD] *Collier²;* not in F 63 Treacherous] F; Thou treacherous F2; Though treacherous F3 67 trusted] F; trusted now F2 71 most accurst] F; accurst *Hanmer;* most curst *Johnson*

57 at arm's end at sword's point (with bawdy innuendo).

61 fashion kind, sort. A reference to 'the kind of friendship now fashionable' (62–3) has been suggested.

62 common Onions glosses the word as 'ordinary, undistinguished'. Leech adduces such usages as 'a common homicide, common liars'. The idea of a heroic friendship, however, demands exclusiveness. Even writers with a less exalted conception of friendship advise restriction to a small number of friends.

67 The line is not deficient if one assumes a missing accent at the caesura. F2 and later emendations have tried to regularise the metre.

67–8 one's...bosom The 'right hand' image, referring here to Proteus, comes rather unexpectedly since never in this play is Valentine seen to rely on Proteus's skill or support. The

complaint about the failing union of bosom and hand as an image for heroic friendship is clearly inferior to the usual verbal representation of the union of souls, which in this play is reserved for the description of Valentine's relationship to Silvia. In the literature of friendship the 'right hand' image stresses the argument for the practical utility of friendship, which in the concept of heroic friendship plays a quite secondary role.

71 private i.e. inflicted by a person from the same intimate group.

73 confounds ruins, destroys. Another case of a singular verb following two singular subjects.

74 hearty sorrow contrition. The religious aspect is resumed with 'repentance' at 79. Compare for the same combination *H8* 4.2.27–8: 'full of repentance, / Continual meditations, tears, and sorrows'.

Be a sufficient ransom for offence, 75
I tender't here; I do as truly suffer
As e'er I did commit.

VALENTINE Then I am paid;
And once again I do receive thee honest.
Who by repentance is not satisfied
Is nor of heaven nor earth, for these are pleased; 80
By penitence th'Eternal's wrath's appeased.
And that my love may appear plain and free,
All that was mine in Silvia I give thee.

JULIA O me unhappy – [*Swoons*]

PROTEUS Look to the boy.

VALENTINE Why, boy?
Why, wag; how now? What's the matter? Look up, speak. 85

JULIA O good sir, my master charged me to deliver a ring to Madam
Silvia, which out of my neglect was never done.

PROTEUS Where is that ring, boy?

JULIA [*Offers a ring*] Here 'tis; this is it.

PROTEUS How? Let me see.
Why, this is the ring I gave to Julia. 90

JULIA O, cry you mercy, sir, I have mistook;
This is the ring you sent to Silvia.
[*Shows another ring*]

---

84 SD] *Pope; not in* F   84] *As Staunton;* Oh…unhappy / …Boy / …Boy F   88] *As Var. 1803;* Where…boy /
…it F   88 SD] *Sanders; not in* F   92 SD] *Johnson; not in* F

---

75 ransom Here an offer of expiation and atonement. Later at 81 taken up by 'penitence'.

77 commit sin.

77–81 Valentine's quick change from outrage and despair to forgiveness has often been criticised as psychologically untrue; but what seems to be aimed at is not realism. The sequence of contrition, offer of ransom and forgiveness conforms to a tenet of Christian doctrine (R.G. Hunter, *Shakespeare and the Comedy of Forgiveness*, 1965, pp. 85–7).

78 receive thee honest accept you as honourable.

82 love amity.

82 free generous.

82–3 For the underpinning of these lines in the literature of heroic friendship, see pp. 10–14 above. Silvia's silence here can only be accounted for by her absence or distance from the present action or, less likely, by a theory of an abridgement of the text. It has also been interpreted as an acceptance and support of the theory of heroic friendship (Ralph M. Sargent, 'Sir Thomas Elyot and the integrity of *The Two Gentlemen*', *PMLA* 65 (1950), 1166–80).

84–5 This device to bring about Julia's discovery is possibly suggested by Sidney's *Arcadia*, where extreme weakness caused by grief leads up to the discovery of Zelmane by Pyrocles (Bullough, I, 255–6).

85–7 These three lines of prose most likely present a compositorial corruption of the text. See Textual Analysis, pp. 143–5 below.

85 wag mischievous boy (often as a term of endearment).

91 cry you mercy beg your pardon.

PROTEUS But how cam'st thou by this ring? At my depart I gave this
    unto Julia.
JULIA And Julia herself did give it me,   95
              [Discovers herself]
    And Julia herself hath brought it hither.
PROTEUS How? Julia!
JULIA Behold her that gave aim to all thy oaths
    And entertained 'em deeply in her heart.
    How oft hast thou with perjury cleft the root!   100
    O Proteus, let this habit make thee blush;
    Be thou ashamed that I have took upon me
    Such an immodest raiment, if shame live
    In a disguise of love!
    It is the lesser blot, modesty finds,   105
    Women to change their shapes than men their minds.
PROTEUS Than men their minds? 'Tis true. O heaven, were man
    But constant, he were perfect! That one error
    Fills him with faults, makes him run through all th'sins:
    Inconstancy falls off ere it begins.   110
    What is in Silvia's face but I may spy
    More fresh in Julia's with a constant eye?
VALENTINE Come, come, a hand from either.
    Let me be blessed to make this happy close;
    'Twere pity two such friends should be long foes.   115
PROTEUS Bear witness, heaven, I have my wish for ever.
JULIA And I mine.

        [Enter DUKE, TURIO *and* OUTLAWS]

OUTLAWS   A prize, a prize, a prize!
VALENTINE Forbear! Forbear, I say! It is my lord the duke.

95 SD] *Collier² (after 97); not in* F   117 SD] *Rowe; not in* F

93 **depart** departure.
98 **gave aim to** was the aim of. The metaphor
from archery is taken up again at 100.
100 **root** i.e. bottom of the heart. With an
allusion to the cleaving of the centre pin of an
archer's target.
101 **habit** dress, i.e. her page's costume.
Synonym of 'raiment' (103). Julia is the only
Shakespearean heroine who expresses feelings of
guilt for dressing as a male. Shakespeare possibly
took his cue from Zelmane's complaint in *Arcadia*

(Bullough, I, 254–6). Silvia follows Valentine
without adopting a male costume, but she has
Eglamour to accompany her.
103–4 **if shame…love** i.e. if there need be
shame for a disguise put on for love.
106 **shapes** costumes.
110 Riverside glosses: 'an inconstant man
begins to be faithless even before he has declared
his love'.
114 **close** (1) union, (2) conclusion (of a piece
of music).

                    Your grace is welcome to a man disgraced,
                    Banishèd Valentine.
DUKE   Sir Valentine!   120
TURIO Yonder is Silvia, and Silvia's mine.
VALENTINE Turio, give back, or else embrace thy death.
                    Come not within the measure of my wrath.
                    Do not name Silvia thine; if once again,
                    Verona shall not hold thee. Here she stands;   125
                    Take but possession of her with a touch –
                    I dare thee but to breathe upon my love!
TURIO Sir Valentine, I care not for her; I,
                    I hold him but a fool that will endanger
                    His body for a girl that loves him not.
                    I claim her not, and therefore she is thine.   130
DUKE The more degenerate and base art thou
                    To make such means for her as thou hast done
                    And leave her on such slight conditions.
                    Now by the honour of my ancestry,   135
                    I do applaud thy spirit, Valentine,
                    And think thee worthy of an empress' love.
                    Know then I here forget all former griefs,
                    Cancel all grudge, repeal thee home again,
                    Plead a new state in thy unrivalled merit,   140
                    To which I thus subscribe: Sir Valentine,
                    Thou art a gentleman and well derived;
                    Take thou thy Silvia, for thou hast deserved her.
VALENTINE I thank your grace; the gift hath made me happy.
                    I now beseech you, for your daughter's sake,   145
                    To grant one boon that I shall ask of you.
DUKE I grant it for thine own, whate'er it be.
VALENTINE These banished men, that I have kept withal,
                    Are men endued with worthy qualities.
                    Forgive them what they have committed here,   150

---

122 give back retreat.

123 measure reach. Technical term for the distance of a fencer from his opponent.

125 Verona Another instance of the confusion in place names, perhaps due to the influence of Brooke's *Romeus*.

127 breathe upon The general sense 'speak to' seems here to bear the specific meaning 'to tarnish as if with breath' (see *OED* Breathe *v* 9).

133 means efforts.

137 worthy of an empress' love Compare 2.4.69. Again this is more likely a reference to the highest standard of courtly love than an original intention to mark Silvia as an imperial princess and heir apparent.

139 repeal recall (from exile).

140 state status.

148 kept withal lived with.

And let them be recalled from their exile.
They are reformèd, civil, full of good,
And fit for great employment, worthy lord.
DUKE Thou hast prevailed, I pardon them and thee;
    Dispose of them as thou know'st their deserts.   155
    Come, let us go; we will include all jars
    With triumphs, mirth and rare solemnity.
VALENTINE And as we walk along, I dare be bold
    With our discourse to make your grace to smile.
    What think you of this page, my lord?   160
DUKE I think the boy hath grace in him; he blushes.
VALENTINE I warrant you, my lord, more grace than boy.
DUKE What mean you by that saying?
VALENTINE Please you, I'll tell you as we pass along,
    That you will wonder what hath fortunèd.   165
    Come, Proteus, 'tis your penance but to hear
    The story of your loves discoverèd.
    That done, our day of marriage shall be yours,
    One feast, one house, one mutual happiness.

                             Exeunt

FINIS

151 exile Accented on the second syllable.

152 reformèd...good Although the attempt to include as many figures as possible in the happy ending seems forced in view of Valentine's complaint at 13–17, it fits in with the Outlaws' characterisation as pastoral men. Compare pp. 15–17 above.

156 include conclude.

156 jars (1) quarrelling, (2) musical discord.

157 triumphs public festivities. Also more specifically 'tournaments'.

157 solemnity celebration of special importance.

161 boy...blushes Alluding to the proverb 'Blushing is virtue's colour' which takes bashfulness as a sign of grace (Tilley B480).

162 more grace than boy rather one of the graces than a boy. A distinct reference to her female charms.

165 fortunèd happened.

167 discoverèd revealed, made known.

TEXTUAL ANALYSIS

The only authoritative text of *The Two Gentlemen of Verona* is found in the Folio of 1623, usually called the First Folio. Printed on pages 20 to 38, it follows *The Tempest* and precedes *The Merry Wives of Windsor*. The book is called a Folio because the sheets on which it is printed are folded only once. These folded sheets are gathered into quires. In this Folio a quire consists of three sheets, folded and placed one inside the other, resulting in twelve pages. Just as the sequence of pages is marked by the pagination, using digits, quires are indicated by their signatures, using letters. In the Folio text of *The Two Gentlemen*, a signature at the bottom of p. 25 column b shows the beginning of quire C; pp. 27 and 29 carry the signatures C2 and C3 respectively in the corresponding places. This means that p. 25 represents the right side of a sheet, the left side of which becomes, as a result of folding, a verso page numbered 36, since the sheet serves as the envelope for quire C. Correspondingly, p. 27 represents the right side of the sheet forming the middle part of this quire and p. 29 the right side of the sheet forming the inner part. The beginning of quire D is signalled on p. 37. Pages 20 to 24, which carry the initial parts of the text of *The Two Gentlemen*, are, as is to be expected, unsigned but belong to quire B.

The printing of the Folio text

Printing, of course, precedes the folding of sheets and their gathering into quires. A sheet is printed off from a forme which yokes together the metal type for two pages. When the ink has dried, the sheets are turned and again sent through the press to receive the imprint of another forme, also consisting of two pages. It is part of the compositor's skill to know which pages have to be yoked together on the front and back of the sheet. The sequence of the printing-off of formes is not determined by technical necessity, but the researches of Charlton Hinman[1] have shown that for reasons of economy the printing usually began with the inside forme of a quire and proceeded outwards, which may be shown by table 1. The pages carrying text from *The Two Gentlemen* are distinguished by bold type.

quires	1st forme	2nd	3rd	4th	5th	6th
B	**18:19**	**17:20**	**16:21**	**15:22**	**14:23**	**13:24**
C	**30:31**	**29:32**	**28:33**	**27:34**	**26:35**	**25:36**
D	**42:43**	**41:44**	**40:45**	**39:46**	**38:47**	**37:48**

Table 1: The composition of *TGV* by quires and formes in the First Folio

[1] Charlton Hinman, *The Printing and Proof-Reading of the First Folio of Shakespeare*, 2 vols., 1963.

The printing of *The Two Gentlemen* began with the second forme of quire B, combined with forme-mates presenting pages from the foregoing play *The Tempest* till the printing of quire C. The printing of p. 37 in quire D did not immediately follow that of p. 36; it was done only after the printing-off of five formes that, for the most part, carry text from the following play *The Merry Wives*, and after the printing of p. 38 on which the text of *The Two Gentlemen* is completed. This sequence of printing explains the wrong running titles topping pp. 37 and 38. The *Merry Wives of Windsor* titles had been used in the printing of formes 1 to 4 in quire D, and it would have been necessary to reinsert the proper running title last used in the printing of the sixth forme of quire C. This was probably neglected for lack of time. There are, as we shall see later, other signs on this page which indicate that the workmen were pressed for time here.

In modern book production one can expect the compositor to set up his type following the sequence of his manuscript or copy. In the production of the Folio this would have meant that considerably more type would have been necessary than the printing office could afford. Charlton Hinman has shown[1] that the normal relation between typesetting and printing in this case can be described as follows: while one forme was worked off at the printing-press, compositors had to break up the type of the forme previously printed, redistribute the letters into the letter cases and set up the next forme, thus limiting the type needed to six pages at the utmost. This is indubitably the most economic procedure, but it demands that the setting copy be subdivided into pages of print by preliminary estimate, a process which is called casting off copy. Various kinds of copy-text would present the compositor with different degrees of difficulty in reaching an accurate estimate. Printed copy can be more easily cast off than handwritten copy; verse would be less difficult to cast off than prose or a mixture of verse and prose. A handwritten mixture with perhaps unclear distinctions between verse and prose and marginal or interlinear corrections and revisions would offer the greatest resistance to accurate casting off. Mistakes made in casting off copy could lead either to 'overcrowded pages', where the text exceeded the space available for it, or to so-called 'open pages', where there was not enough text to fill the page in the usual manner. An over-crowded page results from a compositor's trying to make an excess of copy fit the available space by tightening the unprinted areas, changing the lineation or print-ing verse as prose. Folio compositors have been shown to have remedied the faulty casting off of copy even by suppressing speech headings or stage directions or other kinds of text material. If, on the other hand, inaccurate casting off left the compositor with too little text material to fill the page normally, he would widen the unprinted areas and sometimes print one line of verse as two or set up prose in short lines as if it were verse. Each of these measures would contribute in its own way to make a page appear unusually open.

The sequence of pages within the printing process has also to be taken into account, since it may be that compositors could remedy difficulties arising from inaccurate casting off more easily when they occurred within sequences of printed

[1] Charlton Hinman, 'Cast-off copy for the First Folio of Shakespeare', *SQ* 6 (1955), 259–73.

pages following each other in rising numbers – except of course on pages where such sequences end. The first line of table 1 above shows that pp. 20 to 24 were printed in sequence. Ideally they would have been set up by the same compositor while a colleague was working on the corresponding forme-mates. Within such a sequence, an excess of copy on one page could be evened out by using a smaller amount on one of the following pages. If not, the resultant accumulation of material would then have to be dealt with when setting up the type for the last of those pages, in this case p. 24. The second line of table 1 again shows a sequence of pages in rising order – if we confine our attention to the right side of the sheet or forme, coming to an end with p. 36. Pages 24 and 36 would therefore deserve special attention. Within sequences of pages set up and printed in descending order, problems resulting from faulty casting off would have to be dealt with immediately on each individual page. The special significance of pp. 24 and 36 of our text depends, of course, on the supposition that the whole of the text of the play was cast off in advance. If merely enough copy to fill a quire was selected, problems of accommodating the text on pp. 24 or 36 could have been solved when casting off the pages of the following quire. But since the unit of casting off copy is not known, we cannot be sure about any supposed relative lack of difficulties on pages in sequences of rising numbers.

Copy-casting, however, seems not to have presented great problems in the case of *The Two Gentlemen*. The potentially critical p. 24 shows two scene headings with ample space around them and a stage direction at the end of 2.2 set as a separate line, which means that the compositor could accommodate the text comfortably on the page. But p. 36, which also ends a sequence of pages in ascending order, looks tighter (see fig. 1). The word 'Farewell', which should have a line by itself, has

> *Sil.* She is beholding to thee (gentle youth)
> Alas (poore Lady) defolate, and left ;
> I weepe my felfe to thinke vpon thy words ;
> Here youth : there is my purfe ; I giue thee this   (well.
> For thy fweet Miftris fake, becaufe thou lou'ft her. Fare-
> *Iul.* And fhe fhall thanke you for't, if ere you know
> A vertuous gentlewoman, milde, and beautifull.   (her.

Fig. 1 4.4.164–71 (TLN 1992–8)[1]

been squeezed into TLN 1996, causing a turnover into the line above. A stage direction indicating the exit may have been suppressed here by the compositor. This seems all the more likely as there are other signs of 'crowding'. Though the spacing of the three scene headings on this page and the setting of the final stage directions in line with the last lines of text are normal, the three opening stage directions have been fitted more tightly to their first lines than usual and betray at least some lack of space.

A more serious textual problem due to possible casting-off errors appears on

---

[1] The numbers in brackets refer to the through line numbering of *The Norton Facsimile*, prepared by Charlton Hinman, 1968.

> *Iul.* Oh me vnhappy.
> *Pro,* Looke to the Boy.
> *Val.* Why, Boy *?*
> Why wag:how now ? what's the matter?look vp: speak.
> *Iul.* O good sir, my master charg'd me to deliuer a ring
> to Madam *Siluia* : w (out of my neglect) was neuer done.
> *Pro.* Where is that ring *?* boy *?*

Fig. 2 5.4.84–8 (TLN 2208–14)

p. 37. Column a is very comfortably laid out, but there seems to be irregularity in the last quarter of column b. One explanation might be that the compositor, after having justified TLN 2208–10 and perhaps put them in the galley, may then have seen that he had more copy on his hands than could be accommodated in the remaining space (see fig. 2). There are several signs indicating lack of space: TLN 2211 shows no spacing after 'wag:' and after 'matter?'; in TLN 2212 the expletive 'Oh' possibly lost the 'h' and no space follows the comma after 'sir,'; in TLN 2213 an abbreviation for 'which' is used. Moreover, TLN 2211–13 are treated as prose. Since there is no other prose passage in this scene, it is not unreasonable to conjecture that the compositor changed the verse lines of his copy into prose. In doing so, he may even have suppressed words he did not deem strictly necessary, or he may have replaced longer words with shorter words of similar meaning. Previous editors have sensed the irregularity and have either rearranged the wording or at least tried to explain the situation. Capell, for instance, arranged Julia's speech as verse. Though the result of his reconstruction fails to convince, his basic approach seems more appropriate than explaining F's prose as demonstrating the psychological condition of a person slowly recovering from a swoon. Assuming compositorial tampering, the suppression of two speech headings in TLN 2211 and mislineation are also not unlikely since the arrangement of Valentine's speech and the variation from 'boy' to 'wag' is curious. In any case, the short TLN 2210 deserves more attention than it has received from those editors who simply disregard the space after 'Boy?' and connect it with the line immediately following. This edition follows Staunton in interpreting the space as a sign that TLN 2208 to 2210 have to be read as one line of verse. This is possible if we allow for an epic caesura, but the solution still does not take account of the fact that the speech is continued in the next line as prose. The attribution of TLN 2211 to Valentine alone makes him, as he sees the 'boy' now for the first time, so much more solicitous than Proteus who, after all, is Sebastian's master. This may be another indication that speech headings have probably been suppressed. But the assumption of rather drastic changes in the text should be considered together with the other alternatives open to the compositor faced with accommodating a possible surplus amount of text at this point. One might think that the most natural solution would be to shift a few lines on to the following page, on which the text of the play ends and where enough space could have been found. But, as table 1 shows, the concluding page was already in the process of being printed while p. 37 was being set. Alternatively, a conscientious compositor could have tried to find room in column a of p. 37, where a scene heading and its box are quite normally spaced and the foregoing final stage direction takes a line for itself – contrary to normal practice. But revision of column a would certainly have taken more time, and the wrong running title (see p. 142 above) already suggests that the compositor was in a hurry. The general reader may be appalled at the thought of such dabbling with Shakespeare's text by compositors, though this play suffers less from it than others.

Modifications made by the compositor are not always as conscious as in the case conjectured above. Far more often they are made unconsciously and vary according to the individual workman. Bibliographers, therefore, have tried to identify the work of individual compositors who set up the type for the printing of the Folio. With regard to the pages bearing the text of *The Two Gentlemen*, the work of Charlton Hinman and T.H. Howard-Hill suggests the following division between two workmen:

Folio pages	20–2	23–30	31–6	37–8
compositors	(A)F	C	(A)F	C

Hinman, by identifying distinctive spelling habits as well as by observing the occurrence and recurrence of individual types which allowed him to specify which type-case was used in the setting of a particular page, attributed the setting of our text to the two Folio compositors A and C.[1] Howard-Hill, extending the criteria for compositor identification by attending to variations in the spacing of commas and the spelling of elided forms of 'will', 'shall' and 'the' (he'll, hee'll, hee'l, o'th, o'th', etc.), confirms Hinman's division of the text between two compositors, one of them C.[2] But he divides the work done on the Folio hitherto attributed to A into that of the early comedies and that of the plays printed later, beginning with *The Winter's Tale*. He found that the Compositor A of the earlier plays prefers the spellings 'deere', 'diuell', 'sodaine' and 'yong', whereas the A of the later plays rather chooses 'deare', 'deuill', 'suddaine' and 'young'. Howard-Hill therefore identifies the earlier A as a new Compositor F. The distinct differences in their spelling habits, he thinks, are supported by differences in their spacing of commas and in the tolerance they show for copy spellings. Howard-Hill's identification of the work attributed to Compositor F has been confirmed by John O'Connor.[3]

Several studies have been devoted to qualitative analyses of Compositor C's work, as some of it is believed to have been set from quarto text. If a compositor's stint can be correctly identified and editorial changes in the quarto copy be correctly separated from compositorial changes, comparison of variants between quarto copy and the Folio would allow some insight into a compositor's individual

[1] Hinman, I, 352–71.
[2] T.H. Howard-Hill, 'The compositors of the Shakespeare First Folio comedies', *SB* 26 (1973), 61–106.
[3] John O'Connor, 'Compositors D and F of the Shakespeare First Folio', *SB* 28 (1975), 81–117.

habits, into the kinds of mistakes he was prone to make and into the extent to which his work could corrupt a text. Of course, setting from printed texts would involve fewer errors due to misreadings than setting up the text from handwritten copy, as in the case of *The Two Gentlemen*. Compositor C's tendency to make trivial errors – such as omissions, additions and the transposition of one or two letters – has been found to be less marked than, for instance, Compositor D's, as the studies by both O'Connor and Jackson demonstrate.[1] These errors should be relatively easy to detect without knowledge of the compositor's copy, whereas such transpositions as involve the change of place between two monosyllabic words are more difficult to locate since they are often not likely to change the sense in a way that the textual corruption will be immediately felt. But it is to this kind of error that Compositor C has been shown to be especially prone. Such errors are usually due to the compositor's habit of carrying too much copy in his head, wrongly remembering the exact wording when setting up his lines and failing to check his work frequently against the copy-text. This kind of memory failure seems to be responsible for many of Compositor C's substitutions. These show up in the confusion of words of common root like 'willingly' and 'wilfully' or of roughly synonymous words like 'can' and 'should'. Substitution due to misreading of copy is far less common with C than the replacement of words by others of nearly the same meaning but often differing widely from the typographical image of the original word. A more 'photographic' memory would also have prevented his habit of expanding and contracting elisions and other forms. But Compositor C does, on occasion, deliberately substitute a shorter word for a longer one of similar meaning in order to shorten a line. He also seems prepared to attempt to correct his copy on his own initiative: he corrects, for example, one of Dogberry's malapropisms in *Much Ado About Nothing*. Since C's errors are often either lapses of memory or conscious sophistications which do not result in nonsense, they are difficult to detect. He is less prone than other compositors to interpolate words, but he has been found in some cases to add articles, prepositions and pronouns. He seems to show greater sensitivity towards metre than his fellow compositors. O'Connor found only four of Compositor C's interpolations in verse lines, three of which regularise the metre. Two of these verse interpolations emphasise parallel grammatical constructions. He has also been found to justify lines occasionally by the substitution or omission of words. It seems more than likely that, when confronted with space problems due to faulty casting off, he would tamper with the text – as, possibly, in the case of p. 37.

Since Compositor (A)F seems to have set only from manuscript copy, the study of the quality of his work has to rely almost exclusively on the emendations and conjectures that editors have found necessary or desirable on such pages of the text as have been attributed to him. If the number of emendations is a reliable guide, he should not be called an especially meticulous workman. On p. 31 we find

---

[1] John O'Connor, 'A qualitative analysis of Compositors C and D in the Shakespeare First Folio', *SB* 30 (1977), 57–74, and MacDonald P. Jackson, 'Compositor C and the First Folio text of *Much Ado about Nothing*', *PBSA* 68 (1974), 414–18.

a piece of his work which was possibly proof-read against copy.[1] The page shows twenty variants representing almost every kind of minor error. The substitution of 'heauily' for 'grieuously' (3.2.14) shows that Compositor F was capable of memory error. The same habit is probably responsible for the omission of the word 'last' (3.1.337) and the addition of a final *s* to 'haire' (3.1.334). The omission of the speech heading for 3.2.13 is only explicable if we assume that F occasionally tried to carry greater chunks of text in his head than he could memorise. His punctuation shows signs of carelessness in the omission of two question marks (3.1.295 and 3.2.12). Lines 3.1.336, 3.1.355 and 3.2.1 also show that he was not bent on faithfully reproducing the commas of his copy-text; he shifted one, omitted one and added one as he saw fit. He could, moreover, add *-es* to a verb where the singular is clearly wrong as, for example, at 3.1.308. All these errors (plus a collection of such literal mistakes as writing 'thy' for 'try', 'take' for 'talke', 'villanie' for 'villaine', 'lone' for 'love') prove that he did not always check up carefully what he had produced on his composing-stick. From the insight Hinman gained into the frequency and quality of the proof-reading of the Folio, he finds reason to conclude that the proof-reader thought this page 'an adequate job of composition' since after this painstaking test little proof-reading of any kind (and none whatever that implies reference to copy) was made anywhere else in the later pages of the comedy section of the Folio.[2]

The copy-text for the printing of *The Two Gentlemen of Verona*

The texts of the various plays collected in the Folio were printed from different sorts of copy. Some were reprinted from previously published quartos, partly prepared by adding corrections from other sources; others are believed to have been printed from manuscript material in various stages of development: foul papers, clean drafts or even prompt-books. For yet another group of plays, a special handwritten transcript seems to have been prepared to serve as copy for the printer. It is now assumed that Ralph Crane, a scrivener known to have copied theatrical manuscripts for various purposes, was commissioned to carry out the task. This view has been corroborated to a great extent by the painstaking studies of T.H. Howard-Hill.[3] The chief sign of Crane's intervention is now seen in the appearance of the so-called 'massed entrances', which means that all the characters appearing in a scene are listed together at the beginning.[4] 'Massed entrances' are used in *The Two Gentlemen* as well as in *The Merry Wives* and *The Winter's Tale*,

[1] The other proof-read page of *The Two Gentlemen* is p. 20 (B4ᵛ).
[2] Hinman, I, 255–6.
[3] T.H. Howard-Hill, *Ralph Crane and Some Shakespeare First Folio Comedies*, 1972.
[4] Former attempts to explain the 'massed entrances' as being derived from 'plots' used in the theatre, in combination with theories of texts assembled from actors' 'parts', have been discarded, since 'plots' clearly distinguish between characters that enter at the beginning of the scene and those that enter later, and it is unlikely that assembly from 'parts' and 'plots', with the possibility of mistakes in fitting together speeches and cues, would result in such a clean text (F.P. Wilson, *Shakespeare and the New Bibliography*, revised and edited by H. Gardner, 1970, p. 75).

texts which are all believed to have been transcribed by Ralph Crane. The adoption of this kind of stage direction may have been influenced by the prestige of the 1616 Folio edition of the works of Ben Jonson, which followed the practice of the continental publishers of classical dramatists.

About the accuracy of Crane's work as a transcriber of texts that served as copy for the compositors of the Folio no direct judgement is possible, but inferences can be drawn from the quality of those of his other transcripts that can be compared with their originals or from passages that editors have found reason to believe were corrupted by him. James M. Nosworthy summarises such a study as follows: 'Crane's work was variable and never entirely reliable, and the foregoing collations are disturbing since, when all adjustments and allowances have been made, they suggest that he was capable of one error per ten or twelve lines.'[1] Howard-Hill concludes from his own study based on a wider and more varied textual corpus that this view is decidedly too pessimistic.[2] He finds that Crane occasionally substitutes small words (pronouns and prepositions) and exchanges singular and plural forms. Among substitutions of greater significance Howard-Hill found a ratio of eight cases of substitutions of words that are broadly synonymous to three cases where the meaning is seriously affected. Furthermore, Crane would occasionally insert words – either by expanding an elision or by intensifying a phrase. For *The Two Gentlemen* it is interesting to see that various of his transcripts involve errors concerning speech headings, since two little speeches (5.2.7 and 13–14) need to be reattributed. Of course, the possibility that the confusion here was due to the copy from which he transcribed cannot be entirely excluded. Some corruptions undoubtedly entered the text by Crane's omitting letters or his altering the person and tense of verbs, others as the result of his misreading the handwriting in front of him; some would be memory errors leading to synonymous substitutions. There is no evidence that Crane carefully reread the text in order to submit it to extensive revision and correction. He felt free to substitute elisions different from those of his copy, greatly influenced punctuation and introduced his own kind of word compounds. These together with substantive errors, the number of which Howard-Hill found relatively small, affect the authority of texts printed from Crane's transcripts. Even a thorough knowledge of Crane's habits cannot ensure that all errors brought into the Folio by his transcriptions can be detected.

A closer analysis of the initial stage directions of *The Two Gentlemen* reveals that Crane must have invested some thought in the construction of his 'massed entrances'. The order of the characters given follows roughly the order of their taking part in the dialogue, which is usually also the order in which they come on to the stage. There are minor inconsistencies: in 2.1 where Speed speaks before Valentine, in 2.4 where Silvia is given a word before Valentine and Speed has a line before Turio, in 4.1 where the Outlaws open the discussion rather than

[1] James M. Nosworthy, *Shakespeare's Occasional Plays, their Origin and Transmission*, 1965, p. 230.
[2] Howard-Hill, *Ralph Crane*, pp. 56–7.

Valentine and in 5.3 where the Outlaws address Silvia first. In 3.1 even the non-speaking part of Turio is incorporated in the list at the place where he takes part in the dialogue as an addressee. The stage direction for 4.2 is a special case. If the term 'Musitian' refers to the musicians accompanying the song on their instruments, they must enter the stage on the heels of Turio, who addresses them at 4.2.24. They should therefore precede the Host and Julia in the list. It is possible, of course, that the compiler took his cue from the term 'Musitian' at 4.2.54, which undoubtedly refers to Proteus and marks him as at least one of the serenaders.

A further study suggests that groupings within the lists may originally have been indicated by means of punctuation and connectives. In scenes involving only two characters, for instance, the two names are either connected by 'and' (1.2, 2.5, 2.7) or separated by a comma (2.3, 4.3, 5.1). This distinction corresponds in the first case with simultaneous and in the second with successive entrances on to the stage, although in one of the simultaneous entrances the two characters must enter by different doors (2.5). In the stage directions to scenes involving more than two characters, there are also remnants of indicators for groupings – 1.3, for instance, where the connective 'and' joins the simultaneously appearing Antonio and Pantino and a full stop separates Proteus who enters later; and 4.1 where an 'and' signals the joint entrance of the whole group. But the stage direction to 1.1, which reads *'Valentine: Protheus, and Speed.'*, seems mixed up as the colon and the connective should exchange places to indicate the correct grouping. The lack of the introductory word *Enter* reflects Crane's style rather than printing-house practice. Otherwise, those scene headings that involve three or more characters separate them by commas, irrespective of simultaneous or successive entrance. The problem of whether the observed indications of groupings are purely coincidental or expressive of the care of the inventor – and how many of these features may have been obliterated by the compositor's intervention – would need an investigation of the massed entrances in the other plays for which Crane provided the copy; but it is quite certain that in this play these features do not coincide with compositors' stints. There are also variations in typeface from italic to roman within some of these stage directions (2.5, 2.6, 2.7) which are characteristic of the transcriber. Again, the preservation of these does not coincide with compositors' stints. Since stage directions involving longer lists of characters regularly use only italic type and commas as means of separation, these seem to be the ones with which compositors are most likely to have tampered.

The system of 'massed entrances' does not mark the points where individual characters enter within a scene. At the end of scenes exits are regularly provided – with the exception of 4.2, where the final stage direction is entirely missing, probably owing to an oversight. The stage direction to 2.4 reads *Exeunt* although only one figure is left on stage. This wrong plural possibly derives from a faulty reading of the abbreviation *Ex.*, perhaps in combination with the compositor's use and reuse of units of type. Exits within a scene appear only before monologues, as at 1.1.62, 1.2.49, 2.1.118, 2.4.184. The special attention given to monologues also shows up in the superfluous *solus* in the initial stage direction to 2.6. There are, however, other cases where the beginnings of monologues are not marked by a preceding stage direction, though at 4.4.169 a stage direction in the manuscript could have been dropped by the compositor because of a distinctly visible lack of space.

Added to the text of *The Two Gentlemen* is a list of characters. There are eight such lists in the Folio. Their provenance has aroused considerable controversy. According to Greg, the only one printed because it was certainly in the copy and not made up in the printing-house for the purpose of filling space, as those at the end of *2 Henry IV*, *Timon of Athens* and perhaps *Othello* apparently were, was that attached to *The Tempest*.[1] Of the five plays held to be set up from Crane transcripts, on the other hand, four are provided with such a table of characters. In the case of *The Merry Wives*, the fifth of these plays, it is plain that there would not have been sufficient space for it on the last page. It therefore seems highly likely that the lists were provided by Crane's transcript. In the table attached to *The Two Gentlemen*, one of the names is set up in roman type, which could reflect copy characterised by various styles of handwriting otherwise obliterated here. Since such lists also appear in non-Shakespearean plays printed from transcripts Crane supplied, the evidence against the printing-house provenance of the list in *The Two Gentlemen* must be deemed to be overwhelming, but whether Crane compiled these lists or merely copied them cannot be finally decided.

The copy-text for Crane's transcription

Coming thus to the difficult question of the nature of the manuscript Crane transcribed, Greg's theory that a playhouse manuscript was copied has to be discussed.[2] Greg based his opinion on the apparent correctness of both the massed entrances and the act and scene divisions. Though both these features are unlikely to be authorial – that is, Shakespeare's – it does not necessarily follow, as Greg concluded, that they were first introduced into a prompt-book and then appeared in the transcript. Indeed, it must be asked whether the chief reason for the use of the massed entrances was not simply the fact that entrances within scenes were not clear or copious enough for Crane to produce a satisfactory script. The theory of the prompt-book provenance of his copy is further weakened by the complete lack of all positive indications: systematic stage directions especially regarding offstage sounds and properties, directions to ensure the readiness of the actors backstage so that they can enter on cue, names of particular actors, etc. The lack of these features alone may not suffice to prove false the assumption that Crane's transcript was based on a prompt-book, but the total absence of all descriptive stage directions in the Folio text of *The Two Gentlemen* would seem to exclude this possibility. Of course, it is theoretically possible to argue that in his transcription Crane deliberately suppressed all descriptive stage directions as well as the indications for individual entries and re-entries. But the researches of T.H.

[1] W.W. Greg, *The Shakespeare First Folio*, 1955, pp. 355 and 418.
[2] *Ibid.*, pp. 217–18.

Howard-Hill have shown that there was in at least one of Crane's transcripts a combination of 'massed entrances' and descriptive stage directions. Howard-Hill saw 'little evidence that he [Crane] omitted stage directions' but rather that 'his tendency was to insert matter which might assist the reader'.[1] It therefore seems most likely that Crane copied from a manuscript which didn't provide them (see Appendix, pp. 153–4 below).

There are also other textual features that point to Crane's having transcribed an early draft of *The Two Gentlemen* rather than a version carefully prepared for theatrical performance. These are the inconsistencies concerning the places of action and the indecision about the rank of the territorial ruler. Though other minor inconsistencies in Shakespearean plays survived stage productions, those in *The Two Gentlemen* are unlikely to have passed even the scantiest rehearsal practice. When Valentine sets out on his journey from home, he suggests that Proteus write to him in Milan (1.1.57). A little later Pantino mentions that Valentine is attending the emperor at his court (1.3.26–7). Proteus pretends that he has received a letter from his friend there (1.3.56–8), and Don Antonio determines that Proteus shall join Valentine at the emperor's court to complete his education (1.3.67). But when the two young men meet again, it is at the court of a certain duke (2.4.42). Lance, who follows his master, meets Valentine's page Speed, who welcomes him to Padua (2.5.1). Later we seem to get it straight from the Duke that he thinks himself in Verona (3.1.81). But when the banished Valentine falls into the hands of outlaws, he states that he has come from Milan and is on the way to Verona (4.1.16–19). The third of the Outlaws reveals to him that he was banished from Verona, which may be taken to mean that they are both suffering from the same ruler (4.1.47–9). Valentine's threat (5.4.125) again implies that it is a duke of Verona on whose protection Turio has relied all the time. There are various other minor inconsistencies, the most important of which concerns Julia's father. At the beginning of the play, his main function – like that of Valentine's father – is to motivate the clearing of the stage at the end of a scene (1.2). But when in 2.7 Julia prepares to leave Verona, 86–7 suggest that the author has forgotten that his Julia ever had a father.

Having argued that there are no positive signs that characterise Crane's copy as prompt-book material, we might ask whether there are any of the usual indicators of foul papers: the absence of directions for necessary entrances, calls for entrances that are not necessitated by the text or actors' names in speech headings, etc. The answer can only be that such indicators are not visible here because of Crane's intervention. His 'massed entrances' solve, as it were, all the problems relating to entrances connected with foul papers. To regularise speech headings would also have been one of his tasks. And Crane can also be expected to have obliterated a supposedly light punctuation of his copy-text by putting in his own.

To sum up, then, there is good reason to assume that the copy for the Folio was a Crane transcript, probably from an unfinished draft version of the play. If the

[1] Howard-Hill, *Ralph Crane*, pp. 24 and 113.

play was enacted before 1623, though we have no evidence for this, we can be sure that the Folio text is not derived from a prompt-book. In the absence of other copy-texts, this edition follows the Folio as closely as possible. Where F is clearly wrong, defective or inadequate, emendations, with few exceptions, follow standard editorial practice. To supply the missing stage directions, prompt-books of nineteenth- and twentieth-century productions have also been consulted.

APPENDIX: A FURTHER NOTE ON STAGE DIRECTIONS

The absence of all stage directions in the Folio text of *The Two Gentlemen* is especially regrettable since they would have cleared up the meaning of several passages. 1.1.105–10 is an example, where editors have tried to bring light into the enigmatic 'noddy' business almost from the beginning (see collation). Both Cam. and Sisson find a way of rendering the text acceptable as it stands, but they fail to make Proteus's obtuseness understandable and convincing. Assuming no textual corruption, it seems that the task of supplying the missing stage direction has yet to be worked at.

Act 1, Scene 2 also offers a series of instances where stage business is needed to make specific bits of the text intelligible. Editors, stage-adapters and producers have copiously supplied stage directions which affect character conception and motivation in this scene (see 1.2.69–71 n.; 86–97 n.).

Another case in question is 2.2.7. Though no editor has hitherto found it necessary to provide a stage direction here, presumably because all thought that this line's internal direction is sufficient to indicate the following stage business, A.P. Slater (*Shakespeare the Director*, 1982, pp. 84, 214 n.7) maintains that the line requires merely a 'marriage handshake' or 'palmer's kiss' as in *Romeo and Juliet* 1.5.93 ff. and 4.1.43, and *Love's Labour's Lost* 5.2.806. But none of the parallels drawn upon is really convincing. Much, of course, depends on character conception. The impulsive Julia is not likely to speak the line in question with her hand stretched out for the 'marriage handshake', nor is Proteus, the later would-be rapist, likely to avoid a proffered kiss. The best solution would be the enactment of both kiss and 'handshake' as the lovers complete the three steps outlined by the priest in *Twelfth Night* when testifying to Olivia's marriage:

A contract of eternal bond of love,
Confirm'd by mutual joinder of your hands,
Attested by the holy close of lips,
Strength'ned by interchangement of your rings ...   (5.1.156–9)

The symbolism of the joined hands is the basic sign of unity here, followed by additional less important gestures. The complete inversion of the ritual sequence in *The Two Gentlemen* must be deemed deliberate. If it had been clear that the 'holy kiss' merely described the joining of hands, the adapter Victor would hardly have seen the necessity of taking this line away from Julia and attributing it to Proteus.

A further case is offered by the metrically incomplete line 'There, hold.' (4.4.118). An authorial stage direction would have made clear whether Silvia's two words are directed to Julia/Sebastian in the meaning 'Take this letter' or perhaps addressed to herself in the sense 'Let me think.' But perhaps the most important of all these cases concerns Silvia's silence after 5.4.59. Here a plausible motivation has proved to be beyond every editor's ingenuity.

READING LIST

This list includes some of the books and articles referred to in the Introduction and in the Commentary and may serve as a guide to those who wish to undertake further study of the play.

Beckermann, Bernard. 'Shakespeare's dramaturgy and binary form', *Theatre Journal* 33 (1981), 5–17

Berry, Ralph. *Shakespeare's Comedies: Explorations in Form*, 1972

Bradbrook, Muriel C. *Shakespeare and Elizabethan Poetry: A Study of His Earlier Work in Relation of the Poetry of the Time*, 1951

Brooks, Harold F. 'Two clowns in a comedy', *E&S*, 1963, pp. 91–100

Ewbank, Inga-Stina. '"Were man but constant, he were perfect": constancy and consistency in *The Two Gentlemen of Verona*', in *Shakespearian Comedy*, Stratford-upon-Avon Studies 14, 1972, pp. 31–57

Gabler, Hans W. 'Experiment and parody in Shakespeare's early plays', *Studia Neophilologica* 46 (1974), 159–71

Godshalk, William L. 'The structural unity of *The Two Gentlemen of Verona*', *SP* 66 (1969), 168–81

Harrison, T.P., Jr. 'Shakespeare and Montemayor's *Diana*', *Texas University Studies in English* 5 and 6 (1925–6), 72–120

Holmberg, Arthur. '*The Two Gentlemen of Verona*: Shakespearean comedy as a rite of passage', *Queen's Quarterly* 90 (1983), 33–44

Honigmann, E.A.J. *Shakespeare: The 'Lost Years'*, 1985

Hunter, G.K. *John Lily: The Humanist as Courtier*, 1962 (see his chapter 'Lily and Shakespeare')

Hunter, R.G. *Shakespeare and the Comedy of Forgiveness*, 1965

Leggatt, Alexander. *Shakespeare's Comedy of Love*, 1974

Lindenbaum, Peter. 'Education in *The Two Gentlemen of Verona*', *SEL* 15 (1975), 229–44

Morse, Ruth. '*Two Gentlemen* and the cult of friendship', *Neuphilologische Mitteilungen* 84 (1983), 214–24

Muir, Kenneth. *Shakespeare's Comic Sequence*, 1979

Phialas, Peter G. *Shakespeare's Romantic Comedies: The Development of Their Form and Meaning*, 1966

Priest, Dale J. 'Julia, Petruchio, Rosalind, Viola: Shakespeare's subjunctive leads', *Massachusetts Studies in English* 9 (1984), 32–51

Rossky, William. '*The Two Gentlemen of Verona* as burlesque', *ELR* 12 (1982), 210–19

Slights, Camille W. '*The Two Gentlemen of Verona* and the courtesy book tradition',
    S.St. 16 (1983), 13–31
Small, S. Asa. 'The ending of *The Two Gentlemen of Verona*', *PMLA* 48 (1933),
    767–76
Tillyard, E.M.W. *Shakespeare's Early Comedies*, 1965
Vyvyan, John. *Shakespeare and the Rose of Love*, 1960
Wales, Julia G. 'Shakespeare's use of English and foreign elements in the setting
    of *The Two Gentlemen of Verona*', *Transactions of the Wisconsin Academy of
    Sciences, Arts & Letters* 27 (1932), 85–125
Wells, Stanley. 'The failure of *The Two Gentlemen of Verona*', *SJ* 99 (1963),
    161–73